THE LIVING COUNTRYSIDE
HAVENS *of the* WILD

A Reader's Digest selection

HAVENS OF THE WILD

Front cover picture: A young fallow deer finds certain sanctuary
in the dense cover of this sunlit woodland.

THE LIVING COUNTRYSIDE
HAVENS *of the* WILD

PUBLISHED BY THE READER'S DIGEST ASSOCIATION LIMITED
LONDON   NEW YORK   MONTREAL   SYDNEY   CAPE TOWN

Originally published in partwork form
by Eaglemoss Publications Limited and Orbis Publishing Limited

Consultant

Heather Angel

Contributors

Contents

HAVENS *of the* WILD

Introduction

On a world scale, Britain and Ireland are small in area, but they still have a glorious mix of habitats throughout the breadth of the land. Some of these are completely natural, but most have been shaped to some extent by man.

Ever since the Stone Age, Britain's countryside has been exploited by man for living space, farming and industry. Many of our wild flowers and animals have been able to adapt to the new habitats thus created, but most survived only in isolated patches of wilderness – the havens of the wild. Some of these havens were areas remote and inaccessible to man – small islands, mountain-tops and cliffs. Others were regions unsuitable for agriculture, such as some wetlands and heathlands. A few fertile areas were preserved for deer parks or other recreational use, and some parts, originally exploited, reverted to wilderness as a result of dramatic events in history such as the Black Death in the 14th century.

Unexpectedly, some human activities have aided the processes of conservation. Strips of woodland were left to form natural boundaries – hedgerows. The sport of foxhunting has meant that copses were retained as shelter coverts, and woodland management schemes, such as coppicing, have led to the development of rich plant and insect communities.

Such areas as these are now becoming the framework of protected sites and reserves scattered throughout Britain which ensure that many of our more vulnerable animals and plants are able to survive and flourish for appreciation by future generations – an important and truly national heritage for everyone in the country.

Left: White waterlilies and amphibious bistort on open water – a tranquil and secluded English summer scene.

Central Southern England

Chesil Beach to the Chilterns

More than any other area of the British Isles, the wild places of Central and Southern England are under threat – by reason of their very accessibility to large numbers of people. Nevertheless, almost every kind of habitat, with the exception of mountains, is found there, offering sanctuary for many wild forms of wildlife.

On the coast, the sheltered landward side of Chesil Beach in summer is dotted with salt-tolerant yellow horned poppy, sea kale and the rare sea pea, while slightly farther inland, in saltmarsh areas bordering The Fleet, grow sea aster and marsh mallow.

Dorset's Studland Heath, like parts of the New Forest, is also rich in flowers, especially in midsummer when the heathers burst into purple colour. In the drier parts these heaths, vital remnants of a once much larger habitat, support two of our largest reptiles – the sand lizard and smooth snake.

The New Forest and Savernake Forest in Wiltshire, both survivors of ancient woodlands, come to life in May when their huge old oaks and beeches leaf out and spring flowers appear. Autumn, too, is a beautiful season here, when shafts of sunlight pierce the early morning mists and the roar of rutting deer echoes through the trees. Fine beech stands can also be seen at Ashridge Park in the Chilterns, growing on steep chalk slopes.

Unlike these ancient southern forests, the Cotswold Water Park is not steeped in tradition. It is a new wildlife haven – a collection of man-made flooded gravel pits which are now attracting a multitude of plants, birds and insects.

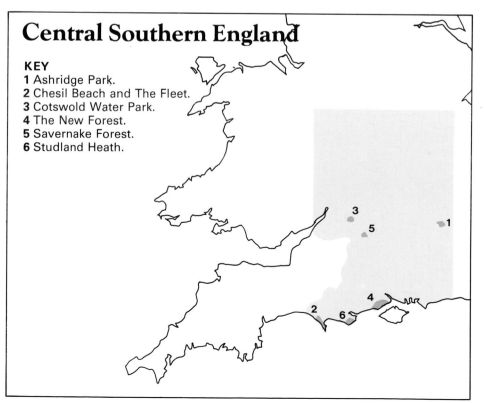

Central Southern England

KEY
1 Ashridge Park.
2 Chesil Beach and The Fleet.
3 Cotswold Water Park.
4 The New Forest.
5 Savernake Forest.
6 Studland Heath.

Left: A tantalizing glimpse of heathland through tall and stately pines in the New Forest. This heathland environment is as important a part of the New Forest as its ancient oak and beech woodland, containing as it does a number of rare and endangered animals and plants. Two that are exclusive to the Forest are the wild gladiolus and the New Forest cicada.

Below: Our southern oakwoods are under constant onslaught from a vast army of insects — these currant galls, for instance, are formed on oak catkins by tiny parasitic gall wasps.

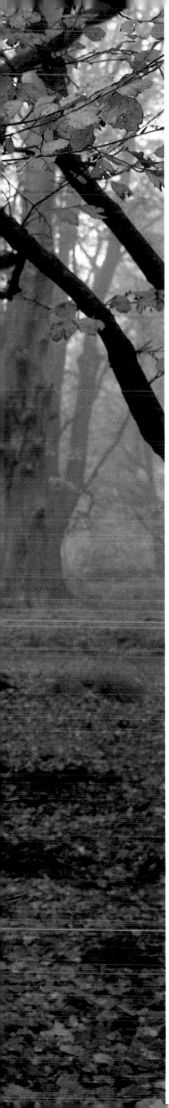

ASHRIDGE IN THE CHILTERNS

Ashridge Park is an estate in the Chilterns with three quite separate habitats—woodland, downland and common land—each with its own assemblage of plant and animal species.

Opposite page: Ashridge Park is justly famed for its beeches. The sparseness of the undergrowth is a common feature of beechwoods, as the dense foliage prevents sunlight from reaching the ground for most of the summer.

Below: An edible dormouse among the autumn leaves of the sweet chestnut. The Chilterns are the stronghold of this charming dormouse, so-called because the Romans regarded it as a delicacy.

Lying only 40km (28 miles) north-west of London, Ashridge Park covers 16sq km (6sq miles), encompassing parts of Buckinghamshire, Bedfordshire and Hertfordshire. This extremely rich habitat for wildlife attracts thousands of weekend visitors from nearby large towns and cities.

When the third and last Earl, Lord Brownlow, died in 1921 his will directed the trustees to dispose of the whole of the Estate to meet death duties. Immediately 4600ha (11,300 acres) were sold, mainly to the National Trust, and in 1925 a fund was initiated for the purpose of acquiring Berkhamsted Common and as much of Ashridge Park and adjacent woods as possible.

This fund eventually enabled the National Trust to buy more than 1200ha (3000 acres) by the early 1930s, and further land has since been bequeathed and purchased.

Wild woodland Some of the woodland at Ashridge dates back well over a thousand years, and it was once part of the vast Saxon forest between the manors of Berkhamsted and Little Guddesden. The two notable ancient woodlands surviving today are Frithsden Copse and Old Copse. These woods still contain most of their native flora and fauna, including magnificent oaks and beeches, the occasional hornbeam and, in spring, drifts of bluebells. The purple helleborine, though localised, is still a fairly common flower.

Among mammals associated with these woodlands perhaps the best known are fallow deer, which are totally wild and have descended from the deer of the original Park. In 1921 the Park contained approximately 150 red deer, 550 fallow and 25 sika. By 1945 one red deer remained, the sika deer had become extinct and the fallow was holding its own. Today there are no sika or red deer, but there are more than 300 fallow deer and muntjac or barking deer are also fairly common, though their numbers fall dramatically in severe winters. As well as the common dormouse, the introduced edible dormouse is also present in small numbers, this area of the Chilterns being its main stronghold.

Beech and bracken The huge commonlands which once covered much of the area are now hardly distinguishable from the woodlands. Remnants remain, however, due mainly to walkers and picnic parties, whose activities prevent the trees from encroaching. Silver birch, hawthorn, gorse, heather and bracken were quick to colonize these areas, making for a time an ideal habitat for birds such as stonechat and nightjar, neither of which are found there now. Nevertheless, interesting birds like the woodcock and redstart are still present, as is the hawfinch, particularly where there is a predominance of wild cherry and hornbeam.

A welcome sight is the lesser spotted woodpecker, which is far commoner than

fescue turf deteriorated, giving way to coarse grasses, principally upright brome, while hawthorn scrub also began to encroach. For a time rabbits held the delicate balance in check, but with the outbreak of myxomatosis in 1953 the hawthorn began to invade in earnest. (It is difficult to imagine that at one time the hawthorn was a rare plant in the British countryside until extensively used as a hedging plant at the time of enclosures.)

The change from downland to scrub is thought to have benefited small mammals by providing them with shelter from predators. In turn, their habit of burying haws during winter may have assisted scrub invasion.

Downland plants Despite the invading scrub the rich downland flora still exists where conditions are suitable, and it is still one of the treasures of the Estate. From March to October there is a succession of plants including hairy violet, rock rose, kidney vetch, pasque flower and six species of orchid. Some of these plants are rare on the Estate–as they are nationally. It is usually easy to find as many as 20 wild plants growing in a square metre on this downland, many–like the three species of gentian–having their own peculiar

most people think. This elusive bird, about the size of a great tit, is often overlooked in the high tree canopies where it spends much of its time.

One of the most attractive features of Ashridge is its beech hangers. These are small stands of mature beeches growing on the steep slopes of chalk downland. They extend along the slopes of the plateau from the village of Aldbury and finally peter out as the clay with flints gives way to the pure chalk downland of Ivinghoe Beacon. Beech woodland has no shrub layer and supports little vegetation, with the result that some of the plants you would expect to find in, say, oakwoods are absent here. However, these woods have their specialities such as sanicle, woodruff, white helleborine, fly orchid, bird's-nest orchid and in a few places spurge laurel. On the lower slopes of the hangers one can often find the whitebeam, perhaps the most beautiful of all the trees of the Estate.

Chalk downland The last and most spectacular habitat of Ashridge is the chalk downland. The best examples can be seen at Ivinghoe Beacon, Incombe Hole and Steps Hill. These areas had been grazed by sheep since time immemorial and as long as this continued the downland's shallow soil supported a close turf of fescue grass with a colourful associated flora.

Grazing ceased in the 1920s and 1930s when sheep became unprofitable. As a result the

Above: Young leaves of whitebeam opening in spring.

Right: The chalkhill blue, feeding on a flower of bird's-foot trefoil.

Below: Primrose and bugle are two spring flowers common at Ashridge.

niche. The early gentian appears in June and is usually only 5cm (2in) in height. It grows only in the short turf. The more robust autumn gentian can be seen over much of the downland in August and September but the Chiltern gentian, which often grows over 15cm (6in) high, is only found where the soil has been disturbed comparatively recently.

Downland butterflies Because of the profusion of flowering plants the downland also supports a variety of insects. Notable are the butterflies that appear in early summer, including the common blue, small blue and Duke of Burgundy fritillary. Late summer brings the marbled white and dark green fritillary and finally, towards the end of summer, the beautiful chalkhill blue. This butterfly roosts at the top of grass stems as evening approaches and may become quite tame as the chill evening air prevents it from flying. The chalkhill blue is still plentiful, although in wet summers it is hardly ever seen on the wing.

The future A bird census of the Ivinghoe hills conducted by the British Trust for Ornithology in 1966 found that on land previously grazed, where hawthorn was beginning to take over, there were no fewer than 37 different bird species breeding in an 80ha (200 acre) sample plot; a far higher density than on arable land or most woodland. The great difficulty for the continued successful management of any area of downland is finding the correct balance: many of Ashridge's rarest species require short downland turf, the maintenance of which needs constant clearance and the introduction of grazing animals. Yet overgrazing would lead to erosion of the soil. Achieving this balance is now the aim of conservation bodies involved with this and other sites.

In the meantime Ashridge Park continues to provide pleasure and recreation for people coming from miles around.

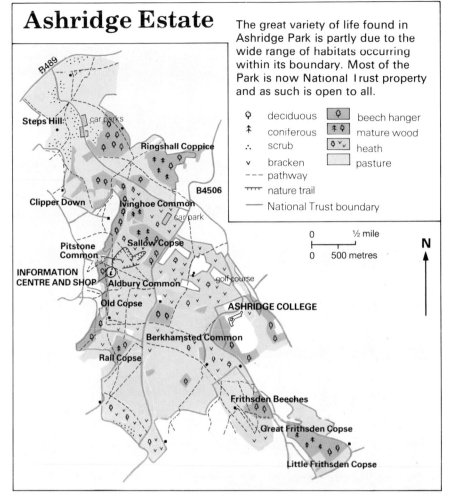

Ashridge Estate

The great variety of life found in Ashridge Park is partly due to the wide range of habitats occurring within its boundary. Most of the Park is now National Trust property and as such is open to all.

- ♀ deciduous
- ♠ coniferous
- ∴ scrub
- ∨ bracken
- --- pathway
- ┰┰┰ nature trail
- — National Trust boundary
- beech hanger
- mature wood
- heath
- pasture

0   ½ mile
0   500 metres

N

Right: The rare Chiltern gentian growing among the short downland turf at Ashridge.

Below: A jay broods three nestlings. Jays hoard large numbers of acorns, some of which they lose—a habit that helps to spread new oaks, thus replacing old felled trees.

CHESIL BEACH AND THE FLEET

Stretching for ten miles along the Dorset coast is Chesil Beach, and behind it a lagoon called The Fleet. Together these make a landform unparalleled elsewhere in Europe. The plants they support are adapted to survive harsh conditions.

Chesil Beach is essentially a simple shingle storm beach enclosing the largest estuarine lagoon system in Britain. The lagoon–known as The Fleet–is 13km (8 miles) long and at its eastern end, at Weymouth, opens into the sea through a narrow bridged entrance less than 75m (250ft) wide. At the western, enclosed end is the famous Abbotsbury Swannery. The Fleet has been designated an area of international importance for the conservation of migrating birds and both it and Chesil Beach are graded as an *Area of Outstanding Natural Beauty* and a *Site of Special Scientific Interest*.

The sheer magnitude of Chesil Beach makes it a unique landform, and it is often quoted as being the finest European example of a tombola–a narrow sand or shingle bar which links a small island to the mainland (Chesil Beach links the Isle of Portland to the mainland).

Since Chesil Beach is so long (16km/10 miles), aerial photographs often give it the appearance of being very narrow. This is not the case. In most parts the beach is 150-200m (500-650ft) wide and up to 14m (45ft) high. The seaward, southern side often takes a battering from the sea but The Fleet side is afforded some protection by the relatively high crest of the beach.

The sheltered Fleet Protected partly from the sea by the beach lies The Fleet, a lagoon composed of a series of narrows and coves. At the Weymouth end, where the lagoon joins the sea, there is a tidal rush of immense power and range, but at the Abbotsbury end the presence of normal tides is barely noticeable. There are extensive mudflats at the Weymouth end which are exposed at low tide, but even at high tide The Fleet is extremely shallow, except for the deep channels between the mudflats.

The Fleet is unique among British tidal lagoons in having a marked difference in salinity (salt concentration) along its length and contrasting conditions along its two main shorelines. The salinity in the lower third of The Fleet, near Weymouth, is much the same as in the English Channel, but in the upper two-thirds it can vary considerably depending on whether drought conditions or floods

Opposite page: A view of Chesil Beach and The Fleet, taken from the Isle of Portland, near Weymouth.

Below: Chesil Beach is an important national site for the yellow-horned poppy (*Glaucium flavum*). The horns are its seed-pods.

prevail. In a drought the salinity might be a quarter that found in sea water, yet during floods this may be diluted to one twentieth of seawater salinity.

The two long shorelines have very little in common, and thus add considerably to the interest of the area. The straight shoreline bordering Chesil Beach is composed predominantly of shingle whereas the opposite, landward edge is convoluted and offers a considerable variety of habitats ranging from saltwater and freshwater marsh to cliffs and cultivated soils.

Hardy beach plants As the beach is so exposed to south-westerly winds and sea spray, vegetation is concentrated on the sloping shingles facing the calmer waters of The Fleet. Plant colonization is also considerably greater at the Abbotsbury end because the finer pebbles which occur here help to trap such organic matter as guano which enriches the soil and helps to retain moisture. Vegetation is still sparse though, and the only plants to survive this harsh habitat are those that are tolerant of sea spray and can either root very deeply or withstand

long periods of drought.

Shrubby seablite and annual seablite are two of the most characteristic, if not the most striking, plants that grow on Chesil Beach. Both have insignificant flowers, but shrubby seablite grows up to 1m (3ft) high and thrives best at the edge of the shingle where it meets The Fleet. The prostrate annual seablite is hardier and grows up the shingle bank.

Chesil Beach is a nationally important site for sea kale, yellow-horned poppy and the even rarer sea pea. The last two plants produce a fine blaze of colour made all the more spectacular because they are in flower at the same time – in mid-summer. The dainty purple flowers of trailing sea milkwort and the fleshy growths of sea purslane and glasswort further add to the contrast of plants on Chesil Beach.

Other plants on Chesil Beach typical of coastal shingle include sea wormwood, Babington's orache, sea beet, sea bindweed and prickly ox-tongue. These plants have all devised ways of withstanding drought and fierce winds: sea wormwood, for example, is covered in a fine down to reduce evaporation,

Above: Rock samphire (*Crithmum maritimum*) is a plant of southern Britain, usually associated with sea cliffs although it also grows on shingle. On Chesil Beach it is found on the loose shingle at the Abbotsbury end (shown here) and on the stable turf at the Weymouth end. Its attractive yellow flowers are in blossom from June to August.

Below: Another typical plant of the shingle beach is shrubby seablite. This thrives mainly at the edge of Chesil Beach by The Fleet, and may grow as high as 1m (3ft). It is a perennial and its flowers, which are small and insignificant, come out in July and August.

and sea beet can store considerable amounts of water in its fleshy leaves. Among the more general coastal plants growing on the shingle are thrift, rock samphire, sand cat's tail and sea campion.

Saltmarsh plants Because the northern shore of The Fleet rises steeply there is only a small area suitable for the development of salt marsh – this is in the coves along the inland shoreline. The most remarkable feature about the saltmarshes here is that plants typical of both freshwater and salt water marshes grow alongside one another.

Reeds, sedges, rushes and grasses are all common along the muddy shores. The ubiquitous common reed occurs along most of the shore but adjacent to the Swannery it forms large reed beds. Interspersed with this, where the water is least salty, is flag iris. Sand sedge, distant sedge, saltmarsh sedge and false fox sedge also grow here, and sea clubrush thrives in the shallow water.

Although these plants are the most abundant and productive of the saltmarsh they are eclipsed in summer by other species with spectacular flowers. Two of the most attractive are the blue sea aster and pink marsh mallow, both sturdy upright plants.

Algae in The Fleet The number of flowering plants that occur in The Fleet is limited, and those that are present dominate only the mudflats. Elsewhere algae thrive. Contrasting physical and chemical conditions in The Fleet have encouraged an unusual array of green, brown and red algae. At the eastern end the strongly salty water and tidal fluctuations encourage species that are normally found on the open seashore. Marine green algae such as *Prasiola* or *Blindingia*, brown algae including several species of *Fucus*, and red algae such as *Ascophyllum*, grow on old walls and boulders.

At the Abbotsbury end the characteristic algae of the Weymouth end are absent, but they are replaced by a mass of entangled species which lie on the mud surface. Sea lettuce (*Ulva lactuca*) is a common species growing alongside shining, tough filaments of *Chaetomorpha*. It is a favourite food of swans. One of the most interesting algae of The Fleet is stonewort (*Lamprothamnion*) which occurs along the shallow northern shore. This alga is confined to coastal areas of southern England, and The Fleet is one of fewer than five sites in which it is common.

Flowers of The Fleet The only flowering plants to be found in The Fleet itself are two species of eelgrass and two species of tasselweed. The rarest is beaked tasselweed which occurs in only a few isolated pockets of The Fleet. Spiral tasselweed is much more widespread and dominates the Abbotsbury end of the lagoon, growing among the algae. It is a particularly attractive plant as the stalk which holds the flowers is long and tightly coiled like a watch spring.

Of the two eelgrasses, narrow-leaved eelgrass is the most widespread and tends to

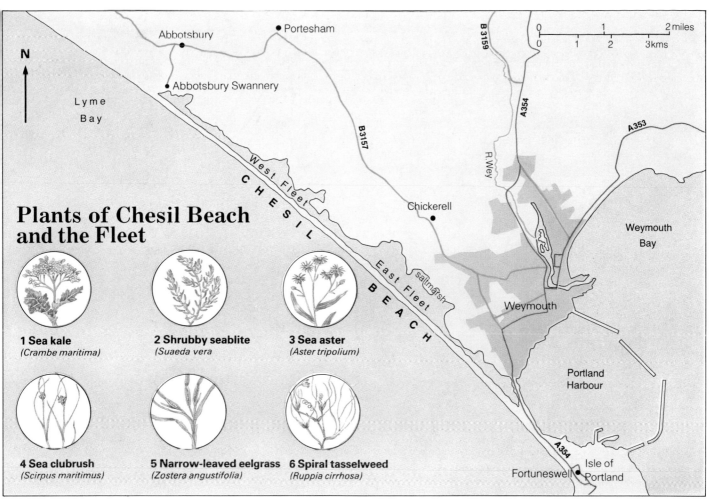

Plants of Chesil Beach and the Fleet

1 Sea kale
(*Crambe maritima*)

2 Shrubby seablite
(*Suaeda vera*

3 Sea aster
(*Aster tripolium*)

4 Sea clubrush
(*Scirpus maritimus*)

5 Narrow-leaved eelgrass
(*Zostera angustifolia*)

6 Spiral tasselweed
(*Ruppia cirrhosa*)

dominate the mudflats whereas dwarf eelgrass, a much smaller species, favours the coves. The success or failure of eelgrass and tasselweed spells joy or disaster for the swans and wildfowl during the winter for this is their main food supply. Without plenty to feed on many will not be tempted to spend the winter on The Fleet and large numbers of swans may die.

The existence of today's wildlife on Chesil Beach and The Fleet has much to do with the fact that the land has been owned by the same family for the last 450 years. Their concern in protecting it may mean that access is limited to certain parts, but at least the plants' future looks promising.

Above: A map of Chesil Beach and The Fleet showing some of the plants growing there.

Right: Prickly ox-tongue (*Picris echioides*) is a coastal plant and is able to withstand both the fierce winds and drought.

Below: The purple flowers of sea pea (*Lathyrus japonicus*) are usually a rare sight but they can be found on Chesil Beach between May and July. The seeds of this plant are dispersed by the sea.

17

THE COTSWOLD WATER PARK

'The new Broads' is how one observer described the Cotswold Water Park, and looking across the dozens of flooded gravel pits it is easy to see why. Like the Broads, the Water Park holds both opportunities and problems for our wild plants and animals.

Below: Summer time on one of the Cotswold lakes. Most are privately owned, and many are dangerous for the unwary visitor, although one lake in the Ashton Keynes section is a nature reserve.

The Cotswold Water Park straddles the Wiltshire-Gloucestershire county boundary and is divided into two sections, one to the west centred on Ashton Keynes and South Cerney, and one to the east between Lechlade and Fairford. Together they comprise an area of about 5700ha (14,000 acres) of gravel-bearing land. The Water Park has been formed around a series of flooded gravel pits.

Before gravel digging began the area was almost wholly agricultural, with scattered small towns and villages. Doubtless many of the fields would have been rich in the plants now found only in old hay meadows or permanent pastures. Some such areas still occur in or near the Water Park and such plants as green-winged orchid, greater burnet, adder's tongue and the local speciality, snake's-head fritillary, grow there. However, as elsewhere, modern agriculture has produced larger fields more intensively farmed for dairying and cereals and these, not the old pastures, now frame the gravel pits.

Gravel lakes The Cotswold Water Park is, fundamentally, an area of sand and gravel deposits. These deposits are 4-6m (15-20ft) thick under a shallow topsoil and subsoil, and are of great economic importance. The site has been worked since the early 1920s and the mineral industry is well established locally—both for the extraction and the subsequent

manufacture of concrete and concrete products. Output has increased several times over since the 1940s, reaching a peak in the mid-1970s (helped by the construction of the nearby M4 and M5 motorways).

Because of the high water table, which is usually 1m (3ft) or less below ground level, the excavated pits readily fill with water and form lakes, the water coming from rainfall and from inflowing springs rising in the calcium-rich limestone rocks of the Cotswolds to the north. The gravels themselves are also largely derived from limestone–consequently the water of the lakes is rich in calcium and very alkaline. Indeed, under certain conditions solid calcium carbonate may be precipitated out of the water forming a deposit called 'marl'. The lakes of the Cotswold Water Park are considered to form the largest area of marl lakes in Britain.

Lake invaders Plant colonization of both the open water and the lake margins can be a slow process, the reason being that modern gravel working methods often produce deep water right up to the bank. Under such conditions no marginal vegetation can develop and instead the bank may become overhung by brambles and dog roses or by branches of hawthorn, willow and alder trees. However, in time the water cuts into these banks and produces shallow gravelly ledges which can then be colonized by plants. Bulrush is one of the first plants to establish in such shallow margins in the Water Park and most of the lakes have some small narrow bulrush beds, while a good number have much larger beds.

The common reed, which is usually a familiar plant on the edges of rivers and lakes, is not as common as might be imagined. Possibly the largest stand of it is associated with the outflow of silt from a gravel-washing plant, showing it requires rather particular conditions to grow well. Large tufts of rushes, notably hard rush, dominate the shore line in some other places while more occasional stands of club rush are found scattered among the bulrush.

Lake aquatics The establishment of truly aquatic plants in the Water Park appears to be related to the chance introduction of seeds or pieces of stem, and also to the depth of water in the lake. Aside from a few microscopic algae, like *Spirogyra* and *Oscillatoria*, the first colonizer is often a species of stonewort. These are primitive flowerless plants lacking roots and with the plant surface made stiff by an encrusting of lime. Several different species have been recorded and the common stonewort is present in many water bodies.

Eight different species of pondweed have also been recorded from the Cotswold Water Park. These include species with broad leaves, such as the shining pondweed (another plant that is often covered with lime), and species with narrow grass-like leaves, such as hair-like and fennel pondweeds. Other aquatic plants noted

Above: An alder tree with its fruits, known as 'cones'. Among the trees found in the Cotswold Water Park, some are naturally established–for example, oak, field maple and common buckthorn, which date from the presence of old hedgerows on the site. Other trees, however, have been planted by man. It is hard to tell whether the alders that occur around the pits fall into the first category or the second.

Right: Hemp agrimony is found in damper ground in the Water Park.

Below: A family of young sand martins. These birds often breed in sandy cliffs, and even the more gravelly ones, in the Park. In one year alone, more than 800 nest holes were counted.

habitats created during gravel extraction provide conditions that attract a wide range of birds throughout the year.

During the winter months the lakes hold large numbers of ducks, especially diving ducks. The wintering populations of pochard and tufted duck are regarded as nationally significant. In most winters there are at least 2800 of the former and 1100 of the latter. In exceptional circumstances, mainly related to particular weather conditions, the numbers of these and other wintering species may be much higher. The most numerous water bird at this time of year is the coot, whose numbers can top 4000 in some winters. Coot, pochard and tufted duck all feed in open water around

from the area are spiked water-milfoil, rigid hornwort and fan-leaved water-crowfoot.

Behind the shoreline The vegetation of the banks behind the shoreline is quite variable. Initially the bare soil surface is colonized by species typical of waste ground–docks, thistles and goosefoot, together with groundsel, colt's-foot and stinging nettle, are common components. After a while the vegetation becomes thicker, and taller grasses such as oatgrass and cock's-foot become abundant. With them, however, grow a variety of taller flowers such as knapweed, hogweed and ragwort on the drier areas and meadowsweet, hemp agrimony and fleabane on the damper ground.

In some places, probably over long-forgotten gravel heaps, a short calcareous turf develops. Growing here are bee orchid, felwort and devil's-bit scabious, all of which also grow on the old limestone pastures to the north and west.

Birdlife Despite the variety of plants in and around the lakes, most naturalists are attracted to the Park by the birds. The variety of

Above: So far, 17 species of dragonfly and damselfly have been reported from the area; this is about 40% of all the species recorded in Britain. One of the dragonflies you are most likely to see is the common sympetrum.

Right: Many thousands of black-headed gulls pass the winter at the Park, particularly at one of the lakes in the western part near South Cerney. Here you can sometimes obtain good views of the gulls flighting in to roost from the disused railway bridge near the main road through the Park.

Below: Great willow-herb, a common species around the margins of the lakes.

1-3m (3-10ft) deep.

Other water birds frequently seen in winter include mallard, wigeon and teal, mute swan and great crested grebe. There is also a large winter roost of gulls on one of the biggest lakes near South Cerney.

Some of these wintering birds remain in spring to breed on the lakes. Mallards are certainly quick to use suitable localities and both tufted ducks and great crested grebes have nested in increasing numbers over the last ten years. The breeding requirements are rather different to those needed for overwintering. The presence of sheltered shallows and bays, islands and marginal vegetation is all of considerable importance for successful breeding. Tufted ducks prefer the islands for nesting and they and the mallard need sheltered water for raising their young. The emergent vegetation, such as the bulrush beds, are essential for great crested grebes and coots to nest, while other water birds like moorhens also make use of these plants but may in addition nest in the low branches of trees.

Land birds The thickets of bulrush, willows and other plants also provide nesting sites for sedge and reed warblers and for reed buntings. Some scrub areas attract breeding passerine species, among which the nightingale and lesser whitethroat are the most noteworthy. Sandy cliffs, and even rather gravelly cliffs, often attract breeding sand martins, but such cliff faces are often transitory affairs, being associated with a certain phase in the sequence of operations in gravel working: they may soon be dug away again or, if not, become colonized by vegetation, making them unsuitable for the birds.

Another species that breeds on temporary features is the little ringed plover. A few pairs nest in most years on bare gravel areas but such features are quickly lost under vegetation unless positive steps are taken to keep them open.

Also of interest to the birdwatcher are the small pools and wet patches in the muddy bottoms of actively dug pits. In such pits there is a constant flow of water coming in, which the pit operators have to remove by pumping. In practice, however, it is impossible and unnecessary to remove all the water, hence the wet pit-floor, which is a great attraction for waders during the migration seasons of spring and autumn. Seen almost every spring are black-tailed godwit and sanderling, while late summer and autumn may well produce little stint and wood sandpiper. Other scarce birds which have been recorded in the Water Park in the last decade include gannet, scaup, osprey, black tern and water rail. However, the chances of seeing these depend on regular visits to likely areas and good luck!

Other animal life The Cotswold Water Park has, of course, its share of more sedentary creatures. Various species of fishes are taken by anglers, roach, perch and pike probably being the most widely occurring, though there is much variation between the lakes.

Those who sit on the banks in the summer cannot fail to notice the numbers and variety of damselflies and dragonflies that fly around the pits. The common blue damselfly lives up to its name and is very abundant in places while two of the commoner dragonflies are the brown aeshna and the common sympetrum. Most of the other groups of insects have been little studied but some of the more familiar butterflies and grasshoppers may often be seen in the longer grass around the pits.

The future The Cotswold Water Park was created by man, yet its habitats have a future as uncertain as many of our more natural areas. Many of the features of particular interest are transitory, such as the muddy pit-floor, open gravel area and sandy cliff, and depend on continued gravel working. Ultimately, perhaps a nature conservation body may have to simulate those conditions if the wildlife is to be maintained. Likewise many species of plant, bird and insect only establish themselves dependably if large

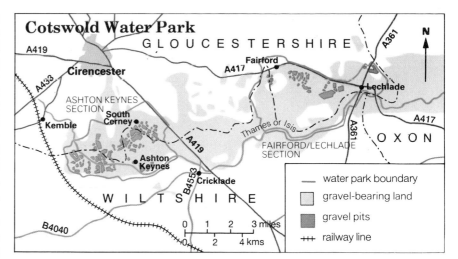

enough areas of, for example, reed bed or willow thicket can be created. Conservation is badly needed here.

Of course, a wide variety of flora and fauna manages to flourish alongside many of the current uses of the lakes–sailing, windsurfing, angling and so on. But the full potential of the area will not be realised, nor the present value maintained, without active provision of the necessary conditions.

Above: The Cotswold Water Park is divided into two parts, the Ashton Keynes section to the west and the Fairford/Lechlade section to the east.

Below: The big fruiting head of bulrush in the middle here shows why this plant got its name.

THE NEW FOREST

The New Forest in Hampshire is a magnificent example of ancient unfenced woodland; it also includes some of Europe's finest extensive heath and valley bog habitats.

Above: Bratley Wood in the New Forest – beeches in spring leaf. This wood is unfenced, but the New Forest also has large areas of enclosed mixed woodland.

Opposite page: Of the three species of deer found in the Forest, the fallow is the most common. This buck sports a magnificent set of antlers.

Between Southampton and Bournemouth in south-west Hampshire lies the New Forest, a stretch of mixed countryside covering an area of 366sq km (145sq miles). It is made up of a magnificent range of woodland, dry and wet heathland and farmland. The local community derives many benefits from the New Forest – from farmers and forestry workers to those in search of relaxation, for whom the forest is full of colourful walks and nature trails. Local people are also owners of the New Forest ponies, which provide an attractive sight in many areas of the Forest.

This is the last of the old Royal hunting

beech trees may be due to the fact that they colonize clearings faster than oaks. In former times some areas were felled to provide wood for the Navy and these tended to be taken over by beech. In other places, the increase of beech was helped by deliberate planting.

Occasional specimens of whitebeam and the rare wild service tree are also found in the open woods. Less rare are rowan and hawthorn, while clearings are also colonized by birch. Fine examples of alder woodland are found in the moist valleys, with ash and field maple growing at the edges of these valleys.

The ground flora of the open woods includes two characteristic species: wood spurge and butcher's broom, which survive because cattle, ponies and deer do not like to eat them. Open areas where bracken spreads provide the habitat of one species that is found nowhere else in the British Isles – the wild gladiolus. This lovely plant, which produces purple spikes of flowers in June, can be difficult to find under the bracken. This probably gives it much needed protection from being picked.

Woodland animals Three species of deer roam in the New Forest. The commonest is the fallow deer, with numbers in the region of 1700. There are also some 300 roe deer, while the magnificent red deer, never the dominant species in the Forest, numbers about 160 in the New Forest and environs.

Domestic animals from the New Forest

forests, having gained this status under William the Conqueror. Today two-thirds of the New Forest are still Crown Land and a sizeable part of this is designated 'Ancient and Ornamental' woodland. This is an open type of woodland where deer, cattle and ponies roam freely as they used to in the Middle Ages.

Open woodland The 'Ancient and Ornamental' woods are almost certainly the remnants of the original forest that covered most of lowland Britain in prehistoric times. In the course of their long history, they have been thinned in certain areas; but there are many woods where no felling has taken place for nearly 300 years.

If you look carefully at the trees in these woods, you can see that those of certain ages are more common than others. These age groups date back to a series of periods when there were less grazing animals in the Forest, so more seedlings were left undamaged and grew to maturity. In some of the woods there are signs that when trees were removed by felling, the foresters sowed acorns to ensure that new trees replaced them.

The acorns were planted in threes, forming a triangle with sides of about a metre. Holly berries were sown around this triangle, so that a prickly barrier would grow to protect the young oaks from grazing animals. In Frame Wood, near Beaulieu, you can still recognise pairs of oaks, now 200 to 250 years old, with the centre of their trunks a metre apart; and in some places the complete triangle has survived.

The oaks of the New Forest are mainly pedunculate and sessile, with some hybrids. In prehistoric times these were the Forest's dominant species, while beech was restricted to limited areas. Through the ages, beech increased in numbers and today roughly half the mature trees are beech, with the oaks making up most of the rest. The increase of

Above: A buzzard with nesting young in the top of a birch tree. This is a common bird of prey in the New Forest.

Below: The New Forest pony is an ancient breed that dates back to before the Norman Conquest.

farms are often seen in the open woods. A characteristic sight in autumn is a herd of pigs, browsing through the leaf mould beneath the mature trees, feeding on acorns and beech nuts. This form of feeding is known as pannage and the New Forest is one of the few remaining places in Western Europe where this ancient practice survives.

Forest lichens The old woodlands are renowned for the rich variety of lichens that grow on the oaks and beeches. An astonishing total of 278 species of epiphytic lichens (species growing on trees) are known to be present in the Forest, including some great rarities, for example the spectacular lungworts – *Lobaria pulmonaria* and *Lobaria laetivirens* – which spread in great mats on trees here and there. These and some other lichen species are found only in ancient forests and therefore testify that these woods date back to prehistoric times.

Enclosed woods These incorporate a variety of habitats, all protected from the grazing and browsing of ponies and cattle, though not from deer, which are able to leap over most of the fences. Some enclosed areas are similar to the 'Ancient and Ornamental' woods, and others are 18th and 19th century plantations. A large proportion are more recent conifer plantations. Waymarked walks lead the visitor through some of these pleasant conifer woods. Although these are not as rich in plant and animal species as

Above: Typical lichens on a beech tree in the New Forest. The one that hangs down is a beard lichen (*Usnea*), while the leafy ones are *Hypogymnia* and *Parmelia*.

Right: The wild gladiolus, exclusive to the New Forest, growing among bracken.

the broadleaved woods, they contain grassy rides where wild flowers grow and nesting sites for the many conifer-dwelling species of birds.

The ground flora in the enclosed broadleaved woods is richer than that of the open woodland, due to the protection from grazing. There is also a greater variety of butterflies and of rare moths such as the triangle, the marble pug and the light crimson underwing; this is mainly because there are more species of food plants for the caterpillars.

Large heathlands Although called the New Forest, the most extensive habitat there is open heathland. The wildlife that is found today on the heaths owes its character to a process which began in the Bronze Age, when early farmers cleared the trees from certain areas, turning them into pastures. Later these pastures were abandoned and went through a gradual change: rainwater washed most of the plant nutrients down from the topsoil into lower levels, resulting in a soil formation known as a podsol. The pale, rather acid upper soil supports only a few plant species, heather being the most typical.

Most of this heathland survives today and

provides grazing for deer, ponies and cattle. The ponies and cattle belong to the people of the area, who have for centuries had grazing rights in the New Forest.

These heaths are the largest remaining in Western Europe. Their size makes it possible for certain endangered species to survive here. In smaller fragments of heath, local communities of a particular species become isolated and have less chance of successful breeding. Rare animals that survive on the New Forest heaths include the sand lizard and the smooth snake. The Dartford warbler and the stonechat are among breeding birds of the heaths, while insects include the silver-studded blue butterfly and many species of beetles found only in a few heathy places.

Wet heaths Richer in species than the dry heath areas are those that are waterlogged in winter – the wet heath areas. These are the

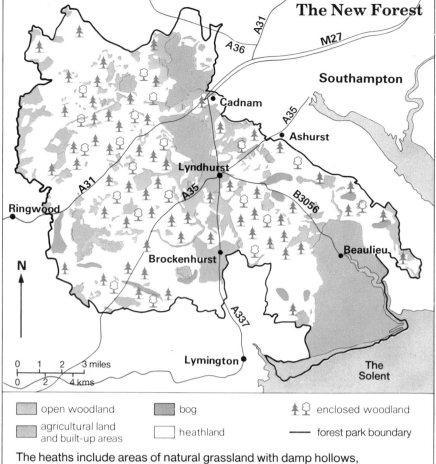

The New Forest

Southampton

Cadnam
Ashurst
Lyndhurst
Ringwood
Brockenhurst
Beaulieu
Lymington
The Solent

N

| 0 | 1 | 2 | 3 miles |
| 0 | 2 | | 4 kms |

- ☐ open woodland
- ☐ agricultural land and built-up areas
- ☐ bog
- ☐ heathland
- 🌲🌳 enclosed woodland
- — forest park boundary

The heaths include areas of natural grassland with damp hollows, occurring on clay or loam, that are too small to show on this map.

Left: The New Forest cicada, another species unique to the Forest.

Below: Dry heathland north-west of Burley in the New Forest. On the left in the small pit you can see a typical podsol profile, with a bleached sandy layer and the reddish 'iron pan' below.

home of the lovely marsh gentian, the rare marsh club-moss and the less rare deer-grass.

Valley bogs The valleys on the heaths are largely treeless bogs – the finest, most varied and extensive series of such lowland bogs anywhere in Western Europe. Here you can see carpets of sphagnum mosses – the green, yellow or brown species growing mostly in wet hollows, and the red species forming distinctive low hummocks. The valley bogs are the main stronghold, in southern Britain, of the tiny green bog orchid as well as various insect-trapping plants – two species of bladderwort, the pale butterwort and the three sundews. These bogs are almost the only remaining habitat of several rare dragonflies, especially *Ischnura pumilio*, and rare damselflies such as *Coenagrion mercuriale* and *Coenagrion tenellum*. These insects are highly sensitive to the effects of pollution or drainage of their habitat.

Future of the Forest The Forestry Commission has organised an excellent system of well concealed car-parking areas. From any of these, ten minutes' walk into the woods brings you complete solitude, where you can follow the interesting nature trails or just walk for hours without seeing anybody else.

Pressure of tourism is largely under control and a major review of the New Forest as a heritage area is currently underway, the conclusions of which will take the Forest into the 21st century.

SAVERNAKE FOREST

To speak of Wiltshire is to conjure up images of rolling downs and skylarks soaring through the sky. For the most part this picture is true, yet there are also more shaded, woodland places. One such is Savernake Forest: once an ancient royal hunting ground, it is now the only privately owned forest in England.

Lying just south-east of Marlborough, Savernake Forest once provided a convenient and diverting stop-over for hungry kings and princes en route between London and the West Country. Indeed, the attractive market town of Marlborough continued to provide the same break in journeys until the M4 motorway arrived to change the habits of

Above: Some of Savernake's splendid beeches in early spring foliage.

Right: Wood sage is one plant that flourishes in the sunlight dappled glades.

27

centuries. In the middle ages an unbroken tract of forest extended from the town of Marlborough to the Solent in Hampshire. Today, Savernake occupies some 930ha (2300 acres), of which 375ha (930 acres) have been designated as a *Site of Special Scientific Interest*.

The Forest The underlying geology, like that of the nearby Marlborough Downs, is chalk but is here overlaid for the most part by superficial deposits of clay-with-flints and, in some places, sand. Ancient forests typically encompass a wider range of habitats than just woodland, and Savernake is no exception. Open areas occur in shallow valleys which bisect the Forest. In the west they are calcareous but in the east deposits of sand give rise to heaths.

The woodland itself is predominantly oak and beech, but with quantities of birch and hawthorn as well. Magnificent beech-lined avenues, laid out by 'Capability' Brown in the 18th century, radiate out from the centre of the Forest along the cardinal points of the compass, dividing the woodland into eight segments. On the map they appear to be a monstrous human imposition upon the ancient oak woodland, but at ground level the lofty beeches, themselves now two centuries old, merely keep prying eyes away from the many hidden glades out of which roe and fallow deer slip at dusk or in the early morning light to feed.

The most stately of these 18th century accomplishments is the Grand Avenue. Listed in the *Guinness Book of Records* as the longest beech avenue, it runs for some four miles in a north-west/south-east direction across the Forest. Planted with elm and beech, an impressive vista is provided from Tottenham House, the former home of the Marquesses of Ailesbury, to the tall column which was erected to celebrate the return to sanity of George III.

The ownership of the Forest goes hand in hand with the wardenship and both hereditary positions are now held by the Earl of Cardigan, the son of the present Marquess. Large areas of the Forest are now leased to the Forestry Commission.

Above: The nuthatch is one bird to look for among the trees in Savernake Forest. Its slate-blue upperparts and orange-buff underparts make it easy to identify. The long, sharp beak is very strong and is used to break into nuts and seeds with a hammering motion. A characteristic of this bird is to hop up and down tree trunks at speed – it feeds upside down just as easily as it does in an upright position. Male and female are alike.

Over the last fifty years the Forestry Commission has been responsible for a substantial amount of afforestation with conifers. However, recently they have been persuaded to respect the broad-leaved character of Savernake and plantings now include oak and beech.

Two species of oak occur–the common or pedunculate oak and some very ancient and massive stands of sessile oak, of which the 'King' and 'Queen' oaks are the best known specimens in the Forest. (The pedunculate oak differs from the sessile in possessing stalks on its acorns, but hybrids also occur.) An extremely rich lichen flora of over 100 species is associated with the sessile oaks, whose epiphytic flora also includes mosses and polypody ferns. Silver birch thrives in the sandier areas of the Forest.

Flourishing fungi Among the birches in late summer you may find the poisonous fly agaric fungus. With its handsome, white-spotted red cap this picture-book toadstool is instantly recognisable, yet far more deadly is its less familiar close relative, the death cap. whose streaked greenish-yellow cap is to be found beneath beech and oak.

The realistic-looking beefsteak fungus, on the other hand, while not exactly a chef's delight, is at least edible. The flesh-coloured lobes of this bracket fungus not only have the colour, weight and fibrous texture of raw beefsteak, they even exude a red juice for

Seedling stages

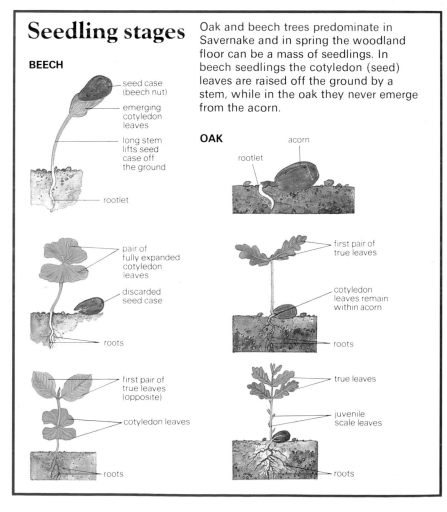

Oak and beech trees predominate in Savernake and in spring the woodland floor can be a mass of seedlings. In beech seedlings the cotyledon (seed) leaves are raised off the ground by a stem, while in the oak they never emerge from the acorn.

BEECH

seed case (beech nut)
emerging cotyledon leaves
long stem lifts seed case off the ground
rootlet

pair of fully expanded cotyledon leaves
discarded seed case
roots

first pair of true leaves (opposite)
cotyledon leaves
roots

OAK

acorn
rootlet

first pair of true leaves
cotyledon leaves remain within acorn
roots

true leaves
juvenile scale leaves
roots

good measure. This species is found on the stumps or around the bases of older oaks.

Savernake Forest is, indeed, renowned for the variety and abundance of its fungi, but unless identification is certain, they are best left untouched. Apart from the interest they provide, fungi perform a vital function in assisting the decomposition of organic material to provide humus, without which the life of the Forest would cease.

Savernake flowers and insects In contrast to the abundance of lichens, mosses, ferns and fungi, the herbaceous flora is generally sparse within the wooded areas. This is partly due to grazing by deer and partly to the tree cover. Under beech, in particular, the flora may be restricted to ivy, sanicle and the graceful, shade-loving wavy hair grass.

In the more open glades and rides an

Above: The fallow deer is one of three deer species inhabiting the Forest in the wild. (The other two are roe deer and Chinese muntjac or barking deer.) Of the Forest's 250 fallow deer, about 100 live in the deer park, but the remainder run wild. Savernake's population of about 120 red deer live exclusively in the deer park.

Below: Among the many different fungi found in Savernake is the attractive – but poisonous – fly agaric.

exuberant growth of bracken and foxglove predominates, along with purple moor grass, wood sage and several species of bramble. Herbaceous species are most abundant in the open areas, where they range from such typical calcicoles (lime lovers) as kidney vetch and wild strawberry on the exposed chalk in the west, to such familiar calcifuges (lime haters) as ling and gorse on the sandy heathland to the east. In recent years, however, these open patches have diminished in extent as trees and shrubs have come in to colonize. Birch, in particular, can rapidly take over what was once a heath of yellow gorse and purple heather.

Gorse is represented in Savernake by two species–the common gorse or furze, which flowers throughout the year but is at its best from April to June, and the smaller, more prostrate dwarf gorse, which does not flower until July. Smaller still is another yellow-flowered relative, the petty whin, a spiny, almost hairless undershrub with wiry stems and small pointed oval leaves.

As its ponds have silted up and become overgrown, the wet places of the Forest have also tended to decline. Where they persist a refuge is provided–not only for such specialised plants as blinks, water purslane and shoreweed, but also for the amphibian population of frogs, toads and newts.

Like the flowering plants, most butterflies favour the rides and glades or the more open areas of heath and down. Wild violets provide the foodplant for several species of fritillary butterfly, while the kidney vetch caters for the small blue and gorse supports the green hairstreak. Other butterflies, such as the speckled wood, marbled white, meadow brown and ringlet, are content with coarse grasses. Like many of Savernake's

rarer butterflies, the purple hairstreak is dependent upon the oak for its survival and rarely descends to ground level. Rare beetles and flies also rely on the mature oaks, single trees having yielded over 600 different species of invertebrates.

Bird life Just as the plant life of the Forest provides for the insects, so the insects in their turn become food for the many woodland birds. As you might expect, all three species of woodpecker are present–these being the handsome great spotted woodpecker, its smaller relative the lesser spotted woodpecker, and the green woodpecker, whose laughing call betrays its presence as surely as does the harsh chatter of the jay. Sharper eyes are needed to spot the small brown treecreeper as it deftly climbs a tree trunk in search of insect larvae.

Summer migrants include the redstart. A shy bird, similar to the robin in size, the male redstart is dark grey above but with a bright chestnut-red rump, tail, breast and flanks. The woodcock, on the other hand, is a true Savernake resident, secretive by day and feeding mainly by night. Large, brown and well-camouflaged, the males are occasionally encountered at dawn or dusk when they circle their territory issuing a strange 'wizzick' call.

Hideaway deer Dawn and dusk are also the best times to see the equally secretive deer, of which four species are represented in

Savernake. The largest of these is the native red deer, whose population of about 120 survives in the deer park just to the south of Tottenham Park. Only the stags bear antlers, using them to fight for females in the autumn rut, prior to which they can be heard roaring furiously, usually on the first clear frosty nights of late September.

The fallow deer, a long-established introduction to Britain (presumably by the Romans), is a native of southern Europe. Somewhat smaller than the red deer, its summer coat is a splendid reddish fawn ('fallow'), dappled with white spots which are lost in October when it acquires its drab winter coat.

Our other native species, the roe deer, predominates in the woodland; here individuals lie up during the day. A small graceful species, the largest bucks stand no more than 64cm (25in) at the shoulder.

Savernake Forest

wooded areas

꙼꙼꙼ deciduous woodland

🌲🌲🌲 coniferous woodland

--- paths and rides

If you approach Savernake Forest on the M4 motorway, leave it at Junction 15 and travel the eight miles south to where the Forest lies like a green wedge between the A4 and the A346 (to Andover).

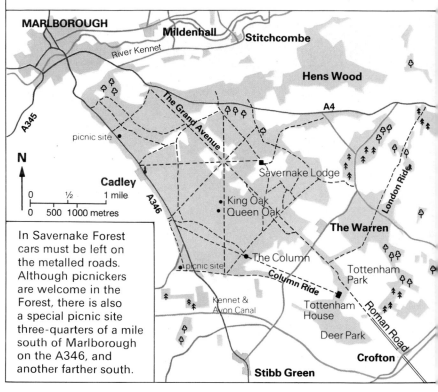

In Savernake Forest cars must be left on the metalled roads. Although picnickers are welcome in the Forest, there is also a special picnic site three-quarters of a mile south of Marlborough on the A346, and another farther south.

Left: A widespread plant of damp grassy places is the lady's smock or cuckoo flower, whose lilac flowers grace many a woodland path from April to June; it is the principal foodplant of several of Savernake's many woodland butterflies, including the orange-tip (shown here) and the green-veined white. Only the male orange-tip has the brilliant orange wing colouring; the female can be mistaken for one of the cabbage white butterflies.

Right: Savernake's rides and glades are favoured by the lovely but poisonous meadow saffron, whose pale mauve flowers have a crocus-like appearance which belies its membership of the lily family. The vigorous tufts of its large bluebell-like leaves precede the flowers, which do not appear until August or September–a feature which has given this plant its other common name of autumn crocus.

The Chinese muntjac is a more recent introduction. Smaller even than the roe, it is identifiable by its white underside and short tusks in the upper jaw.

If the deer are shy of daylight, then the small mammals of the Forest are true night-dwellers, coming out after dark to feed on nuts, berries, slugs and insects. Perhaps the most endearing of the rodents in Savernake is the dormouse, which hibernates through the winter in a nest of moss and leaves.

STUDLAND HEATH NATURE RESERVE

Studland in Dorset is one of the finest examples of lowland heath in the British Isles. It is endowed with a rich variety of rare animals and plants whose futures are assured so long as Studland remains a protected nature reserve.

Below: A view of the nature reserve from the south. Nearest lies a large area of heath, with the peninsula further away, its freshwater lake gleaming in the middle. In the distance are Poole and Bournemouth.

At the beginning of the last century much of the land between Dorchester and Southampton was covered with heath, about 30,400 hectares (75,000 acres) lying within the modern boundaries of Dorset. Less than one fifth of that now remains, and the losses continue at the startling rate of over an acre a

day. Heaths have disappeared under the towns of Bournemouth and Poole. Others have been converted into pastures, conifer plantations and rubbish tips, and some have been ravaged by army tanks or the excavation of sand and clay. Now there is another hazard—oil exploration.

The remaining fragments of heath are widely dispersed. Many of them are too small to hold significant populations of the rarer wildlife species, and too isolated to be re-colonized from elsewhere. A few comparatively large blocks, however, survive in the Isle of Purbeck, to the south of Poole Harbour, and the largest of these is Studland Heath National Nature Reserve, with an area of about 720 hectares (1800 acres). It is in the care of the Nature Conservancy Council.

Nature reserve Over a third of this area has been a reserve since 1962, most of it forming part of what is known as the South Haven Peninsula. This name was coined by the late Captain Cyril Diver, who carried out an

Above: The grayling is a handsome butterfly, its brown and buff wings marked with eye-like spots. It is seen here on flowering bell-heather, but when it settles on bare ground it seems to vanish as soon as it alights; showing little more than the underside of one dull-coloured hind wing, it melts perfectly into the background. The grayling adds the final touch to its disappearing act by leaning over at exactly the right angle so that it casts no shadow.

excellent ecological survey here in the 1930s, and it applies to a finger of land lying between the saltings of Poole Harbour and the sandy beach of Studland Bay. It extends northwards almost as far as South Haven Point, where a ferry takes motor traffic across the narrow harbour entrance to Sandbanks, now the southern tip of the greatly expanded Poole and Bournemouth conurbation.

Only a part of the peninsula is heathland. Broadleaved and coniferous woodland, scrub, sand dunes and wetlands make up the rest, while in the centre lies the Little Sea, a freshwater lake bordered by reedswamp, acid marsh and sallow carr. It is an important refuge for wildfowl, especially in winter, when over 2000 duck of 12 or more species can be present. Captain Diver's research showed that the sand dune system, which lies to the north and east of the lake, has only developed over the last four centuries. Building against the northern and southern ends of the narrower original peninsula, it gradu-

ally enclosed a saltwater lagoon, which eventually became the freshwater lake we see today.

In November 1980 the reserve was extended to include a much greater expanse of heath, containing several valley bogs of great botanical and entomological interest.

Dry heath On the better-drained ground, heather or ling is the dominant plant, mixed here and there with the earlier-flowering bell heather, and dwarf gorse, which flowers in late summer and autumn. The much taller common gorse, which also occurs here, is usually considered to flower the whole year through – hence the saying that kissing is in season when gorse is in bloom – but in Purbeck it makes a somewhat poor show in August and September. This, however, is the time when dwarf gorse is at its best, and it is joined by a second autumn-flowering species, the western gorse. This is mainly found on the west side of Britain, but in East Dorset its range overlaps with that of the dwarf gorse.

Gorse and heather are important to many of the heathland animals. Heather flowers are much visited by ants and bees, and one species of ant, *Tetramorium caespitum*, collects and stores the seeds. In the spring it feeds them, after chewing them into a soft pulp, to its grubs. The heather shoots are consumed by caterpillars of the silver-studded blue butterfly and several kinds of moth, including the oak eggar, fox moth, emperor moth, common heath, beautiful yellow underwing and true lover's knot.

Heather also supports plant life. One of the many heathland lichens, *Parmelia physodes*, grows on its woody stems, and sometimes whole tussocks are festooned with the reddish threads of dodder, a plant parasite which may also be found on dwarf gorse.

In spring the gorse flowers attract the green hairstreak butterfly, which lays its eggs on the petals, and on autumn mornings the bushes are hung with hundreds of dew-laden webs of the hammock spider, one of the many species of spider that prey on heathland invertebrates.

Left: A sand lizard displays its attractive markings. It is an inhabitant of the dry heaths and the sand dunes, for it cannot live in a place where there is no access to sand in which it can lay its eggs. The lizard feeds on the plentiful insect population of these habitats. It occurs in Dorset, Hampshire and a remote colony surviving in the north-west of England.

Lasius alienus, another heath-dwelling ant, collects the seeds of dwarf gorse and may well help to spread the plant. It eats a part of the seed which contains oil, leaving the rest undamaged and still able to germinate.

Ants play a vital part in the heathland ecology. Not only do they exploit the vegetation directly, but also indirectly by taking honeydew from sap-sucking aphids. In the absence of earthworms (which are not so numerous in the acid soil of the heaths as they are elsewhere), the ants are the most important soil excavators on the heath, and their mining activities improve the soil structure, to the benefit of the vegetation. They prey on a wide range of invertebrates, including other ants, and they can dispose of the occasional dead mammal, bird or reptile which they might find lying on the heath.

Bare ground Here and there are areas of bare sand – trackways, eroded slopes, excavations or the site of a serious fire. Such places are haunted by that fierce and fast-moving predator, the green tiger beetle, by various mining bees and sand wasps which burrow into the banks, and by the grayling butterfly.

Bare ground is often a convenient spot for reptiles to bask in the sunshine: the rare and beautiful sand lizard, which also needs bare sand in which to lay its eggs, and Studland's other reptilian speciality, the smooth snake. Both these animals are on the danger list, and have been given protection under the Wildlife and Countryside Act of 1981. Smooth snakes are, of course, harmless, and it is particularly sad that they should sometimes be killed in mistake for adders – which themselves became protected under the Act in 1991.

Birds A small bare or lichen-covered patch on the dry heath might provide a nesting site for the nightjar. This is a bird of the twilight. It spends the day time resting on the ground or perhaps a fallen tree branch, looking exactly like a piece of dead wood, but after sunset its low-pitched 'churring' song vibrates across the heath, and its silhouette may be seen gliding, floating and even hovering, in pursuit of moths, beetles and craneflies.

Birds are far from numerous on the heath, and the only species one is certain of seeing is the meadow pipit. Stonechats frequent some of the gorse patches, whereas the Dartford warbler, also found here, tends to conceal itself.

Wet heath The main botanical interest of the Dorset heathland lies in the wetter ground – the valley bogs, the bog pools, and the ill-drained slopes and hollows where the underlying deposit is of clay. Cross-leaved heath is the characteristic plant of these areas, but the rare Dorset heath is also found, often hybridising with the former species. In a number of places in Purbeck the Dorset heath is near to being abundant, but nationally it is an

Above: Resplendent with its green back and pink legs, the green tiger beetle is a fast running hunter of insects and other small animals on the heath.

Below: The bog asphodel is a member of the lily family, and grows from a rhizome in the wet ground of the hollows and in the valley bogs. It can spread into extensive patches, colouring the bogs with bright yellow in July.

extremely uncommon plant. Outside a restricted area in Dorset it occurs (in the British Isles) only at a few places in Cornwall, at one site in Devon, and in Connemara, Ireland. It is seen at its best in August and September, when the marsh gentians also appear. These are usually similar in colour to the spring gentian, with their deep blue trumpets, but occasionally a white one may be seen. The popular name is inappropriate, for this is not a plant of marshes, but of damp heath. At Studland it has a long flowering period, lasting from mid-August to early November.

The wetter ground is often covered with purple moor-grass, which provides nest-sites for the harvest mouse, the charming animal

Left: The Dartford warbler, breeding in the gorse thicket, is one of the most interesting species in Studland. It stays here and in other lowland heaths of southern England all through the winter. However, this is only the northernmost tip of its European range and an unusually hard winter can cause a catastrophic fall in numbers.

Opposite page: A green leaf hopper caught on the sticky hairs of a sundew. All three species of sundew are to be found on Studland's acid bogs.

usually shown in pictures clinging to a corn stalk. It is in fact an animal of tall grasses of all kinds, and not only the ones that we cultivate as cereals. The stems of the purple moor-grass are too weak to support the nest in the usual way, and it is therefore constructed in the yellow mass of dead leaves at the crown of the grass tussock.

Where there is a mixture of cross-leaved heath and purple moor-grass, you are likely to find two bush-crickets, the rather attractive brown-and-green bog bush-cricket and the short-winged conehead. They look superficially like grasshoppers, but have long antennae and the females have an ovipositor (egg-laying organ) shaped like a sword scabbard. Close examination of the flower-heads of cross-leaved heath may reveal the presence of a pink crab-spider, *Thomisus onustus*. Its colouring matches that of the flower, and it is ready to seize any unfortunate insect that is deceived by this resemblance. Amongst the predators operating at a lower level in this environment is a metallic green-and-red ground beetle, *Carabus nitens*.

Acid bogs Wet heath grades into bog, a spongy, shaking expanse of sphagnum moss with occasional pools. Bog cotton and the pleasantly aromatic bog myrtle grow here, and in July large areas are yellow with bog asphodel. Here are Britain's three species of sundew, plants which compensate for the poverty of the soil by digesting animal matter: they trap invertebrates with the sticky, enzyme-secreting hairs on their leaves. Other carnivorous plants which occur at Studland are the pale butterwort, which grows on the wet heath, and bladderwort, which is found in the bog pools.

These pools are inhabited by palmate newts and by various aquatic insects and their larvae. Dragonflies and damselflies are well represented, and of particular note are the handsome, but not uncommon, black sympetrum (*Sympetrum scoticum*) and, a southern rarity, the small red damselfly (*Ceriagrion tenellum*). While these and others patrol the air above the pools, the water surface itself is the hunting preserve of the raft spider (*Dolomedes fimbriatus*). This, in body size though not in leg-span, is the largest of our spiders, and it makes short work of any insect falling into the water.

Access The Studland Heath National Nature Reserve is freely open to visitors, but it is as well to keep mainly to the paths and trackways, some of which have been made by the resident roe deer. In this way you can avoid the discomfort of walking up to your knees in the bog, or causing unnecessary disturbance to ground-nesting birds and other wildlife. You should always be aware, too, of the serious fire hazard. There is so much of value in Studland that needs the watchful protection of warden and visitor alike, for this beautiful heathland deserves our greatest respect.

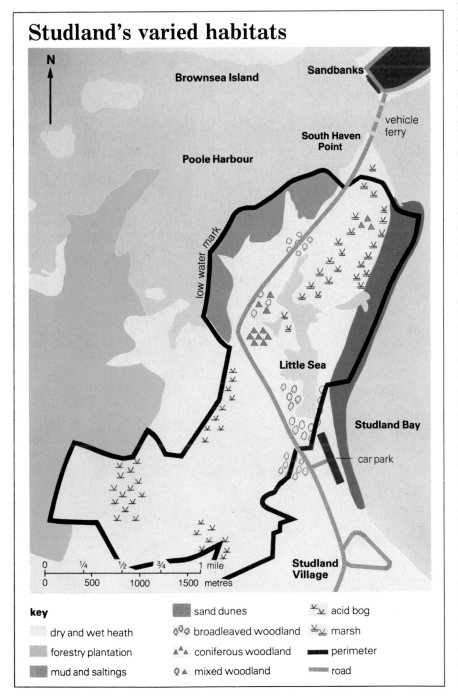

Studland's varied habitats

N

Brownsea Island

Sandbanks

vehicle ferry

South Haven Point

Poole Harbour

low water mark

Little Sea

Studland Bay

car park

| 0 | ¼ | ½ | ¾ | 1 mile |
| 0 | 500 | 1000 | 1500 | metres |

Studland Village

key

dry and wet heath

forestry plantation

mud and saltings

sand dunes

broadleaved woodland

coniferous woodland

mixed woodland

acid bog

marsh

perimeter

road

South-West England

Land's End to the Mendips

The West Country has a rugged splendour all its own, for it can claim some of Britain's finest coastlines, along with extensive stretches of bleak moorland, lush fens and dramatic gorges.

There is nothing subtle about the bleak, treeless, high moorland landscape of Dartmoor. The last great wild haven in southern Britain, Dartmoor extends to over 2000ft in height and is buffeted repeatedly by tearing south-west gales; its most prominent features are the granite outcrops weathered into tors. Apart from lichen, nothing much survives on the granite, but buzzards use the tors as lookout posts and kestrels and ravens breed on them. Golden plovers and dunlin nest on the higher moors, while snipe, lapwing and red grouse settle on the lower sites.

The West of England's other National Park – Exmoor – is much smaller than Dartmoor, but it has a rich mixture of upland and lowland habitats which support abundant wildlife; it is, for instance, one of the few places remaining in southern England where red deer can be seen in any numbers in the wild.

The unique flat landscape of the Somerset Levels presents a dramatic contrast to the wild uplands. In winter these lush wet meadows attract vast flocks of wildfowl – among them Bewick's swans and a host of wild ducks.

Rising sharply to the north-east of the Levels are the Mendip Hills, bisected by yet another different landform – the series of deep gorges running through the Carboniferous limestone. The most famous is Cheddar – home of the lovely Cheddar pink.

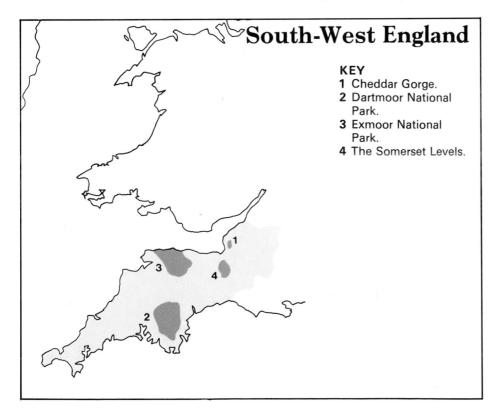

South-West England

KEY
1 Cheddar Gorge.
2 Dartmoor National Park.
3 Exmoor National Park.
4 The Somerset Levels.

Left: The ancient gnarled oaks festooned with ferns and hanging lichens and the huge moss-clad boulders of Wistman's Wood on Dartmoor carry an air of solitude and remoteness that is deeply mysterious — here birdsong and the trickle of running water are the only sounds to break the stillness.

Below: Pennywort, growing in cracks and crevices of rocks and walls, is particularly common in the West of England. Its round, fleshy leaves are easily recognisable from the little dimple in the centre of each.

CHEDDAR: NATURE'S ROCK GARDEN

Apart from its national fame as a beauty spot, Cheddar Gorge in the Mendips is renowned for its wealth of unusual and rare plants, but there are many insects and birds to be seen there as well, dwelling in a wide range of different habitats.

Below: Cheddar Gorge from the south side. Cheddar is special in having habitats never touched by man—the cliffs and cliff ledges in particular—in which such species as the rare Cheddar pink can flourish.

The Mendip Hills rise like a wall to the north of the Somerset Levels and, though they barely reach 300m (1000ft), they contain some of the most impressive rock scenery in Britain. The hills themselves are formed mainly from Carboniferous limestone—a much harder, older limestone than chalk—and in places have been eroded to form deep gorges or coombes, the most famous of which are the Avon Gorge, Ebbor Gorge, Burrington Coombe and, best-known of all, Cheddar Gorge. Among the dramatic cliffs and slopes of these gorges are the series of famous Cheddar Caves.

The Gorge The gorge itself is about 2.5km (1½ miles) long and runs almost east-west through the valley, continuing up into the hills and gradually becoming shallower and less dramatic. The road follows the gorge through its most spectacular part, but turns away at Black Rock, leaving the upper part of the main valley quiet and peaceful.

The cliffs in the lower part tower almost sheer to a height of about 120m (400ft) above the valley floor, and are particularly impressive from the south side. Where they are not sheer from the top to the road, the cliffs on the south side drop in a series of spurs and ledges. The north or north-west slopes are gentler, though broken by frequent smaller cliffs and rock slopes. Both north and south sides provide a wide range of habitats, many of them quite inaccessible, and the result is a natural rock garden on a grand scale.

Cliff-top plants The inaccessible ledges are rich with a mixture of limestone grassland, cliff and woodland plant species. They are now the main (if not only) home of the lovely Cheddar pink, which still grows in fair numbers but which was once much more widespread. Since 1975 it has been one of the elite group of totally protected species—it is now illegal to pick any part of the plant (including the seeds), or to uproot it, without a licence. Some of the other plants of this habitat are almost as rare. Particularly notable species include several of our very rare native whitebeam/wild service tree hybrids (some of which occur only in the British Isles), though the common whitebeam is found here, too.

One of the most interesting species of these cliff areas is the cut-leaved self-heal, discovered for the first time in the wild in Britain at Cheddar in 1906. This species is still very rare, found in only a few localities in Britain, yet it is still not really certain whether it is a native plant or not. The particular feature giving rise to this uncertainty is the odd fact that, though the plant often occurs as the pure species, it gradually hybridises with the widespread common self-heal, until only the hybrid occurs, with none of the original rarer species remaining. The presence of the original species suggests that it has not been in Britain very long, and that new populations are arising from garden escapes, or from other sources.

A species widespread and common on the cliffs (and elsewhere in the gorge), though absent from the rest of Somerset, is the lesser meadow-rue, an inconspicuous plant though one that is attractive on closer inspection of its maidenhair fern-like leaves and delicate wind-pollinated flowers. There are many other species of interest in these upper cliffs as well, including the beautiful bloody crane's-bill, orpine, rock-rose, Welsh poppy and nettle-leaved bellflower.

The north slopes are much less dramatic than the south, being more akin to steep, limestone grassland, albeit with outcrops of rock and scree. Many of the plants are the same as on the south side, though the rare yellow rock stonecrop is particularly abundant here, and many uncommon scrub and grassland species, such as the green-winged and early purple orchids, the pale St John's wort and the mountain sedge, are at their finest here.

Parasitic speciality Another plant that can be found on the cliffs of Cheddar is a peculiar little species called the ivy broomrape. Ivy tumbles down parts of the limestone cliffs in great curtains, and in a few places where its roots are near the surface the rare ivy broomrape grows on it. The broomrapes are a group of parasitic plants that attach themselves to the roots of their host, deriving the whole of their nutritive requirements from them. Consequently they have no need of green leaves and their visible parts consist simply of a brownish or pinkish spike of flowers.

Woodland and caves Higher up, around and above Black Rock, the gorge becomes more wooded, with fine, though rather stunted, ash, oak and wych elm woods with quite a different range of species. A few plants—orpine and spotted orchid for instance—grow both in the woods and on the cliff ledges, but there is also an abundance of the more specialised woodland plants, such as herb paris, hart's tongue and other ferns, and rarities like the narrow-lipped helleborine and

Above: One of Cheddar's many caves, with stalactites and stalagmites. Note the green algal growth flourishing on the walls.

Left: Cheddar's cliffs are frequented by a variety of birds, although the pressure of visitors keeps their numbers down. Jackdaws fly in large flocks over the gorge, ravens breed sporadically there, peregrine falcons have had an eyrie on the cliffs for many years, and sparrowhawks (shown here) can also be spotted.

A gorge/cave system

There are various theories about the origin of Cheddar Gorge. It could be the result of a collapsed cave system, or a chasm caused by earth movements. However, it is now generally thought to have been formed by stream or river erosion, probably in two stages. The initial gorge may have been formed by a river flowing from the Mendip plateau and eroding the limestone, eventually finding its way down a swallow hole and carving through the porous limestone until it developed caves (right) and sank underground to follow a new course. Then, during and soon after the most recent glacial periods, the caves filled with silt and froze solid, the melt water from the snows and ice of the hills being channelled down the gorge every spring and summer and cutting it deeper and deeper.

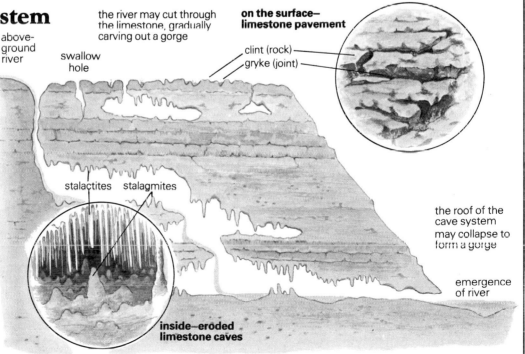

the river may cut through the limestone, gradually carving out a gorge

on the surface—limestone pavement

above-ground river

swallow hole

clint (rock)
gryke (joint)

stalactites stalagmites

the roof of the cave system may collapse to form a gorge

emergence of river

inside—eroded limestone caves

Above: Among the riot of flowers on Cheddar's upper cliffs can be found the small but attractive rock-rose. Accompanying it may be the Welsh poppy (also with yellow flowers), orpine, bloody crane's-bill and nettle-leaved bellflower.

Opposite page: Cheddar's vertical cliffs are made of carboniferous limestone and reach up to 120m (400ft) high. Here ash, ivy and several species of *Sorbus* are widespread.

Left: The species for which Cheddar is justly famed – the beautiful Cheddar pink.

Below: The limestone-rich grasslands of Cheddar are frequented by a variety of butterflies – including this marbled white.

quarter of a mile in from the entrance, depending entirely on illumination from the artificial lights provided to guide visitors.

Too many visitors, too little grazing In spite of the tremendous level of natural history interest throughout the gorge, the area has certain problems, deriving essentially from two main sources – the vast number of visitors and the lack of grazing on the slopes.

Remarkable numbers of people visit Cheddar every year, and though most stay around the main attractions and developments in the lower gorge, many find their way on to the cliffs and slopes. The problems this has caused for rarities like the Cheddar pink are numerous – including casual picking, and the devastating wholesale uprooting and removal to gardens and nurseries. Although the pink has been protected since 1975 and is beginning to recover, it is unfortunate that not everyone observes the law concerning it, nor is necessarily even aware of the prohibition. The slopes of the gorge are deceptively steep – not only is climbing dangerous, it causes serious soil erosion and damage to the ledges. Another rare species, the mossy saxifrage, has not been seen in Cheddar since before the drought in 1976. Although it was the drought that caused its final demise, there is little doubt that previous collecting reduced its population to a size where it was very vulnerable.

The slopes of the gorge were once grazed heavily by sheep, rabbits and goats, but now there is virtually no grazing at all. The result is that coarser grasses and scrub are steadily replacing the species-rich grasslands and ledges which have depended on grazing for their existence in the past. There is no immediate danger of all the rarities disappearing, but the changes are considerable and seemingly inexorable.

the parasitic toothwort here and there. Woodland birds include redstarts, wood warblers, all three woodpecker species, nuthatches and many others.

The uppermost valley is a beautiful mosaic of woodlands, scrub and sheltered, species-rich limestone grasslands which, not surprisingly, support abundant butterflies and other insects. Some 30 species of butterflies have been recorded for the valley as a whole, two of the most attractive and conspicuous in the upper valley being the dark green fritillary and the marbled white.

There are many small caves throughout the area, but the best-known ones are the two open to the public – Cox's Cave and Gough's Cave, of which Gough's is the larger.

The caves are of particular interest to the naturalist for two main reasons. The first is their population of bats, including the greater and lesser horseshoes, which find sanctuary in the vast system of constant-temperature caves. The second point of interest to look out for is the way that ferns, mosses and liverworts have colonized the caves as far as a

DARTMOOR: HIGH, WILD AND REMOTE

The largest and highest of south-west England's upland regions, Dartmoor–a wild, bleak area of bog and moorland with few settlements–is best known for its granite tors and literary associations which have given it a mysterious and dangerous character.

In 1951 some 945sq km (365sq miles) of Dartmoor were designated as Britain's fourth National Park. This area includes the whole of the old Royal Forest, the common lands around it and also areas of 'in-country' (often of great beauty) which are transitional between moorland and lower-lying agricultural land. Large parts of the north of the moor are military training areas and firing ranges (though the area covered by these used to be much larger), only open to the public when not in use by the military.

A granite landscape Dartmoor is largely made up of granite. In fact, the granitic core represents the stumps of a range of much higher mountains into which the granite was intruded in molten form as the mountains were uplifted by folding. All that remains today is the hard core, since all the overlying rocks have long since eroded away; even the granite core is gradually being whittled down by chemical and physical erosion. The great heat of the molten granite when it was intruded melted or baked the surrounding

Below: There are not many places left in the British Isles where you can see wild daffodils–collectors and tourists have picked too many of them in the past–but Dartmoor National Park is one of the favoured few sites. Steps Bridge, in particular, is a good place to look for them. Spring, of course, is the time to seek these lovely wild flowers. If you see any, make quite certain that you don't harm any of the plants. This rule does, of course, hold good for any wild plants you may come across–even if the plants appear in a particular spot in profusion, they may be extremely rare–or even non-existent–elsewhere.

existing rocks, and this circle of altered rocks–the 'metamorphic aureole', as it is called–can still be detected in the rocks around the moor.

At about the same time, or a little later, numerous vapours pervaded the surrounding rocks and the cooling granite, giving rise to many mineral deposits, as well as the vast deposits of china clay around the moor which consist essentially of altered granite.

The granite has a number of peculiar properties that account for many of the moor's characteristics. It weathers rather easily into a moderately fertile to infertile soil called 'growan' where the granite is particularly rotten, though this soil becomes acid and

infertile in the high rainfall conditions of the moor. Because the rotted granite is quite soft, it does not weather into cliffs, so steep-sided valleys are rare, except where bands of harder granite pass across a valley, such as at Tavy Cleave. Harder patches of granite stand out as 'tors', usually at the top of hills, and are often weathered into fantastic shapes. Here and there are outcrops of different rocks which may provide a sharp contrast–for example, the steep hill of Brent Tor (345m/1130ft) on the western edge of the Park, crowned by its ancient church, is an eroded mass of hard volcanic lava.

Altitude and climate The two other related features of Dartmoor, which give it its distinctive character and which have allowed it to survive for so long, are its altitude and its climate. Much of the moor consists of an undulating dissected plateau at about 400-460m (1300-1500ft), although it rises to over 610m (2000ft) in two places in the north–Yes Tor lies at 619m (2030ft) and High Willhays lies at 621m (2038ft)–and many of the hills around Cranmere Pool in the north-west lie at about 580m (1900ft). The south and east of the moor are generally lower, though even there are occasional hills reaching 490m (1600ft) or 520m (1700ft) in height. One such is Ryder's Hill, at 515m (1690ft). Although hardly comparable with the mountains of northern Britain, this represents the highest

Above: A view of the River Dart in May–with the young leaves on the trees still fresh and light green in colour. Although most people associate Dartmoor with bleak, exposed moorland, there are numerous wooded river valleys which have rich soils on which a wide variety of plants can flourish. The woodland trees provide numerous birds with nesting holes and the clean air permits the growth of a host of lichens, liverworts and mosses.

land mass in southern England.

Inevitably, this high altitude has given rise to a climate markedly colder and wetter than that of the surrounding lowlands. In general, this part of south-west England is very mild, so the climate of Dartmoor is not as severe as in areas further north, though it is harsh enough to make agriculture very difficult. The rainfall at Princetown, for instance, at a height of 414m (1359ft), averages about 2160mm (85in) per year. The higher parts of the moor on the west side probably have an even higher rainfall, while the lower eastern areas probably have considerably less.

Dartmoor's upland bogs Although many parts of the moor have been cultivated at some time in the past, the greater part of the moor is now covered by heathland, acidic grassland and bog, with patches of woodland in the deeper valleys, especially around the edge of the moor.

The high hills and plateaux are mainly dominated by huge areas of bog, with heathland or moorland on the drier areas. The bogs, immortalised (not to say exaggerated!) in Conan Doyle's *The Hound of the Baskervilles*, tend to be dominated by a few

species of plants–the bog mosses, two species of cottongrass, various rushes, and cross-leaved heath. The general appearance is one of uniformity, though in fact many of the moor's most interesting plants occur in, or associated with, bogs. The yellow lily-like spikes of bog asphodel, for instance, may be abundant and obvious, often growing with bog pimpernel and the common and intermediate sundews.

In the wetter 'flushes', where the level of

Above: Wheatears can be found in the stonier parts of Dartmoor's heather-clad moorland. Shown here are three juveniles outside their nest hole.

Below: Dartmoor ponies grazing, with Haytor rising grim and menacing in the distance.

Left: A typical view of Dartmoor's heathery hill slopes. This view looks over Headland Warren near Birch Tor.

Below: Underneath the South-west Peninsula of England lies an enormous elongated core or batholith of granite which was pushed up, or intruded, into the overlying sedimentary rock some 290 million years ago. In six places this great batholith apears above the land surface in the shape of huge plateaux or upland areas of granite which, because they are harder than the surrounding rock, have tended to withstand the forces of erosion better. Dartmoor is the largest of these, while the offshore Isles of Scilly form the smallest.

nutrients is higher and there is a greater flow of water, the beautiful pale butterwort occurs, with its pale lilac flowers and rosettes of pale green insect-trapping leaves. The rare bog orchid is very occasionally found on the wettest bog moss areas, though it is so inconspicuous that it could easily be over-looked. An even rarer orchid was found some years ago—the Irish lady's tresses; it is confined to just a few places in western Britain, although it has not been seen on Dartmoor for several years now. One other uncommon western species occurring along some of the high streams, as well as lower down in the valleys, is the attractively named (though rather disappointing looking) Corn-ish moneywort, which trails over the ground in very humid areas.

The bird life of these high bog areas is limited though interesting. The collection of breeding birds consists mainly of curlew, skylarks and meadow pipits, though golden plover and dunlin are recorded very occasion-ally, and common sandpipers nest sparingly along the streams.

Insects, too, are limited, though the lower valley bogs have a more varied fauna, among which dragonflies are prominent. The hardiest is the large golden-ringed dragonfly, which can be seen high up the moorland streams, while the hawkers, darters and common damselflies tend to stay lower in the valleys, away from the windswept tops.

Heather moorland and tors The drier areas of the high moor are usually covered by wet or dry heath, grading into bog on the wetter areas, and changing gradually to grassland where the peat is more fertile and less waterlogged. There are extensive areas of

Granite in the SW Peninsula

Scilly Isles   Land's End   Carnmenellis   St Austell   Bodmin Moor   Dartmoor

INTRUDED GRANITE BATHOLITH

Tor formation

The granite of Dartmoor is heavily jointed, the joint pattern including closely spaced and widely spaced areas (**1**). About 25 million years ago the area that is now Dartmoor was under the influence of a much warmer (almost tropical) climate than that of Britain today (as shown by fossil remains).
This produced very deep weathering of the granite, but it was not uniform, the closer joints weathering more rapidly than the wider (**2**). The tors were formed largely underground in the area of the widely spaced joints and were exposed by later (possibly Ice Age) erosion (**3**).

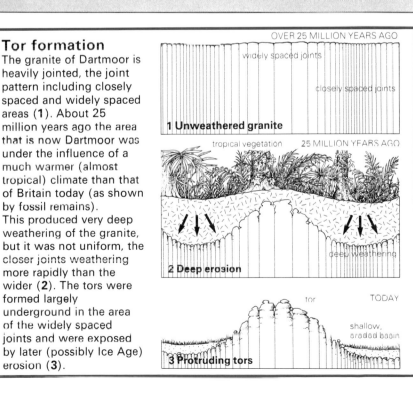

OVER 25 MILLION YEARS AGO

widely spaced joints

closely spaced joints

1 Unweathered granite

tropical vegetation   25 MILLION YEARS AGO

deep weathering

2 Deep erosion

tor   TODAY

shallow, eroded basin

3 Protruding tors

Above: Dartmoor (and Exmoor too) is fortunate in being largely pollution-free. This is particularly evident in the crystal clear streams of the area. This moorland stream near Belstone is a perfect example. (The red-berried tree in the centre is a rowan, or mountain ash.)

Below: A plant to look for in the woodland valleys of Dartmoor National Park – the attractive ivy-leaved bellflower.

heather moor, though it is rarely uniform, and there are usually some patches of grass, bracken, gorse, bog or rock with it, according to the conditions and its past management. Some parts are a riot of colour in late summer as the ling, bell heather and western gorse all flower together, and the whole impenetrable sward is often densely covered by the pink strands of the parasitic dodder. Here and there among the heather there are patches of clubmosses, particularly the stag's-horn club-moss.

The commonest birds by far on the heather moor are the meadow pipits and skylarks: for example, one survey of 132 hectares (326 acres) revealed 94 meadow pipits, 78 skylarks

and nothing else–except one stonechat and one cuckoo (which regularly uses meadow pipit nests here). In fact, both stonechats and whinchats are reasonably widespread where there is taller vegetation, and wheatears occur as well, particularly in the stonier areas or along walls. Ring ouzels breed sparingly, often where there are rocky outcrops at the heads of valleys, and wrens are common in the same habitat.

Walkers on the moor occasionally come across a large bright green and black caterpillar. This is the larva of the beautiful emperor moth, which flies on the moor during the spring. Almost as striking, and rather commoner, are the bristle-covered caterpillars of the fox moth, frequently parasitised by ichneumons. One of the most conspicuous insects is the attractive bumble bee *Bombus lapponicus*, a northern species which comes this far south only on the highest hills. Dor beetles are frequent and obvious as they bumble about searching for dung, usually in the evening but occasionally during the day. The butterflies most often found are the small heath, meadow brown and common blue.

The tors, which rise above the moors, are virtually devoid of life, except that they provide an ideal substrate for numerous lichens, a foothold for a few ferns and cover for various invertebrates such as bristletails and harvestmen. Below them there are often extensive areas of scree or 'clitter'; these may be almost completely bare where they are new or very unstable, while in other places they provide the ideal habitat for woodland to develop, with the seedling trees temporarily sheltered from grazing.

Dartmoor's woodlands Although the moors and tors are the most obvious and best known features of Dartmoor, there are numerous woodlands, particularly around the edge of the moor, which are havens for wildlife. There are a number of high altitude oakwoods, such as Black Tor Copse and Wistman's Wood, which are exceptionally interesting ecologically as examples of woods growing under extreme conditions. Lower down, though, where the valleys deepen as they leave the moorland, there are extensive and beautiful oakwoods, around the Bovey Valley for instance, where Yarner Wood National Nature Reserve lies, and also in the middle reaches of the Rivers Dart and Webburn. The higher parts of these woods are usually sessile oak, while lower down the soil is richer and common, or pedunculate, oak becomes dominant, together with a richer ground flora.

Most of these woods are excellent habitats for breeding birds, with plenty of holes for such species as redstarts, stock doves and pied flycatchers, while other species—from buzzards to wood warblers—are common. They are enthralling places in the early summer, alive with bird-song and flowers. Perhaps not surprisingly in the clean humid air of south Devon, they are also rich in lichens, mosses and liverworts, often growing in profusion over the trees as well as the ground.

So, although one's first impressions of Dartmoor may be of uniformity and barrenness, in reality it is a varied landscape providing habitats for an enormous range of plants and animals. However, the landscape is not quite as stable and unchanging as it first appears. Extensive forestry planting has altered the character of many an open hillside, while the combination of overgrazing and overburning is progressively altering areas of moorland towards grassland or bracken. Nevertheless, Dartmoor substantially remains an unspoilt wild island high above the soft farmland of Devon.

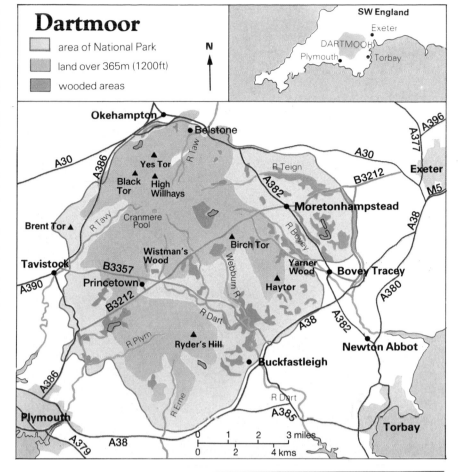

Dartmoor

area of National Park

land over 365m (1200ft)

wooded areas

N

SW England

Exeter

DARTMOOR

Plymouth   Torbay

Okehampton

Belstone

Yes Tor

Black Tor   High Willhays

Brent Tor

R Tavy

Cranmere Pool

Wistman's Wood

Birch Tor

Yarner Wood

Tavistock

B3357

Princetown

Haytor

Bovey Tracey

B3212

R Plym

Ryder's Hill

Newton Abbot

Buckfastleigh

R Dart

Plymouth

R Erme

A38

A385

Torbay

0   1   2   3 miles

0   2   4 kms

Moretonhampstead

R Teign

R Bovey

Webburn R

R Dart

R Taw

Above: A map of Dartmoor National Park, showing some of the places of interest. Remember that Dartmoor is a bleak, exposed and lonely place and never set off for picnics or walking tours without a good map, suitable footwear and adequate clothing and other provisions. Beware, in particular, of the treacherous upland bogs and the mists that can fall with frightening rapidity.

Right: This slug, *Arion ater*, does well in the damp, mild atmosphere of Dartmoor and is easy to find on the high moors in damp weather.

Left: A female emperor moth resting on gorse; she most often flies by night. The males of this magnificent moth are on the wing in daylight, and can be seen flying at speed among the heather on Dartmoor in April and May. The emperor moth caterpillar—bright green with black markings—feeds on a variety of plants, including sloe, sallow, heather and bramble.

Above: A view of Exmoor, near Five Barrows Cross.

HEATHERY EXMOOR

Exmoor National Park, on the borders of Somerset and Devon, is a beautiful compact area of hilly country with a very definite upland character, even though it has no mountains.

Right: The insect life of Exmoor is rather sparse but interesting: a number of northern species find their southernmost locality here, and in some cases there exists both the northern race (persisting as a 'glacial' relic) and the southern race (occurring as a later colonizer). For example, the typical oak eggar moth occurs in the lowlands, while the northern eggar appears on the moors.

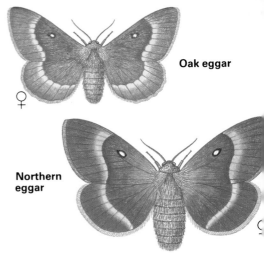

Oak eggar

Northern eggar

Collectively this National Park includes the whole of Exmoor, with the old Royal Forest, together with much of the Brendon Hills which lie to the east of the main mass. Exmoor is probably best described as a dissected plateau, with large areas of undulating moorland at between 365m and 455m (1200-1500ft) in height, rising to 520m (1708ft) at Dunkery Beacon, and deep, steep-sided valleys carrying the rivers north to the Bristol Channel or south to the English Channel.

The contrast between the high, treeless moorland and the deep, usually wooded valleys is one of the chief attractions of Exmoor. In addition, though, it has a feature which is unrivalled elsewhere in England – a 46km (29 mile) coast stretching from Minehead to Combe Martin and consisting of an almost unbroken line of hog's back cliffs, rising in places to over 365m (1200ft).

The high moorlands The high plateau and hills support a mixture of heather-dominated moorland or *Molinia* grass moorland, much of which has been converted, over the last 150 years, to rather poor pasture; the process is still continuing, giving rise to considerable controversy. The heather moorland consists mainly of ling, with smaller amounts of gorse of two species – common gorse and western gorse. The dwarf western gorse grows to the same height as the heather, and many of the coastal hills support a patchwork of gorse and heather – beautiful to look at in summer but almost impossible to walk through.

One high remote area of the moor is known evocatively as 'The Chains', it is a wild, lonely area with a rainfall of over 1980mm (80in), and consists of extensive stretches of bog and some 60ha (150 acres) of deer sedge – the largest such area of deer sedge in southern England. It is the source of most of the moor's rivers, including the Exe and the Barle.

Oak woodlands and river valleys Where the moorland drops steeply into the valleys, or towards the coast, the vegetation frequently changes dramatically. Most of these steeper slopes are clothed with beautiful ancient oak woodlands, although in places they have been 'reclaimed' or planted with conifers. The abrupt ending of the woodlands at 305-365m (1000-1200ft) is partly a natural tree-line, but it is also caused by heavy grazing and burning on the high moors.

The woods consist mainly of oaks – sessile oak towards the top and common oak lower down, and hybrids between the two – although in places there are stands of wych elm, ash, birch and rowan, with other trees such as small-leaved lime, maple and some rare whitebeams occurring very sparingly. The soils are almost all acid, deriving from the parent sandstones and slates, which limits the range of species that can do well.

The rivers that flow down the valleys are beautiful clear, clean streams full of small brown trout. There are virtually no sources of pollution here, especially in the northern

Right: Although acid tolerant species such as heather and gorse dominate Exmoor, there are also many rarer plants such as the pale butterwort pictured here, which occurs in several bogs or hillside 'flushes' on Exmoor. Flowering from June to October, the insectivorous butterwort has long-stemmed flowers and distinctive yellow-green leaves which form a basal rosette. The leaves are covered with thousands of microscopic hairs. Any insect landing on the leaf is trapped by the sticky hairs while the leaf margins roll inwards to enclose it. A thick digestive fluid is then produced to break down the insect's body so the plant can absorb the nutrients. Once the digestive process is completed, the leaf re-opens.

Below: A buzzard with its prey – a rabbit. Buzzards can be seen almost everywhere on Exmoor.

the area of interesting habitat has contracted steadily over the years as agricultural activities have eaten into it, but it is still a fine bird haunt and the home of a number of coastal plants, though many less than there used to be. Hurlestone Point, to the east, is a good site for coastal lichens.

Flora and fauna The animal and plant life of Exmoor is an intriguing mixture of upland and lowland. It is not excessively rich in rare species-for example, there is no limestone of any significance where rare plants might occur-but there are many species growing here that barely occur elsewhere in southern England, and a few specialities that are virtually confined to Exmoor.

Among the mammals, two are particularly notable. First-and probably most famous-is the red deer. An indigenous population of 600-1000 animals occurs on the moor, separated into a number of more or less distinct herds. They behave here as woodland animals-their traditional haunt-unlike the Scottish red deer which have had to move out into the open. The other well known mammal is the Exmoor pony which, though by no means abundant, is probably the most interesting of our 'wild' ponies. Otters, too, can be found but are difficult to spot.

The bird life is sparse, except in the combes (valleys), but fascinating. Merlins still nest on the high moorlands, though they are now very rare. Black grouse are native but rare and declining, while red grouse were introduced many years ago and have persisted here and there. Buzzards are everywhere, and ravens are by no means uncommon, their deep 'honking' call often being heard on fine spring and summer days, while the clear call of ring ouzels can be heard in some of the high rocky valleys. In the deep wooded valleys, such as Horner Combe, or near Tarr Steps, the air is

rivers which arise on the high moor and flow straight into the sea a few miles away. The rivers therefore support caddisflies, mayflies, stoneflies and dragonflies-just as an upland river should. They are also notable spawning grounds for salmon and trout, and there are many small falls where salmon can be watched leaping their way up to the gravelly redds to spawn.

Coastal riches In many ways the coast is the most exciting of the habitats that make up Exmoor. It is clothed for part of its length by beautiful woodland that is slightly more species-rich than the inland woods because of the eroding, less acidic soils. The more open areas support heather moorland, usually with bell-heather rather than ling because of the better drainage, and often with banks of rhododendron or clumps of gorse. The cliffs themselves, mostly of red sandstone, are broken and eroded and make poor seabird breeding sites, with just a few colonies in one or two places along the coast.

Here and there the coast is broken by a valley, the largest and most interesting of which is the vale of Porlock. Porlock used to be a port but is now a mile or so inland and parts of the former sea-bed are now used to grow arable crops. The outer margin of the vale is formed by an enormous coarse shingle bank, virtually devoid of life; just inland, however, lies an area of tiny saltmarshes, reed-beds and lakes, and old pasture. Sadly,

Above: There is a native population of some 600-1000 red deer on Exmoor.

Below: A dipper at the edge of a swift stream. Often seen along Exmoor's rivers, this bird nests under bridges or overhanging rocks.

Above: Heather moor under Dunkery Beacon. This beacon is the highest point on Exmoor, reaching 520m (1708ft), but it is rounded and smooth rather than craggy, and is dissected by myriads of small streams. In late summer Dunkery Beacon is purple with the blooms of heather.

Below: This map shows the extent of the National Park, with some of the main features of interest.

alive with birdsong in spring and summer. The gnarled old trees provide nest sites for many less common birds, such as redstart, pied flycatcher, stock dove and wood warbler, as well as for many of the more usual woodland birds.

The plant life is dominated by the widespread common species that are tolerant of acid conditions; they include heather, gorse, flying bent, cottongrass and so on, but here and there, usually in small numbers, there are many plants of interest. The flora in general has elements of northern, southern and western species. Pale butterwort can be found in several boggy areas, while Irish spurge, another western species, occurs here in one of its

few mainland localities. Crowberry, lesser twayblade, Welsh poppy, and stag's-horn clubmoss are examples of northern species with small populations on Exmoor, though the clubmoss has been declining for many years. The parsley fern, a former inhabitant, appears to have succumbed to the 1976 drought—such events are a common problem to plants at the edge of their range. Other species of interest include bastard balm, now confined to one or two localities, and wood vetch, which is abundant in places along the coast. There is also a rare whitebeam growing along the north coast and nowhere else in the world, and the attractive rock stonecrop, too, is common along parts of the coast.

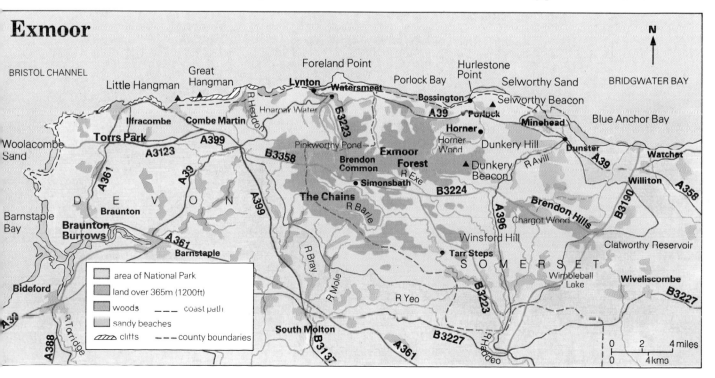

Exmoor

N

BRISTOL CHANNEL

Little Hangman
Great Hangman
Foreland Point
Lynton
Watersmeet
Porlock Bay
Hurlestone Point
Selworthy Sand
BRIDGWATER BAY

Ifracombe
Combe Martin
R Heddon
Hoaroak Water
Bossington
Selworthy Beacon
A39
Porlock
Minehead
Blue Anchor Bay

Torrs Park
A399
B3223
Horner
Horner Wood
Dunkery Hill
Dunster
Watchet

Woolacombe Sand
A3123
A361
Pinkworthy Pond
Exmoor Forest
Dunkery Beacon
R Avill
A39
Williton
A358

D E V O N
A39
B3358
Brendon Common
R Exe
B3224
Brendon Hills
B3190

Barnstaple Bay
Braunton
A399
Simonsbath
Chargot Wood
Clatworthy Reservoir

Braunton Burrows
A361
The Chains
R Barle
Winsford Hill
A396

Bideford
Barnstaple
R Bray
Tarr Steps
S O M E R S E T
Wimbleball Lake
Wiveliscombe

R Mole
R Yeo
B3223
B3227

R Torridge
South Molton
B3131
A361
B3227
R Haddeo

A388
A388

area of National Park
land over 365m (1200ft)
woods --- coast path
sandy beaches
clitts --- county boundaries

0 2 4 miles
0 4 kms

SOMERSET'S FLOOD MEADOW COUNTRY

Between the Mendips and the Quantocks there is an enormous area of low-lying marshy land known as the Somerset Levels. It consists of the flood plains of the Rivers Parrett, Brue and Axe, that together form one of the most important wetlands in Britain.

Strictly speaking, the area generally known as the 'Somerset Levels'–covering some 57,000 hectares (140,000 acres)–consists of two quite distinct areas: the Levels themselves are an 8-9½km (5-6 mile) wide belt of land running along the coast, while the remaining low-lying valleys inland of this, mainly covered by peat, are known as the Somerset Moors.

The greater part of the Moors is barely above sea-level, except for the various hills and 'islands' (including Glastonbury Tor) within them, yet the coastal levels are some 2-3m (7-10ft) higher, because of a thick capping of marine clay laid down during Roman times. Inevitably, this capping acts as a

dam, hindering the free drainage of water from the Moors into the Bristol Channel a difficulty made greater because of the huge tidal range of the sea here (the second highest in the world). High tide levels can be over 3.6m (12ft) higher than the level of much of the moors, and – although the sea is prevented from actually flooding across nowadays – this stops the rivers from discharging their load for up to four hours at a time.

The obvious consequences of this unusual physical situation are, first, that the rivers are prone to flooding in times of heavy rainfall, especially if this coincides with a period of high tides; and secondly, that the water table throughout the Moors is kept high and often very close to the surface. Although the rainfall on the Moors and Levels themselves is quite low, their catchment area is much larger and includes such areas as the South Mendips which has quite a high rainfall. The volume of water reaching the moors during a wet period can, therefore, be very large, and the existing network of rivers, channels and ditches (known as rhynes) is simply inadequate to hold it.

Parts of this huge area were once acidic raised bog, well above the level of the more calcareous ground water, but now only small, incomplete fragments of this occur, at Shapwick Moor, for instance.

The value of the area to wildlife and nature conservation lies in two spheres, one par-

Above: Parts of the Somerset Moors consisted of acidic raised bog, and there has been a long history of peat cutting in the area. Peat is still cut today, using modern methods and machines.

Left: Bog pimpernel, easily identifiable by its small, pale pink flowers, is one of the rarer plants worth searching for on the Moors.

Opposite page: Flower filled meadows bordering a rhyne – a drainage channel – in Sedgemoor in June. Perhaps one of the most striking features of the present-day landscape, this vast interconnecting system of rhynes is of great value to wildlife. Although some are very old in origin, the great majority date from the 18th century, as part of the general pattern of enclosure. The total area of this unusual wildlife resource, including the main ditches and rivers, is estimated to be about 610 hectares (1500 acres).

Right: Another plant to look for on the Levels is the adder's tongue fern. This strange-looking plant, which flourishes on damp grassland, bears spore cases on the top 4–6cm ($1\frac{1}{2}$–$2\frac{1}{2}$in) of the stem. Its supposed similarity to the tongue of a snake led people to believe that this plant could cure snake bites – unfortunately not true.

ticularly dependent on winter flooding, the other on a high summer water table, though naturally the two are interlinked.

Winter flooding In winter parts of the Moors flood frequently. This can happen either because the rivers become full and water from the adjacent land can no longer be pumped into them; or because they become overfull and burst their banks. The net result is broadly similar, except that the latter is more devastating to agriculture and tends to be deeper over a wider area.

In a good year (ornithologically speaking) these vast flooded areas over pasture attract enormous numbers of birds, feeding both on the invertebrates brought close to the surface and on the seeds of submerged plants. The area was once particularly important for wildfowl, though it is somewhat less so now. Today, the area as a whole still attracts sizeable numbers of Bewick's swans, together with large flocks of wintering teal, mallard, shoveler and wigeon feeding particularly on the meadow plant seeds. At the same time, huge numbers of waders, especially lapwings, golden plover, whimbrel, snipe, dunlin and ruff, are attracted to the shallow flooded areas by the invertebrates close to the surface. There are also large wintering flocks of thrushes over the Moors, feeding along the hedges or in the drier pastures.

Flower-filled meadows As the winter floods subside, and the wintering or passage birds

leave for their summer breeding grounds, the Moors take on a new aspect. The main land use of the meadows is for hay, followed by grazing, and by late May or early June the richer meadows are a blaze of colour.

Because of the differences in soil (particularly whether there is clay over the peat, its depth, and if it is calcareous), and in water levels and past management, no two meadows are exactly the same. Some may be full of orchids, including the southern marsh, fragrant, frog and green-winged orchids. Others may be dominated by tussocks of purple moor-grass and bushes of bog myrtle, often with masses of meadow thistle and heath spotted orchids poking through the green carpet. Elsewhere, where remnants of the old raised bog still exist, a more acidic, heathy vegetation has developed, varying from acid grassland through heath to areas of wet bog. In these situations a whole group of uncommon plants occurs, including marsh pea, marsh fern, lesser bladderwort and milk parsley. The richer parts of the Moors also support sizeable concentrations of breeding birds, particularly waders, for which it is reckoned to be the best area in south-west England. The main species seen there are lapwings, redshanks, snipe and curlews, though there are rarer waders, too. At the same time the Moors are important for their sizeable breeding populations of whinchats and yellow wagtails.

Above: A flock of Bewick's swans overwintering on the Somerset Levels near Long Sutton. They, and a whole host of other birds, come to the Levels in winter to take advantage of the mass of invertebrates brought up near the surface by flooding.

Below: Pollarded willow trees line the banks of rhynes all over the Somerset Levels and provide a safe habitat for insects, birds and even small mammals.

The drainage ditches The rhynes between the fields are another vital part of the tapestry of the Moors. Traditionally, they are managed by being cleared of vegetation every four or five years. This is ideal for wildlife, providing a patchwork of vegetation at different stages. Some are almost stagnant, while others are faster-flowing, and overall almost all of the water plants that could occur in southern Britain do so somewhere or other in the rhyne or river systems of the Moors.

Of particular interest are sizeable populations of the rare rootless duckweed, the beautiful flowering rush, frog-bit, fine-leaved water dropwort and the water violet, making the ditches teem with flowers.

farmers have not considered it worthwhile to drain their fields, although a number have done so in areas that are flooded less.

It is, however, now technically feasible to reduce the flood risk considerably by complex (and extremely costly) schemes, which will prevent all but the most unusual of floods. In recent years, large-scale works have taken place, embanking rivers, pumping ditches and gradually drying out the area. Because of this work, the general water levels have dropped and individual farmers have tended to remove their own pumps from the fields as they are no longer necessary. Although wildlife has not been strictly monitored, the wildfowl numbers are very low and virtually all wading birds have now disappeared from the site as there are no longer the floods to attract them.

The main cause for optimism now, is the fact that, after pressure from various wildlife protection bodies, the water authorities in the area are now looking at plans to reverse these trends.

At the same time, many areas are undergoing change as the large-scale mechanised peat industry takes its toll and turns areas of old, herb-rich grassland or heath into shallow lagoons. Although peat extraction on this scale gives rise to the possibility of the creation of new habitats – such as the much-publicised Avalon Lakes scheme – many of the habitats it destroys are irreplaceable.

Above: Birds like this brightly coloured shoveler are attracted to the Levels to feed on the seeds of meadow plants.

Left: A wet grazed meadow on the Levels. Growing here are devil's-bit scabious, bog myrtle and purple moor-grass. Fields such as this will disappear if modern drainage and agricultural schemes are allowed to take over.

Not surprisingly, this extensive aquatic system, with its myriad plants, is an excellent place for invertebrates. Work is still going on to ascertain the total range of species, but the Moors are well-known as a nationally important site, and there are particularly good numbers of dragonflies and damselflies, water beetles and spiders. The wealth of invertebrate and fish life, together with the lack of disturbance, has enabled one of Britain's rarest mammals – the otter – to survive. The Levels and Moors seem to be one of the main strongholds for the otter in England, though it is heavily dependent on the present agricultural regime and water levels for its food and cover.

Agricultural change Wetlands throughout Europe are threatened by changes, mostly deriving from agricultural improvements, and the Moors and Levels of Somerset are no exception. Although their strange physical situation might seem to preclude major improvements, this is, regrettably, not the case, and several major drainage schemes have recently been proposed.

Much of the soil of the area is potentially very fertile, and could support more intensive use if it was drier. It is a relatively simple matter to under-drain fields to lower the water table locally, and grow a more productive crop, but if that area is liable to flooding at any time during the cultivation period, the valuable crop will be destroyed. Hence, most

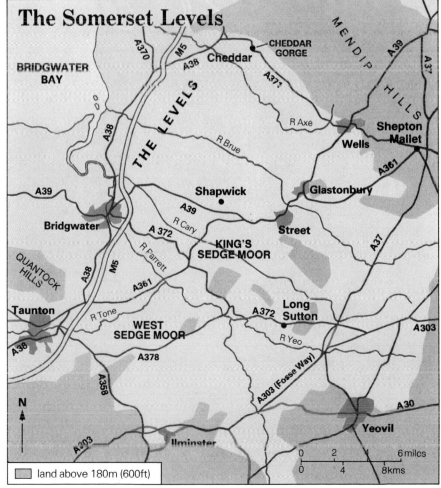

The Somerset Levels

land above 180m (600ft)

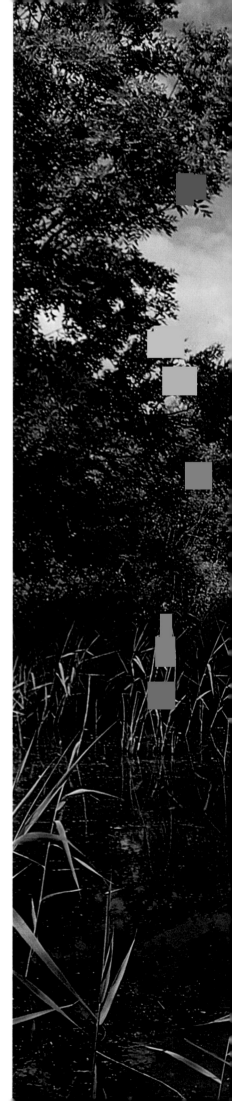

East & South-East England

Sandwich Bay to the Broads

What Eastern England lacks in craggy coastlines and wild mountains it more than makes up for in fascinating wetland and saltmarsh areas. East Anglia is the driest part of Britain, yet the Norfolk Broads and the Fens are essentially liquid landscapes.

The Norfolk Broads look natural enough today, but they are in fact flooded medieval peat diggings. Even though pressure from boat traffic in recent years has destroyed submerged and floating aquatic plants in many Broads, the whole area is an extremely rich wildlife haven. The most extensive reed beds in Britain occur in Suffolk and Norfolk, where rare birds such as the bearded tit, marsh harrier and bittern breed, while a notable insect, the swallowtail butterfly, is now confined chiefly to the Broads.

By way of contrast, the Breckland is a habitat of sandy heathlands and chalk grasslands. This unique area, though greatly influenced by man, has a very special flora. Centred on Thetford and spilling across into both Norfolk and Suffolk, the natural deciduous Breckland was cleared by man, who introduced sheep and rabbits which overgrazed the area to expose bare sandy patches. These are conditions favoured by the extraordinary stone curlew and such plants as the mossy stonecrop.

Sand dunes are an important coastal habitat in Eastern England, and a good example is the Sandwich Bay area. Here some of the best botanical gems appear in the rough ground of golf courses, where the scarce clove-scented broomrape and the even scarcer and more bizarre-looking lizard orchid can be sought out.

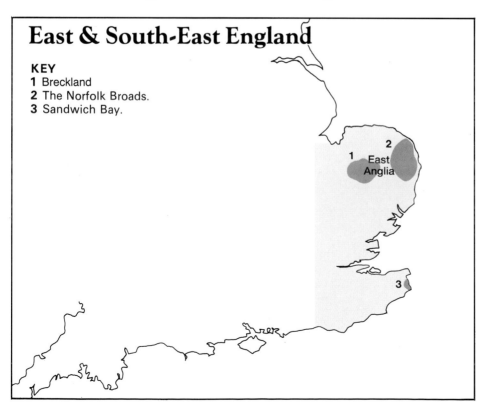

East & South-East England

KEY
1 Breckland
2 The Norfolk Broads.
3 Sandwich Bay.

East Anglia

Left: Although many of East Anglia's waterways are given over to holiday boating and water sports, some are still sufficiently undisturbed to allow natural growth of reeds and other water plants which, in their turn, shelter a wealth of insects, birds and other animals.

Below: The Norfolk Broads are one of the few places where the magnificent swallowtail butterfly can still be found. The green, black and orange caterpillars can be seen in June and July.

57

THE BRECKLAND OF EAST ANGLIA

Like so many parts of lowland Britain, the Breckland is not a natural landscape but man-made–created by forest clearance, land enclosure, sheep and rabbit grazing and forestry planting. Today it is particularly interesting for its special flora.

Below: A rabbit peering out of its burrow, which has been dug in sandy soil. One of the most important factors in the formation and maintenance of the Breckland was the introduction of the rabbit in the 12th century by the Normans for fur and food. The numbers of rabbits increased very rapidly in the 1400s, when managed warrens were an important form of land use, but they became feral (wild) only at the end of the 18th century. In recent years myxomatosis has taken a heavy toll and since 1956 very few rabbits have survived. The consequent decline in grazing by rabbits (and also by sheep, whose numbers are greatly reduced as well) has altered the Breckland landscape.

The word 'breck' was first used in 1674 by John Ray. It applied to an unenclosed area of arable land, which may have been in cultivation for a number of years and out of cultivation for short or long periods. The term 'Breckland' was coined by W G Clarke only as recently as 1894.

Today the Breckland is a mosaic of countryside, chiefly characterised by open, grassy heaths with scattered gorse bushes and some bracken, separated by rows of pine trees or blocks of conifer plantations. The soils are sands and chalky glacial tills overlying chalk, with local gravels and loess. The pH values vary considerably and these variations are reflected in the different vegetation types.

The creation of Breckland The open nature of the Breckland was first created when Neolithic man cleared the mixed oak forest as he colonized the area and worked the flint mines, such as Grimes Graves (now open to the public). In the 12th century the common arable land of the parish was one compact unenclosed area, divided into three shifts for

winter cereal, spring cereal and a fallow. Later, in the Middle Ages, barley was grown extensively. There were permanent grass areas, the more important of which were located on the margin of the fen and the arable shift. Flocks of sheep grazed the heathland and provided the essential fertilisers.

In the 18th century pines were planted as shelter belts for game and later on as protection against wind blow. Sand blows occurred frequently in the past, as is illustrated by the story of one landowner who, when asked in which county his property was situated said, 'Sometimes in Norfolk and sometimes in Suffolk–it blows backwards and forwards'. The last major sand blow was in 1668, when the village of Stanton Downham was buried.

During the Napoleonic period there was a great agricultural revival when chalk and marl digging became prominent (marl being a type of clay soil rich in lime). These materials helped to maintain the soil structure and fertility. After 1820 there was a collapse of farming and game became more important.

Blocks of conifers were then planted as game cover, but it was not until the 1920s that the Forestry Commission began to plant up large areas.

Animal life The largest animals you may encounter in the Breckland are deer. There are four species, three of which are native—red (which occur mainly in the Thetford Forest), roe and fallow. The muntjac was introduced into Britain during the last century and has now spread throughout southern England. The Forestry Commission monitors the native species annually in certain study areas and culls are carried out.

The red squirrel occurs in some of the Scots pine plantations, but is declining. Hares are often seen running across the grassy heaths and their forms, scraped in the sandy soil, provide pitfalls for the unwary. The rabbit, though, must be considered the most influential Breckland animal. From being abundant in centuries past, its numbers have recently been drastically reduced by myxomatosis. The sandy heaths provide ideal territories for common lizards and grass snakes, but the

Above: Typical Breckland scenery—Thetford Warren in Norfolk. The land is fairly flat with gently rising hills up to 60m (200ft) above sea level, and with many tumuli. The area has the lowest rainfall of any inland area in Britain— less than 600mm (24in) annually. The summer temperatures tend to be high, with a relatively high percentage of sunshine. Snow never lies for long, while frost may occur in any month of the year.

Right: The sand cat's-tail is one of several coastal species of plants that occur on the sandy soils found in parts of the Breckland.

Above: A view of Wangford Warren. This, a Suffolk Trust for Nature Conservation reserve, has one of the best examples of lichen heath in Breckland.

Left: Breckland is famous for its speedwell species. This is the spiked speedwell, now restricted to just four sites and protected by law.

Below: The woodlark, though declining nationally, is still found in the area. Here it is at its nest, with not yet fledged chicks.

adder is the most characteristic reptile.

The Breck contains many nationally rare insects associated with the dry heaths and the wetter fens, which occur in the lower-lying ground and by the few rivers. Disturbed ground, a result of arable farming and animal activity, supports an ephemeral plant association which yields a rich community of moths, beetles and bugs, as well as providing nectar for many bees, wasps and flies. Sandy tracks are used by many solitary wasp species as nesting sites—species such as *Episyron rufipes* and *Pompilus cinerus*, both spider-hunting wasps, or *Cerceris arenaria*, which provisions its nest with weevils, and *Ammophila sabulosa*, which preys on caterpillars for the same

purpose. The open, sandy heaths are similar to coastal dunes, so that insects normally found at coastal sites occur here inland at places such as Wangford Warren, a Suffolk Trust reserve.

One of the typical sights in the Breckland is the dipping flight of the green woodpecker, accompanied by a flash of bright green and a cheerful 'cackle'. The glimpse of white on the open ground betrays the presence of the wheatear, but the stone curlew is so well camouflaged against the sandy, stony patches that it is extremely difficult to observe. This species is well protected by wardens and has continued to thrive over the past few years, unlike the red-backed shrike, which was once more widespread and is now virtually lost from Breckland. A species which has increased is the nightjar. The scattered bushes on the heaths and cleared areas within the coniferous forests are particularly suitable habitats for it.

Breckland plants Most of the notable species are those of the 'Continental' element –that is species that prefer warm, dry summers, and can tolerate harsh, cold winters. Many of them are quite small, usually less than 5cm (2in) high, and botanists are often seen on their hands and knees peering diligently for such plants as the annual speedwells–the Breckland speedwell, the fingered speedwell and the spring speedwell. These are all found on arable or disturbed ground where the soil has a high lime content. Although the plants may be small in stature, they do have attractive names, for example the perennial knawel, the Spanish catchfly, shepherd's cress and suffocated clover.

Changes in the landscape Before Neolithic man, much of the area was afforested, mainly with deciduous trees. Now it is the conifer plantations which dominate large tracts. Since 1947, when a Suffolk farmer first used summer irrigation methods, more open heath has been cultivated, and various developments in techniques for spreading lime, fertilisers and pesticides have also meant an increase in arable farming. The demand for sand and gravel continues for the building of houses and roads, and the town of Thetford illus-

Above: Knotted pearlwort is a plant of damp sandy places and peaty areas. This low-growing perennial, though not a rare species, is nevertheless attractive.

Right: Spanish catchfly–one of the Breckland 'specialities'. This species is not found anywhere else in the British Isles.

Below: A heathland soil profile. This soil, which is found over much of Breckland, is sandy and poor, the nutrients quickly leaching through the thin band of topsoil.

trates the amount of urban development and industrial expansion that have occurred in recent years. Together with this is the need for more leisure areas, and several heaths are now in use as golf courses. Because of the flatness of the land, it is an ideal place for aerodromes and the once extensive area of heath that was Lakenheath Warren is now dissected by the USAF base at Lakenheath. Other major events in recent times have been the striking reduction in the numbers of sheep and rabbits.

But these changes do not necessarily mean a drastic reduction in areas of ecological interest. The Breckland was, and continues to be, fashioned by the hand of man. It is a dynamic system and species of interest are

found in the disturbed habitats as well as in the relatively stable ones. Airfields encompass large areas of land, some of which are built upon, but also the need for a clear view means that large tracts are left intact and are continuously mown, a form of management which is a substitute for sheep or rabbit grazing, and so the low-growing plants survive within their boundaries. Golf courses also provide patches of short turf, the 'rough', together with screening patches of bushes, giving a similar diversity to that occurring on the original heaths. The Stanford Training Area north of Thetford is one of the largest remaining areas of Breckland. Access is strictly limited so that destructive fires do not occur and the tank activity provides a certain amount of the disturbed ground which is an essential part of the pattern that is the Breckland.

There is, too, the possibility of discovering something new. The military orchid was found in an old Breckland chalk pit in 1954 – a site at least 80 miles north of any previously known locality for the species.

Within the last few decades the Nature Conservancy Council for England, the Suffolk Trust and the Norfolk Naturalists' Trust have acquired or have the management agreements on many of the remaining fragments of heathland in the region. Breckland continues to be a shifting pattern of land use influenced by man, as it has been since Neolithic times.

Where is the Breckland?

The Breckland is an area of land of approximately 600sq km (230sq miles) in East Anglia, and the town of Thetford is considered to be its centre. There are three administrative counties included within its boundaries – Suffolk, Norfolk and a small part of Cambridgeshire. (This map shows the approximate boundary.)

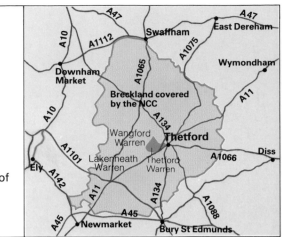

Right: Insects occur in great numbers in the Breckland. The small copper butterfly – seen here on ragwort – is a typical species of sandy heaths. Its caterpillars feed on sheep's sorrel.

Below: Not all of Breckland is heathy – some parts have been planted by the Forestry Commission. This is a view of woodland in Thetford Warren in Norfolk.

THE WILDLIFE OF THE NORFOLK BROADS

Created by peat diggings in medieval times, the Norfolk Broads – embracing Britain's latest National Park – are an outstanding area for wildlife. The scenery and vegetation is very diverse, changing from open water with submerged plants, through marginal beds of reeds and lilies, to alder woodland.

Above: Floating and emergent vegetation on a Norfolk Broads reserve – boats are prohibited here, hence the flourishing plant life.

Below: A male bearded tit, with a morsel of food, among reeds. This species was extremely scarce between the 1860s and the 1890s, due to egg and specimen collecting, but today as many as 200-300 pairs nest in the Broads.

The Norfolk Broads, an extraordinary series of over 40 freshwater lakes dotted about the flat landscape of East Norfolk and Suffolk, nestle in the river valleys of the Ant, Bure, Thurne, Waveney and Yare. There are over 200km (125 miles) of navigable tidal waterways which discharge into a 6km (3½ mile) long estuary known as Breydon Water, before mingling with the waters of the North Sea at Great Yarmouth. These rivers link some of the Broads and make about a dozen of them easily navigable. The largest is Hickling Broad, with 140 ha (350 acres) of water and reed-bed, but the majority are much smaller. Most are not more than 3-4m (10-13ft) deep.

The open water The lime-laden waters of the rivers, streams and dykes flow, or are pumped, into the Broads. Only a few are

partly spring fed, and only four now retain anything like the abundance of water plants inhabiting them before the complex water chemistry changes that began in the 1950s and accelerated in the late 1960s and early 1970s. Most Broadland water is now bereft of its water plants–such species as water soldier, frogbit and water milfoil–and the reasons for the loss are not yet fully understood.

Some 15-20 species of fishes are recorded from the Broadland. The Broads were known nationally for their pike fishing, but 11kg (25lb) specimens are now rare. Perch were another target species for specialist anglers, and Oulton Broad was renowned for them. Ruffe, roach, tench, bream and eel are the typical fishes found now.

Fishing ospreys are annual visitors to the Broads in spring and autumn on their way to and from Scottish and Scandinavian nesting sites. The handsome great crested grebe was almost erased as a breeding species just over a century ago, due to egg collecting and the use of feathers for hats and muffs, but a few pairs remained on private Broads and the species has subsequently returned in strength. Common terns occur around the Broads, feeding mainly on small fish fry. They first nested inland at Ranworth in 1949, when eggs were laid on derelict wherries. These boats– special shallow draft sail craft which carried commercial commodities between the towns

and villages before the days of effective road and rail transport–were sunk to prevent erosion between Ranworth Broad and Malthouse Broad. Over the past 20 years specially constructed platforms and rafts have been used by the terns at Ranworth, Ormesby, Hickling, Crome's, Martham and Hoverton Great Broads, with upwards of 100 pairs now nesting annually on them.

Coot, moorhen, mute swans, mallard, teal, shoveler, gadwall and garganey breed or occur as visitors, while winter weather can still bring a spectacular increase in wildfowl, with tufted duck, pochard, wigeon, pintail, goldeneye and goosander appearing in varying numbers. On the open waters large groups

Above: A flourishing growth of common reeds in Hickling Broad. There are no floating aquatic plants–a situation typical of the Broads that are open to boating and other recreational activities.

Below: A pair of swallowtail butterflies mating. This species is a feature of the Broadland marshes, to which it is restricted. It flies in May and June. The bright green, black and orange ringed caterpillars feed on milk parsley.

of noisy feral-domestic greylag and Canada geese flock at night, accompanied by thousands of roosting gulls. In addition the birdwatcher can hope to spot flocks of black terns on passage, or perhaps a group of pale spoonbills preening their feathers in a shallow reed-fringed bay.

Marsh and fen The most interesting habitat within the Broads is that lying between the water's edge and the point at which the sallow bushes start to invade the otherwise open habitat. The Ant valley probably contains the best assemblage of different plant communities within this habitat type, but most areas can be characterised by their particular dominating semi-natural vegetation. An instance of this is in the Yare valley, with its regular tidal rise and fall; here reed sweetgrass (*Glyceria maxima*) dominates the open fen and invades the dykes and Broads.

The Norfolk reed is characteristic of the Broads and river edges, forming extensive beds where it may be harvested on a one or two year cycle to be bundled up and used to

Above: Reeds and a solitary lapwing reflected in the still water of a Norfolk Broads waterway. Lapwings nest on the grazing levels, though in decreasing numbers.

Above left: The rare and inconspicuous fen orchid retains a last and rather precarious station in the heart of the Broads.

Below: A noctule bat in flight. These bats roost during the daytime in the deserted nests of bank voles and common shrews in the Broadland carrs, as do pipistrelle bats. The noctule is Britain's largest bat, with a wingspan of up to 16 in (40 cm). It is usually found in lowland areas, and flies in steep dives.

thatch many a Broadland barn, farm or cottage. Reed swamp has died back in recent years, while many flowering plants have been shaded out by bushes since regular cutting and burning ceased. The reed-beds are the habitat of many of the Broads' famous birds—the bittern, bearded tit and marsh harrier, for example. The latter has staged a come-back in the past few years, but the bittern is declining in numbers, from over 50 pairs in the mid 1950s to less than a dozen today. Reed and sedge warblers, too, occupy the reed-bed habitat in summer, along with water rails and reed buntings. Grasshopper warblers find the rougher congested fens to their liking, and the similar-sounding Savi's warbler can now be heard calling from at least two localities among dense reeds.

The marsh pea is a locally abundant plant, scrambling among the reeds, while the dampness of the peaty marshes encourages large quantities of the marsh fern. Marsh orchids occur in quantity where the vegetation is not too rank, and among the many other typical plants are ragged robin, yellow flag, greater and lesser reed-mace, saw sedge and tussocks of *Carex*, while the orange balsam, introduced by accident in 1927, is now widespread.

The drier reed-beds and rough grassland probably harbour a greater concentration of harvest mice than any other area in Britain. The aquatic South American coypu, originally imported from the Argentine and bred for its fur, escaped into the wild in the 1920s but is now officially extinct. Another mammal introduced from overseas is the secretive Chinese water deer which is now widespread throughout the Norfolk Broads, with a population probably in excess of 100. The first animals were identified in 1968, but the exact time and place of the original release of these

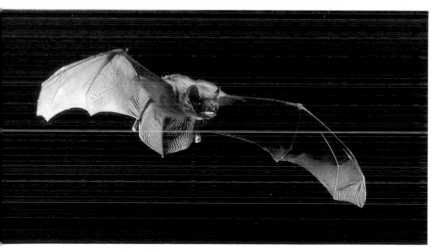

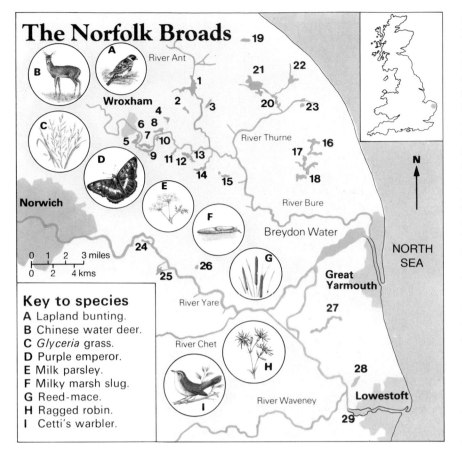

The Norfolk Broads

River Ant

Wroxham

River Thurne

River Bure

Breydon Water

Norwich

0 1 2 3 miles
0 2 4 kms

River Yare

River Chet

Great Yarmouth

NORTH SEA

N

River Waveney

Lowestoft

Key to species
A Lapland bunting.
B Chinese water deer.
C *Glyceria* grass.
D Purple emperor.
E Milk parsley.
F Milky marsh slug.
G Reed-mace.
H Ragged robin.
I Cetti's warbler.

Above: There are more than 40 freshwater broads in East Norfolk and Suffolk—this map shows only some of the larger ones.
1 Barton.
2 Alderfen.
3 Crome's.
4 Burntfen.
5 Wroxham.
6 Hudson's Bay.
7 Hoveton Great.
8 Hoveton Little.
9 Salhouse.
10 Decoy.
11 Cockshoot.
12 Ranworth.
13 Malthouse.
14 South Walsham.
15 Upton.
16 Ormesby.
17 Rollesby.
18 Filby.
19 Calthorpe.
20 Heigham Sound.
21 Hickling.
22 Horsey Mere.
23 Martham.
24 Surlingham.
25 Rockland.
26 Buckenham.
27 Fritton Decoy.
28 Flixton Decoy.
29 Oulton.

Right: A Norfolk drainage ditch or dyke—some of the best populations of plants and invertebrates linger in the dyke systems.

deer is shrouded in mystery. Otters, too, are elusive; only a few pairs live in the Broads, reflecting the general decline of the species throughout Europe.

Apart from the famous swallowtail butterfly, which occurs in the wild only in the Broads, various other Lepidoptera also inhabit the fens; among these are the wainscot moths *Nonagria sparganii*, *Arenostola brevilinea*, *Senta flammea* and *Leucania obsoleta*. Sadly, one fenland insect that has disappeared

recently is the large marsh grasshopper, bu balancing these losses are such species a *Ishnodemus sabuleti*, a brightly coloured plant bug found chiefly on *Glyceria* and firs seen at Wheatfen Broad in 1954—it is now abundant everywhere. Rare water beetle such as *Agabus striolatus* and *Hydroporu scalesianus* still live in the swamps where they were first discovered 150 years ago, and glow-worms still produce their green glow or some marsh banks on warm summer evenings. The larvae of *Lipara lucens*, a small fly produce the 'cigar' galls on reed stems, while several new species of Diptera are being described from the Broads. Among the in vertebrate specialities of the marshes are the milky marsh slug and the slender amber snail.

Alder carrs A Broadland carr in summer i the nearest habitat in Britain to impenetrable tropical jungle. Alder is the predominan tree species, but sallows also occur, whil the slightly drier areas can support birch, ash oak, hawthorn and buckthorn, with honey suckle and hops scrambling upwards to th light. All are shallow rooted and gale frequently topple trees, producing a bottom less hole of black oozy mud, while the up turned roots make a nesting place for wren and kingfishers. The understorey is a thicke of wild currant, raspberry, Duke of Argyll' tea plant and brambles, with masses o nettles. Some tussock sedges are found i swamp carr, as are magnificent royal ferns.

Although these carrs are typically floode under a foot or two of water for several week every winter, small mammals such as woo mice, bank voles and common shrews occu in some numbers. When flood condition prevail these animals retreat to higher ground and river embankments, or to nests con structed in rotting trees. Their deserted holes along with cracks in ash trees, are the day time roosts for pipistrelle and noctule bats.

About 50 species of birds breed in the carrs while a few more occur as migrants or winte visitors. Heronries are important, with 150 pairs of herons nesting in the early 1970 (although numbers have subsequently de clined). Woodcock and mallard nest on the carr floor, while a few long-eared owls re-us old heron nests. Smaller nesting birds includ treecreepers, chaffinches and blackcaps, an the more recently established Cetti's warble can now be found in the brambly edges of th carr. Thousands of rooks and jackdaws arriv in a long noisy black column in the lat winter afternoons from adjacent farmlan feeding grounds to roost in the carrs. delightful sight at this time of year is th groups of siskins and redpolls pecking amon the alder cones for the seeds.

One mature Broadland alder carr has large population of white admiral butterflies while purple emperors have also been re corded, and swallowtail butterflies mate hig in the air over the trees.

The grazing levels In the river valley

one can find large areas of fenland, reclaimed by man in past centuries by digging a criss-cross of ditches or dykes to act as sumps. Some follow old tidal creeks, others are straight cut. They are all linked to a riverside drainage pump which lifts the water into the river.

A flock of 300 wintering bean geese is to be found on the reclaimed fenland in the Yare Valley, but groups of whitefronts or pink-footed geese are an uncommon sight, although several flocks of Bewick's swans now graze the levels. Other regular winter visitors are hen harriers and short-eared owls (which feed chiefly on field voles). These wide open spaces also attract flocks of skylarks and mixed seed eaters such as corn, reed and Lapland buntings.

The breeding season is an exciting time on the levels. Redshank pipe away at any potential intruder, as do the oystercatchers which have begun to nest inland. Snipe bleat over the wetter meadows to proclaim their territory, while in one or two damper areas black-tailed godwits and ruffs linger in haunts where a century ago their ancestors nested. Along the dykes stand herons, while another long-legged bird – the crane – is an occasional autumn and winter visitor to the levels.

No description of the bird-life of these places would be complete without mentioning the two predatory species breeding in the area. By day the kestrel hangs from an invisible 'sky hook', and at dusk the ghostly white barn owl quarters each field for its staple diet of field voles. Barn owls have declined in a spectacular fashion as pasture has given way to arable farming with the consequent disappearance of the voles. Other occasional food items taken by the barn owl include the water shrew and the water vole – both associated with the dykes. Both birds of prey nest amicably together in the same owshed or derelict mill.

The ecology of the dyke systems has a very real intrinsic value, but it has been ignored by most people until very recently. Much of the glory of plants and invertebrates that typified the real Broadlands lingers in some dyke systems. Over one hundred flowering plants are found around the dyke systems, many of them quite rare. Water soldier, bladderwort, flowering rush and arrowhead compete with Canadian pondweed, hornwort, frogbit and bur-reed for water space. The native duckweeds compete on the water surface with the introduced floating water fern (*Azolla* sp.), which turns the dykes red in the autumn. Perhaps the rarest pondweed to occur is *Potamogeton acutifolius*, while rare invertebrates living in the dykes include the Norfolk dragonfly (*Aeshna isosceles*) and two small ram's-horn snails, *Anisus vorticulus* and *Segmentina nitida*.

The invertebrate fauna can be very rich, but the mechanical dredging now practised can totally deplete the fauna and the flora, as

Right: a waxwing perched on a look-out branch. In certain winters small flocks of these colourful birds appear in Norfolk, driven further south than usual by exceptionally hard weather in Scandinavia. Like the larger groups of migrant song thrushes, fieldfares and redwings so frequently seen on the Broads in winter, the waxwings are attracted by the late autumn crop of hedgerow berries.

Below: Reeds being harvested on Hickling Broad. They are cut on a one or two year cycle for use as thatch. Such management is only one of the many conflicting interests in the Broads. One of the more obvious changes in the last 30 years has been a vast increase in the number of boats. It is no surprise to see craft nose to tail on the more congested northern rivers. This disturbance by man and machine has the effect of pushing wildlife away from the rivers – except for the semi-tame coots, ducks and swans that appreciate the holiday-makers' bread supply. The more insidious effects are bank erosion, oil and diesel pollution and muddy water from the spin of propellers – not to mention the spread of litter.

can sheer neglect – allowing the dykes to silt up and disappear as the edges become trodden down and compacted by cattle.

Modern drainage has meant that large tracts of the grazing levels are no longer subject to winter flooding; as a consequence, they have been turned over to arable use. While the occasional arable area among acres of grazing will increase the diversity of habitat, the prairie-like fields created by filling in dykes have limited wildlife potential. A migrant flock of lapwings may congregate, or a group of mute swans may come to graze on the winter wheat, but few species can breed. The dykes, themselves under an arable regime, generally become overgrown with reeds and lack invertebrate diversity.

Among other creatures to find the disappearance of the dykes a problem is the common frog, which lacks suitable areas of water in which to deposit its spawn. Some common toads spawn in the deeper dykes, however, while smooth snakes are widespread throughout the region.

SANDWICH BAY

Sandwich Bay is a haven for a truly spectacular range of wild flowers (some of them extremely rare), and a gathering place for hundreds of wildfowl.

As it exists today, the Sandwich Bay area consists largely of unspoiled duneland which, since pre-Roman times, has slowly been displacing the sea and growing further out into the Bay. This aggregation of land has been created by two agencies: firstly, the carrying and deposition of silt at its mouth by the River Stour, and secondly the carrying of sand and shingle by tidal currents north of the town of Deal, to be deposited in the Bay area. Over the centuries since the Romans departed, the land has been built up on the eastern side of the ancient port of Sandwich, so that today it lies more than 2½km (1½ miles) inland from the nearest point of the shore.

Centuries ago much of the newly formed dune area stabilised and became agricultural land, over which the great mound of the Roman fort of Richborough Castle towers to this day. But to the east of the main Thanet to Sandwich road (A256) a strip of land more than 1½km (1 mile) wide has remained almost untouched by agriculture. Its escape from agricultural 'improvement' is due to the fact that most of the land was purchased for use as golf links, and the land not so utilised was only suitable for grazing by cattle.

The Royal St George's and Prince's Golf Courses, together with the Sandwich Bay Estate, are the most interesting areas for the botanist, while the grazing land lying between Prince's Links and the River Stour, together with the flats to north of the river, is now a

Above: On the seashore at Sandwich Bay the dominant plant is the sea holly — instantly identifiable with its prickly leaves and thistle-like flower heads. On the sand dunes the main plant is marram grass, tall 'forests' of which feed and shelter a host of molluscs, spiders and beetles and, later in the year, provide a haven for bird life. The marram is one of the first stabilizing agents on the dune, colonizing the shifting sand and holding it down with its mass of lateral roots.

Right: Among the clumps of sea holly grow patches of restharrow. The attractive pink pea-like flowers appear in bloom from June to September.

nature reserve of interest to botanists, ornithologists and other scientists. This nature
reserve is administered by the Kent Trust for
Nature Conservation.

Wild flower wealth During the summer
many people pass through the toll gate leading
to the Sandwich Bay Estate, with the sole
intention of swimming and sunning themselves on the dunes by the shore, or perhaps
enjoying a picnic. But to anyone with an
interest in wildlife, the day is enriched a
hundredfold by the profusion and beauty of
the wild flowers, insects and birds to be seen.

Among the plants to be seen along the
footpaths and in the rough grass are the lizard
orchid, the rare clove-scented broomrape
(which is parasitic on the roots of the bedstraw
family), the bright blue viper's bugloss and the
pyramidal orchid. In wetter areas of the dune
slacks, sometimes growing among tall stems
of common reed, marsh orchids can be seen in
profusion. These handsome plants, with their
large rosy-purple flower heads, make a
wonderful splash of colour during the month
of June, and are very attractive to insects,
particularly the brilliantly coloured burnet
moth. A month later, when the fertile flowers
have withered and given way to the ripe
brown seed pods, the same dune slacks bloom
again with the starry flowers of the marsh
helleborine and buzz with the humming
hordes of insects searching for pollen and
nectar.

Moving up from the damp slacks to the
intervening dry and grassy sandy ridges, you
can find a host of wild plants, among them
two outstanding species which have escaped
from cultivation and are now firmly established. These are the evening primrose, whose
red buds open up into bright yellow poppy-
like flowers late in the afternoon, and as-

Left: In a year when orchids
are abundant, you can see as
many as half a dozen
flowering spikes of one of
our rarest plants—the strange
and beautiful lizard
orchid—growing by the
roadsides leading to the Bay,
and up to 150 or more
scattered over the adjacent
areas of coarse grass. Their
numbers are variable,
however, and in a 'bad' year
perhaps only two or three
plants may be found. This
unpredictability is due to the
long germination and
growing period of orchid
seeds, which may need from
six to nine years of
underground development
before the first green leaf
appears above the surface.

Below: In addition to the
stands of orchids found
among the grass at Sandwich
Bay, you may also see tall
clumps of the bright blue
viper's bugloss—a plant that
is in flower from May to
September. The flower buds
start by being pink in colour,
but become a vivid blue
when fully open.

paragus, whose delicate fronds seem too frail
to stand up to the strong, salt-laden winds that
often blow in off the sea. Yet they survive such
windburns better than many of the truly
native plants.

In the same areas and at the same time of
year (June to August) the shrublike, rounded
profile of houndstongue can be seen, with
many purplish flowers on the tips of the
branches. Where the grass cover is less dense
(in the region of a bunker, for instance) the
large pale pink trumpets of sea convolvulus
hug the ground as they turn their faces to the
sun, their trailing stems sprawling on the sand
and holding up the small kidney-shaped
leaves.

On the golf course Even on the well mown
fairways of the golf course, where one would
imagine flowering plants would have little
chance of coming into bloom, there are
interesting flowers to be seen. As early as
February-March the pretty pink starry
blooms of dune stork's-bill shine out from
among the short grass blades, and by April the
tiny, bright blue flowers of the early forget-
me-not peep out among the daisies. A little
later the brilliant yellow flowers of biting
stonecrop can be seen wherever the grass is
short or sparse, accompanied in places by the
white blooms of the closely related English
stonecrop.

Also surviving well in these situations are
various members of the pea family, of which

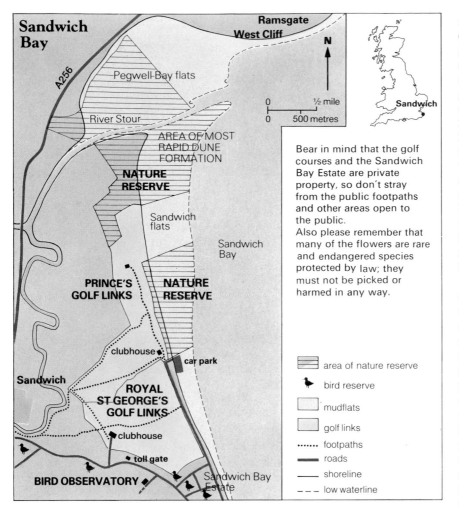

Sandwich Bay

Ramsgate West Cliff

N

Pegwell Bay flats

River Stour

AREA OF MOST RAPID DUNE FORMATION

NATURE RESERVE

Sandwich flats

Sandwich Bay

PRINCE'S GOLF LINKS

NATURE RESERVE

0   ½ mile
0   500 metres

Bear in mind that the golf courses and the Sandwich Bay Estate are private property, so don't stray from the public footpaths and other areas open to the public.
Also please remember that many of the flowers are rare and endangered species protected by law; they must not be picked or harmed in any way.

clubhouse

car park

Sandwich

ROYAL ST GEORGE'S GOLF LINKS

clubhouse

toll gate

BIRD OBSERVATORY

Sandwich Bay Estate

▦ area of nature reserve
🐦 bird reserve
☐ mudflats
☐ golf links
······ footpaths
▬▬ roads
──── shoreline
─ ─ ─ low waterline

the red and yellow flowers of bird's-foot trefoil are familiar to everyone. This group of plants is also parasitised by one of the broomrape species, the lesser broomrape, and in late June and July the fingerlike stems of this plant can be seen thrusting upwards, sometimes in little groups, looking rather like sticks of pink asparagus.

The seashore The dominant plant of the seashore is sea holly, its prickly clumps sometimes interspersed with patches of rest-harrow. On the dunes – out of reach of salt spray – are marram grasses, the first colonizers and stabilizers of the shifting sand.

The fore-dunes area, being the part most exposed to battering by wind and sea, has a

Right: The rare and beautiful clove-scented broomrape can be found on the golf course roughs. This parasitic plant has three colour forms – either pale cream, pale rose or puce. It grows no leaves and taps the roots of the bedstraw family for sustenance. It usually flowers in June.

Below: Keep an eye open for the ringed plover on the shores of Sandwich Bay. Here the bird is guarding some well-camouflaged eggs.

rather unstable plant population. You can expect to find sea couch grass and marram grasses and they may be accompanied by scrubby little plants such as annual sea-blite and sea saltwort. Hugging the sand near the grasses are clumps (sometimes quite extensive) of little greyish-green plants with oval, fleshy leaves and tiny white five-petalled flowers. These are sea sandwort plants, resistant to both salt and dehydration by wind. In the same area grows an equally tough and fleshy plant, though considerably larger and more shrub-like in appearance and bearing handsome four-petalled pink flowers from June to August. This is sea rocket, which is sometimes found growing in colonies of several clumps just above the level of the highest spring tides.

A little further inshore grow sea plantain and buck's horn plantain, in company with the fleshy silvery-green sea spurge. And most silvery of all, growing in the saltmarshes and up the muddy creeks, masses of sea purslane flourish in dense clumps. In late summer this makes a lovely background for the bluish-purple flowers of sea lavender, elegantly arranged in a curving spike at the tip of a tall slim stem. Less spectacular, but equally interesting, are the little tufty, branching plants growing in and often submerged by the muddy sea water. This fleshy, salt-loving species is perennial glasswort; the plants have a strong reddish tinge and produce tiny flowers which must be seen through a magnifying glass to be appreciated. They are one of the few species of land plants which have adapted to a salt-water habitat.

Seashore birds The seashore itself is the area where most birds will be seen, whatever season of the year it may be. Most of the birds are extremely shy and unapproachable. It is

best to sit or lie on the edge of the dunes by the shore, watching with binoculars and waiting for the birds to come closer, rather than to try to approach them. During peak migration periods great flocks of waders may be seen, commonly of oystercatchers, godwits, knot, dunlin, curlew, sanderling and many others. Various species of gulls and terns fly overhead, or come down to feed in company with grey plover and ringed plover, carrion crows and even the occasional rook. Out on the mudflats the goose-like shelduck feed, sometimes with wigeon or teal.

Inshore, the fore-dune area is a rich source of food and shelter during the winter months for wandering flocks of finches and larks. Snow buntings frequently overwinter in the area of the Nature Reserve, in company with linnets, greenfinches, twites and reed buntings. In hard weather thrushes are able to find snails and other creatures among the marram tussocks when the remainder of the countryside is covered with impenetrable snow. Small flocks of shore larks, too, wander up and down the coastline, along with skylarks and meadow pipits.

In the middle dune area, with its more stable vegetation of coarse meadow grasses and dune slacks with dense clumps of the rare sharp sea rush, you may flush out a pair of ground-roosting short-eared owls that spring into the air and then appear to float away with long, lazy wingbeats. Equally unexpectedly,

Above: The wealth of wild flowers in Sandwich Bay attracts an enormous variety of insects – including this six-spot burnet moth.

Below: Tough, resilient marram grass on the dunes.

from the blind side of a clump of rushes or a bed of reeds, a large bird may appear, gliding close to the ground on long uptilted wings. A white ring round the root of the tail proclaims it to be a hen harrier (one of our rarer raptors), which has taken to wintering and hunting in the lower Stour valley in appreciable numbers over the last decade–as many as 30 may be seen in some peak years. The presence of these hunters implies the existence of a population of voles and mice in sufficient numbers to support the raptors for four or five winter months and still to survive as a viable rodent population.

The Bird Observatory In addition to the golf links and Nature Reserve, there is also the Bird Observatory, which has been in operation at Sandwich Bay for many years. Here birds have been trapped and ringed, weighed and recorded, then finally released to travel onward on migration to their summer or winter destinations. Slowly, over the years of patient recordings from this and many other stations like it all round the world, we have learned where at least some of these birds go, and also that many come back again to the same spot year after year.

The Bird Observatory has itself a number of Nature Reserves and provides hostel-type accommodation for up to 12 visitors. Any arrangements for staying at the Observatory should be made well in advance to the Warden, Sandwich Bay Bird Observatory Trust, Guildford Road, Sandwich Bay, Kent CT13 9PF. Up-to-date information and maps of suggested walks can be obtained either by visiting the Observatory HQ or by telephoning Sandwich (0304) 617341. Information about the KTNC can be obtained from the East Kent Reserves Officer, KTNC, 1a Bower Mount Road, Maidstone, Kent ME14 1BR.

Northern England

Derbyshire's Peaks to the Borders

The northern part of England is indeed a naturalist's paradise, containing as it does five magnificent National Parks as well as many Areas of Outstanding Natural Beauty.

The untold riches of the Lake District – including England's highest mountains and largest lakes – mean that it is under constant pressure from ever-increasing visitors. The original woodlands have virtually all gone and in their place coniferous forests have been planted, but deciduous larch forests bring their own shade of golden yellow to the multi-coloured palette of the autumnal hillsides. And up in the mountains, typical upland birds – peregrine, raven and kestrel – nest, while the golden eagle has recently returned to the Lake District to breed.

There can be no finer way of appreciating the impressive moorland scenery of the Peak District, the Yorkshire Dales and the Northumberland National Parks than to walk the Pennine Way – the longest footpath in Britain. The drier parts of the Pennines are grassland areas, while the wetter parts are blanket bogs – areas where the insectivorous sundews and the attractive bog rosemary flourish.

Farndale in the North York Moors National Park, can show just what these northern Parks have to offer. Every April, this area is transformed by the carpets of wild daffodils bursting into flower, while elsewhere, though not in the same profusion, bird's-eye primroses and yellow globeflowers gladden the eye. Grouse call on these Moors, and thousands of seabirds congregate on the coasts.

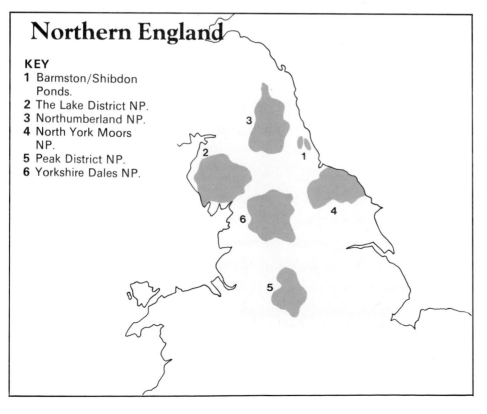

Northern England

KEY
1 Barmston/Shibdon Ponds.
2 The Lake District NP.
3 Northumberland NP.
4 North York Moors NP.
5 Peak District NP.
6 Yorkshire Dales NP.

Left: Not all of the Peak District consists of bleak peat-covered moorland. The limestone dales are a mass of wild flowers in spring and summer, as can be seen here — the meadow is full of buttercups and clover as far as the eye can see. The imposing tree by the drystone wall is a sycamore.

Below: Northern England is still a little too far south for the mountain hare to appear, but its cousin the brown hare, shown here, can be spotted in rough upland grassland and even quite far up the heather-clad moorland slopes of Yorkshire, Northumberland and the Lake District.

BARMSTON AND SHIBDON PONDS

The county of Tyne and Wear in north-east England is named after two rivers that dominate the area, yet away from these the county has few aquatic habitats. Two exceptions are Barmston Pond, a site for many rare passage migrants, and Shibdon Pond, which has been set aside as a nature reserve.

Above: Barmston Pond with mute swans on the water and flocks of wigeon and black-headed gull in the air.

Below: Shibdon Pond in winter. The site was first created a nature reserve by Blaydon Urban District Council, who bought it in 1968 for this purpose. Since 1979 it has been under lease to the Durham County Conservation Trust, who are now responsible for its maintenance.

Shibdon Pond and its surrounding area lie on the south bank of the River Tyne in the middle of the houses and factories of Blaydon. It consists of 4ha (10 acres) of open water and 10ha (24 acres) of wet and dry grassland, marsh and scrub. Barmston Pond lies across the county from Shibdon, being sandwiched between the new town of Washington and the old shipbuilding town of Sunderland. It lies further away from the River Wear than does Shibdon from the Tyne, but it is still near enough to attract birds using the river as a migration route. Barmston is smaller than Shibdon, with an area of about 2.4ha (6 acres) of flooded grassland. The surrounding fields are used mainly for cereal crops, but some dairy farming is also carried out.

The two ponds have several features in

common. Barmston Pond has arisen solely because coal mining in the area has caused the land to subside. Shibdon Pond, though it lies on the old flood plain of the Tyne and is thus a traditional wetland site, has also been greatly affected by mining subsidence. Until recently both ponds had a companion pond associated with them. Unfortunately, both are now lost. The one at Shibdon was used as a tip for domestic council refuse, while Barmston's shallow muddy-edged pond—which was much favoured by birds—was lost when the local farmer drained the corner of the field.

Both of the large ponds are, however, still vitally important as wetlands in a county short of such habitats. Barmston has an important role to play as a 'staging post' for migrating birds in the spring and autumn, and also as a relatively undisturbed area where wildfowl and other wetland birds can pass the winter in safety. Shibdon, with its much more diversified habitats, fulfils the above two roles and also provides living space throughout the year for a whole range of plants and animals not found at Barmston.

Barmston Pond The vegetation of Barmston consists mainly of low-growing aquatic plants, with common spike-rush, common water-plantain and floating pondweed dominating the water margin in the spring and summer. In winter the pond increases in size as it collects more and more surface water. As it does so the water margin spreads out and comes to consist of flooded grassland and cow-puddled mud, a combination that, along with a plentiful supply of seeds and invertebrate animals, has brought many rare birds to Barmston. Of the 136 species of bird that have been recorded so far there, 35 of these have been waders and 22 have been wildfowl. Notable among the rarer birds have been lesser yellowlegs and Wilson's phalarope from North America, broad-billed sandpiper and Temminck's stint from Scandinavia and collared pratincole and spoonbill from southern Europe. Other rarities include black kite, purple gallinule (the first British record of this bird), grey phalarope and red-footed falcon.

Most of the very rare birds were seen in the period when both ponds at Barmston were intact. Since the draining of the smaller, shallower pond the number of waders has dropped considerably. What is doubly distressing is that the small area of land the draining released for farming has shown itself to be very unproductive—though the water has gone from the surface the land is apparently still waterlogged and in most years the crops fail.

The larger, remaining pond still attracts good numbers of birds. Up to 200 wigeon (with an exceptional 250 in 1983) arrive in October and winter on the pond, and shovelers and mallards are usually present in late summer. Large numbers of migrating birds sometimes break their journey at Barmston,

for example ringed plovers in spring and groups of ruff (more than 200), curlew sandpiper and little stint in late summer. As with most stretches of inland water Barmston carries a large population of non-breeding black-headed gulls, with smaller numbers of herring gulls and lesser black-backed gulls. On the short cattle-grazed turf around the

Above: Tansy is a common plant of the dry grassland at Shibdon, while (below) the reed beds there act as assembly points in late summer for thousands of birds such as swallows about to migrate south to warmer regions for the winter.

Above: One of the most exciting of the rare birds seen at Barmston is the black kite, a vagrant from the Continent.

Below: A water vole feeding in a reed-bed.

than 300), tufted duck, wigeon, teal and shoveler. The fishes in the pond attract regular visits from kingfishers, herons, cormorants and goosanders, all of which find the clear water of the pond easy to fish in.

Some of the water of Shibdon Pond comes from a number of natural springs arising at the base of a nearby scarp slope, but the main influx of water comes from an old mine shaft. The water from the shaft is heavily laden with iron which is deposited on the bottom of the pond as an orange-brown layer. No one yet knows what effect this iron is having on the pond's flora and fauna. One of the main problems facing the team of people who look after the site is that the rate of water flowing into the pond is increasing, gradually raising the level of the pond and allowing greater reedmace to spread. There is to be an attempt to control the rising level of the water by installing a weir where the stream flows out of the pond to the Tyne.

Marsh and grassland The marshy area surrounding the pond is dominated by greater bulrush and reed sweet-grass, both plants providing food and breeding sites for coots, moorhens, mallards, and water voles. Various insects, such as water boatmen, diving beetles, dragonflies, damselflies and mayflies, can also be seen in the vicinity. A small area of common reed is being encouraged to spread by the reserve management, who hope it will replace some of the greater bulrush since

pond lapwings and starlings can always be seen feeding.

Shibdon habitats Whereas Barmston consists simply of a pond surrounded by fields Shibdon has a much greater diversity of habitats. The centrepiece is, of course, the pond itself, which attracts large numbers of wintering wildfowl such as pochard (more

common reed supports a more varied animal population.

Over a small section of marsh the bulrush has been deliberately removed to make a 'wader scape'–an area of very shallow water and exposed mud. This, it is hoped, will attract and provide food for waders such as greenshanks, redshanks and wood and green sandpipers. At present these birds explore the reserve but do not stay long because of a shortage of suitable feeding sites.

Shibdon Pond also has interesting areas of wet and dry grassland, particularly the wet grassland, of which there is very little in the rest of the Tyne valley. Two species of orchid are abundant: the common spotted and the northern marsh, the pale spotted flowering heads of the former contrasting with the dark purple heads of the latter. Yellow rattle, lady's smock and great burnet also grow here. Where the wet grassland has been disturbed recently, and pockets of slightly drier soil form, small clumps of heather have become established. Some areas of wet grassland are being threatened by encroaching sallow.

A recent addition to the habitats of Shibdon is dry grassland, which has formed on the site of a colliery that was demolished in 1951. Typical plants of this habitat include common toadflax and tansy. Butterflies such as large skipper, common blue and orange tip are fairly common during the summer. Among birds, goldfinches, linnets, dunnocks, sedge warblers and reed buntings are all common.

Human pressures While Barmston Pond is visited only by dedicated birdwatchers seeking an elusive rarity the Shibdon Pond reserve attracts a large number of visitors, which puts great pressures on the wildlife of the area. To control these pressures and safeguard the areas that are of particular interest to naturalists, the management has constructed a timber broadwalk footpath and nature trail through the various habitats. Thanks to this work the future of the reserve looks comparatively secure. Barmston Pond, on the other hand, is still threatened by attempts to drain it and, until it receives legal protection, its long-term future must be in doubt.

Above: One of several attractive butterflies at Shibdon is the orange tip, which lays its eggs on lady's smock.

Right: Much of the marshy area at Shibdon is dominated by bulrush, though the reserve management is trying to control its spread and replace it with reeds.

Below: Wigeon winter at both Barmston and Shibdon Ponds. In spring they fly to their breeding grounds to the north.

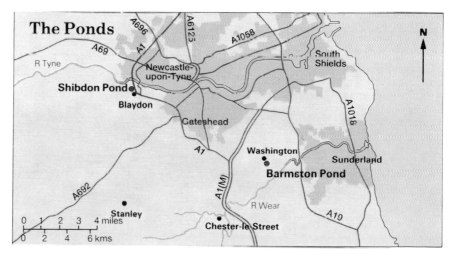

The Ponds

THE LAKE DISTRICT'S LANDSCAPES

Lakeland well deserves its reputation as a treasure store of England's most glorious scenery. It is unfortunate that its landscapes and plant life are severely threatened.

The Lake District National Park includes in its 880 square miles perhaps the finest countryside in England. The lakes themselves lie within a small area: a circle 30 miles across would enclose them all. The combination of high mountains, deep wooded valleys, large lakes and small mountain tarns, open fells covered with smooth grass or waving bracken, and extensive forests provides habitats for a great array of plants, animals and birds.

The landscape The Lake District has three main kinds of landscape, which can be divided into bands running roughly from south-west to north-east. In the north there are the rounded mountains of the Skiddaw slates; south of these are the rugged mountains of the Borrowdale volcanic rocks; and further south still are the lower, gentler hills around Windermere and Coniston.

Skiddaw is vast and rounded in shape. When the whole of the north was gripped by glaciers in ice age after ice age, the toughness of the Skiddaw slates proved to be about the same wherever the ice attacked it, and so the glaciers cut evenly and left a smooth finish. Quite a different outline is seen on the Langdale Pikes, with their swooping cliffs and rugged crags. This is typical of the appearance of the mountains in the zone of Borrowdale volcanic rocks, laid down in fiery primeval times as lava and ash. The different layers and segments of the volcanic deposit were formed out of different flows of lava or beds of ash, so that the mountain has many textures, and its toughness is uneven from one point to the next. When the ice came, the mountain surfaces gave way in some places and held fast in others, and the result is the jagged look of the Langdale Pikes, Scafell and the many other peaks that are visited by rock climbers.

Further south still are the younger rock

Above: Skiddaw's rounded outline rising beyond Derwent Water.

Top right: The Langdale Pikes rise above Grasmere.

Bottom right: Set in a gentle Silurian landscape, Esthwaite's north end is a National Nature Reserve. Into the lakes here flow the waters of Black Beck from the village of Hawkshead. The community of plants make a fine example of the series of waterside plant zones; these include submerged plants, emergent plants such as the common reed, and then the trees — willows, alders, birch and ultimately oak.

formations (the Silurian rocks) which have produced gentle contours and lush, often well-wooded countryside around Windermere and Coniston, the first landscapes which the traveller from the south encounters on a visit to the Lake District.

The fells All hills except the higher mountains are called fells. They are smoothly contoured, usually with enough soil to support grass or low plant growth. Some fells are heather moors, but not many of these remain in Lakeland today: burning and excessive grazing have killed the heather and all that remains is rather poor grassland, or bracken, which sheep do not eat.

The bracken is an unending spread of green from June to September, in autumn becoming a rich tapestry of reds and browns – a heartening sight to the country-goer, but a threat to the farmer, since the bracken is probably about to invade a few more acres of his already sparse grassland.

Drystone walls snake in all directions from valley bottom to the tops of high fells. No mortar is used in building these walls, which are a characteristic feature of the local scene; some have been standing for 150 years and more. Fortunately, when one needs repairing there are still craftsmen to do the job. The walls are not all built to mark boundaries of the pastures; some are designed to channel the sheep from the high pastures to the farms for shearing or lambing, and they provide

Above: Lily Tarn on Loughrigg near Ambleside. The small tarns are not rich in plant life since they have acid water and few nutrients. They often contain the unusual quillwort (*Isoetes lacustris*) which grows underwater with rosettes of quill-shaped leaves; and beaked sedge (*Carex rostrata*) often grows at the margins.
Right: Two kinds of bog moss. The one with the reddish colour is *Sphagnum rubellum* and the other is *S. recurvum*.

shelter from blizzards – much to the benefit of fell walkers as well as sheep.

Growing abundantly on the stone walls are beautiful examples of lichens; these tough organisms cling to the stone and resist being washed or knocked off. A lichen is a partnership of a fungus and an alga growing together for their mutual benefit.

The dominant plants of the better grassland of the fells are sheep's fescue and the two bent-grasses, common bent-grass and fiorin. These grasses form a close sward with little room for other plants, but the tiny yellow flowers of tormentil are dotted everywhere, as well as sheep's sorrel and heather bedstraw.

Heavy grazing causes the sheep's fescue to disappear, the bent-grasses to increase and mat-grass – which sheep will not eat – to thrive. Mat-grass is the foodplant of the caterpillar of the mountain ringlet butterfly, so this alpine species is common on fells above 550m (1800ft), and a speciality of the Lake District since it is rare elsewhere in England.

The wetter areas of the fells are deep in sphagnum mosses, a warning to the walker that a bog is nearby; and the tall golden flowers of bog asphodel are another clue. There are also wide spreads of the carnivorous sundew, a plant with a rosette of sticky leaves. You can sometimes see the remains of insects caught on the globules of sticky fluid held by the leaf hairs.

The butterwort, another insect catcher, is

found in the wetter parts of the fells. Butterwort has shining, bright yellow leaves. In summer the fluffy heads of cotton sedges will tell you if you are near waterlogged ground, or a bog pool.

Relieving the bleakness of the fells are a number of shrubs or small trees. Hawthorn and mountain ash are among these and, in favoured places, juniper, which sometimes occurs in groups. In southern Lakeland juniper was much in demand in the 18th and 19th centuries for charcoal-burning, as it made the best charcoal for gunpowder.

Woodlands The history of the vegetation of the Lake District is revealed by pollens preserved in peat and sediments left over from past ages at the bottom of lakes and tarns. The presence of tree pollens shows that almost all the Lake District was once wooded; then, starting about 3000BC, tree pollens decreased while pollens of grasses increased – evidence that the early farmers were clearing woodlands. The process was continued in later times.

None of the original woods now exists except, perhaps, in two small areas, Keskadale and Birkrigg. In these areas, some 400m (1300ft) up the fells in the Newlands Valley between Derwent Water and Buttermere, there are fragments of almost pure sessile oakwoods.

The present-day woodlands in the valley, apart from recently planted conifer stands, are mostly of mixed species – a high proportion of oak with birch, hazel, alder and ash. These were planted in the last 200 years to provide local needs: oak for building, coppice for fencing and basket making, firewood and wood for charcoal burning.

Sheep have traditionally been allowed to graze in the woods, so there is not a rich variety of plants on the woodland floor. However, wild daffodils, which the sheep find unpalatable, carpet the woods in spring. Lichens, ferns, mosses and liverworts are prolific, and their rich growth is an indicator of clean air and high rainfall. Another reason why these flowerless plants survive is because they too are left alone by the sheep.

Lakes The larger lakes vary in their ability to support plants. Scientists have arranged them in a series according to their productivity, which in its strict meaning is defined as their ability to produce a rich growth of microscopic algae. These are the lowest link in the food-chains of a lake, and so the abundance of all other forms of life, plant and animal, is also covered by the term.

The least productive lakes, such as Wastwater, Ennerdale and Buttermere, which are all in the west of the district, lie within the main mountain masses. Rain falling on their drainage areas runs mostly over bare rock which yields little in the way of chemical nutrients to the water entering the lake. Moreover, there are few farms or other habitations around them to add fertiliser or

sewage effluents to the water.

Lakes at the other end of the series, such as Esthwaite and Windermere, lie on the softer Silurian rocks which break down easily into soil and thus support more settlement.

In productive lakes a reedswamp community may develop, and water lilies may grow. Wave action, even in productive lakes, discourages plants from taking root in the shallow waters of the lake margin; but plants that grow at any depth are less affected by the waves. From a depth of about 2m (6ft) until the water is too deep for adequate light for plant growth, there are swards of quillwort, shoreweed and pondweeds. In deeper waters one of the stoneworts, *Nitella flexilis*, occurs.

Above: Cunsey Beck, which carries the waters of Esthwaite into Windermere. Beck is the usual word in the Lake District for a stream.

Below: The parsley fern (*Cryptogramma crispa*) is characteristic of the Lake District as it grows only on acid rocks in mountain districts. It is found in the valleys growing out of stone walls but it seems more at home on loose rocks and screes on the fellside.

ANIMAL LIFE IN LAKELAND

It can take a lifetime to appreciate the wildlife of the Lakes: rare fish and protected bird and animal species are found in the district's many and varied wildlife habitats.

Any journey in the Lake District will take you through frequent changes of scene from rock, marsh, grass and woodland to water – a profusion of contrasting animal habitats next door to each other.

The district has its characteristic range of insect life and, not surprisingly with its many different kinds of waters, the speciality is in aquatic and semi-aquatic insects. Living by the lakes and running water there are about 25 species of mayfly and 20 of dragonfly. At the same time about 25 species of stonefly, grey-black insects with flat-folded wings, can be found by the water, and a baffling 100 species of caddis flies flit about, some drab and grey, some with beautifully delicate

Below: One of the most famous and endearing views in the Lakes is Tarn Hows. It is in fact a man-made landscape – the stream was dammed to make the lake, and trees were planted that are alien to the Lake District.

colours.

In the rippling waters The brown trout is the Lake District's most common fish and, in a large lake such as Windermere, can grow to a length of 60cm (24in), but in streams trout do not reach more than a third of that size. The sea trout is a migratory form of the brown trout, and swims up from the estuaries to spawn in the upper reaches of streams. This fish has a remarkable life cycle, living both in fresh water and salt.

Nowadays fewer salmon come up the Lakeland rivers to spawn, but the occasional one still appears. The salmon's relative, the charr, is found in eight lakes: Windermere, Coniston, Ennerdale, Wastwater, Buttermere, Crummock Water, Thirlmere and Haweswater.

Two whitefish of the Coregonidae family are special rarities of the Lake District: the schelly (skelly) which smells like cucumber when fresh, and the vendace. The schelly is a plankton feeder, growing to a length of 40cm (16in) and inhabiting Ullswater, Haweswater and the Red Tarn on Helvellyn. The vendace is about half the size of the schelly and its only Lakeland habitats are Derwent Water and Bassenthwaite Water, two lakes that were formerly joined.

In the more productive lakes the characteristic fish are perch and pike, although trout may also occur. Unfortunately in 1976 an unidentified disease wiped out over 98% of adult perch in Windermere, and the species will take years to regain its former numbers. Eels are trapped commercially in various parts of the Lake District and transported live to London. During the 1980 season two tonnes of eels were trapped in Windermere, to become ingredients for eel pie, stewed eel and other traditional East End delicacies.

Of the smaller fish, bullheads are found under stones both in becks and at lake edges; they are small fish that rush away with a flapping of their tails when discovered. Another small fish of the becks is the stone loach. Minnows swim in shoals in gravelly areas at lake edges, and three-spined sticklebacks frequent the weedy areas of lakes.

Snake spotting When out walking or picnicking in the Lake District, always bear in mind the possibility of coming across an adder (viper). These snakes bask on sunny banks or fellsides, so take care not to tread on them or sit on them. It is not that they are a great menace, for they hurry away whenever they have a chance; but naturally they react quickly if surprised.

On the danger list Buzzards, ravens and the magnificent golden eagle have been persecuted almost to extinction in the Lake District in the past, but have now started to stage a comeback. The buzzard is doing fairly well nesting in the woodlands, and the harsh croak of the raven can be heard on the fells once again. Its larger size and wedge-shaped tail distinguish it from the carrion crow.

Above: Perhaps the Lake District's most attractive mammal is the red squirrel, which at the moment is abundant, although the grey squirrel is now encroaching.

Right: Typical of today's Lakeland herds, these sheep at Esthwaite are of mixed breed. The famous old breed of the district is the Herdwick; today Swaledales are gradually replacing them. You can also see Scottish Blackface, Rough Fell and Dalesbred sheep in the Lake District.

There are still very few golden eagles about, and they are protected with great care. The peregrine falcon is another bird that has suffered badly.

The commonest bird on the fells is the meadow pipit, which arrives in March or early April and leaves the district by the end of September. Wheatears are common breeding birds of the fells, and ring ouzels are frequently seen.

Woodland, stream and lake birds The oakwoods do not have a rich variety of bird life, but one species that is rather special to Lakeland is the pied flycatcher, an attractive bird which takes advantage of the nesting boxes provided for it to increase its range. Other woodland dwellers are sparrowhawks, the green and the great spotted woodpeckers, and woodcocks. Nightjars, which were fairly common at one time, have now become extremely scarce.

Dippers seem to prefer wide, shallow rivers in the valleys rather than upland streams. Grey wagtails show the same preference. The yellow wagtail is becoming a familiar sight in summer, in meadows beside lakes and rivers. The kingfisher, however, has declined in recent years.

Nor do the lakes have a great variety of bird life; perhaps this is because the deep water and the frequently bare shores, stony and lacking in plant cover, are not favourable to a wide range of species. The common sand-

piper nests on lake shores that are less open to human disturbance. Great-crested grebes nest on smaller lakes such as Esthwaite and, in recent years, red-breasted mergansers have nested in some numbers on Windermere. The broods of young swimming after their parents are a charming sight for visitors.

In winter the bird population of the lakes and larger tarns increases with the arrival of large flocks of mallard, and the diving ducks: tufted duck and goldeneye come first, and the pochard later. The most spectacular arrivals are the whooper swans from the north, which start arriving in small parties from the middle of October.

Coot occur in large numbers in winter and

Above: The north-west coast of Cumbria is one of the strongholds of the natterjack toad. This rare and protected animal survives in the sand dunes, where large areas are unfrequented because of military use.

on Windermere parties of over a thousand strong have been observed. Cormorants, too, visit several lakes, looking somewhat incongruous in these surroundings. They feed mainly on perch.

The mammals The most common mammal in the Lake District, as almost everywhere else in the country, is the short-tailed vole, whose grassy runs can be seen even on the tops of the highest fells; it is the main prey of all the predatory birds and animals. The Forestry Commission plantations, which exclude sheep, thereby increasing the long grass, have enabled the voles to grow in numbers.

Surprisingly, the blue (or mountain) hare, in spite of its deliberate introduction to the Coniston area before World War I, is today not found in the Lake District; and the commoner brown hare is not found on the fells as often as in the woodland, for the grasslands are inadequate to provide it with enough food.

As elsewhere, badgers have been reduced in recent years by gassing and digging-out. Otters too have declined, as a recent otter survey has shown. The principal cause of their decline is the presence of man: not hunting, which is now illegal, but disturbance, and possibly the use of chemicals in farming which have a toxic effect on the otters.

One mammal which continues to exist in competition with man is the fox. All farmers unite in supporting the fox hunt; they are anxious to prevent depredation of their

Above: One or more pairs of golden eagles have returned to nest in the Lake District with varying success; a major hazard for them is disturbance by people.

Below: The brown trout of the lakes move up into the streams to spawn. The eggs are laid in mid November, and the young fish (alevins) hatch in early March. These remain in the river until they are about two years old, then return to the lakes.

lambs and poultry, but the hunt is not an effective means of keeping down the numbers of foxes, for in a hill country with many natural rocky retreats it is almost impossible to eradicate such a cunning animal.

The Lake District has the only deer forest in England. The wild red deer of Martindale run freely on the fells, without any form of enclosure. Except during the rut in autumn the stags roam on their own, away from the females (hinds) and calves in the main home range. Picnickers are sometimes alarmed by the sudden appearance of a stag, wandering in search of a resting place.

Smaller groups of red deer are found in other parts of the district, such as Thirlmere and at the southern edge of the National Park in Furness. In the forestry plantations at Grizedale, near Hawkshead, high seats have been provided to enable visitors to watch deer.

Roe deer, as in many other parts of Britain, have increased their populations in recent years, and live in small groups in many woodlands throughout Lakeland. During the day they remain sheltered and out of sight, but come out at dusk to browse, and at this time of day they are liable to rush across a road, and can cause accidents. Road signs warn of this danger on roads that pass through the areas where the deer are numerous.

Destruction or conservation? The Lake District is an incomparably beautiful landscape. It is also a rich legacy of wildlife. Great pressures are now imposed on this fragile environment, on the one hand by the demand for more intensive farming and forestry, and on the other by the vast increase of mainly car-borne visitors who infiltrate even the remote areas and leave no place untouched.

The recent histories of the golden eagle, the peregrine, the pine marten, the now absent polecat and the endangered natterjack serve to warn us that the future for wildlife is bleak. Yet we seem unable to resolve the problems of preserving even areas which have been chosen as National Parks. Unless these problems are solved in the near future, the animals and plants people come to see will no longer exist.

Lakeland Nature Trails

There are dozens of beautiful nature trails in the Lake District –
all with something special to offer in the way of wildlife and
spectacular landscape. This map shows just a few of them.

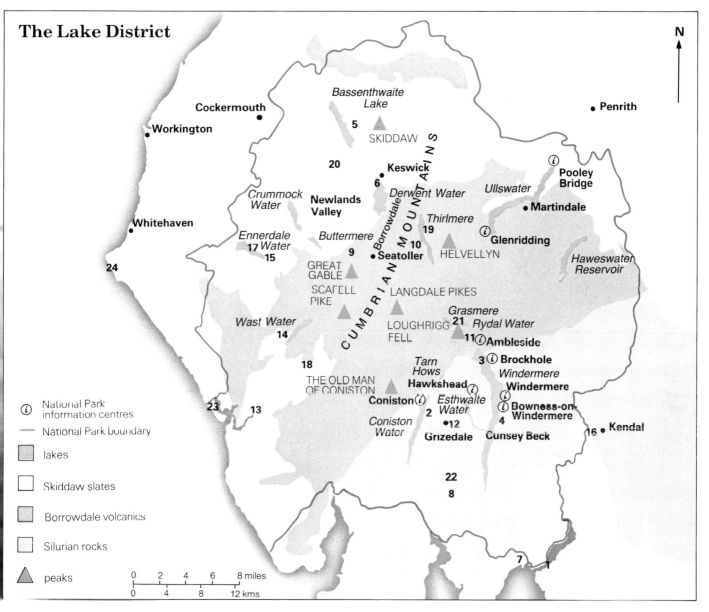

The Lake District

Workington
Cockermouth
Penrith
Bassenthwaite Lake
5
SKIDDAW
20
Keswick
6
Pooley Bridge
Crummock Water
Newlands Valley
Derwent Water
Ullswater
Martindale
Whitehaven
Buttermere
Thirlmere
19
Glenridding
Ennerdale Water
17
15
9
Seatoller
10
HELVELLYN
Haweswater Reservoir
24
GREAT GABLE
SCAFELL PIKE
LANGDALE PIKES
Wast Water
14
Grasmere
21
Rydal Water
LOUGHRIGG FELL
11
Ambleside
18
Tarn Hows
3
Brockhole
Windermere
THE OLD MAN OF CONISTON
Hawkshead
Windermere
Coniston
Esthwaite Water
2
Bowness-on-Windermere
Coniston Water
12
4
23
13
Grizedale
Cunsey Beck
16
Kendal
22
8
7
1

Key:
- (i) National Park information centres
- National Park boundary
- lakes
- Skiddaw slates
- Borrowdale volcanics
- Silurian rocks
- peaks

0 2 4 6 8 miles
0 4 8 12 kms

Key to map numbers

Nature trails:
1 Arnside Knott
2 Brantwood
3 Brockhole
4 Claife Shore
5 Dodd Wood
6 Friar's Crag
7 Hampsfell
8 Hay Bridge deer trail
9 Johnny Wood
10 Launchy Ghyll
11 Loughrigg Fell
12 Millwood forest trail
13 Muncaster
14 Nether Wasdale
15 Nine Becks

16 Serpentine Woods
17 Smithy Beck
18 Stanley Ghyll
19 Swirls forest trail
20 Whinlatter forest trail
21 White Moss Common
Nature reserves:
22 Hay Bridge
23 Ravenglass
24 St Bees

Restrictions on access
Hay Bridge (8, 22) and
Ravenglass (23) have access
restrictions. For details of
these, and of other nature
reserves contact Cumbria
Wildlife Trust.

Information and advice are available to the public at the
National Park Visitor Centre, Brockhole, Windermere.
There are also **National Park Information Centres** in
Coniston, Glenridding, Pooley Bridge, Hawkshead, and
Waterhead, Ambleside, Bowness on Windermere and
Keswick. The **National Park Centre** at Brockhole,
Windermere, holds frequent lectures and displays which
cover natural history, local crafts and literary associations.
The Lake District National Park's **Dalehead Base** at
Seatoller is also well worth a visit, offering various displays
and study facilities housed in a converted barn.
The **Forestry Commission** has a **Visitor Centre** at
Grizedale near Hawkshead. The centre has laid down nature
trails and placed observation towers in the forest for
watching wildlife. There are also two museums, one dealing
with trees and one with wildlife of the forest.
The **Whinlatter Visitor Centre** is at Braithwaite, Keswick.

NORTHUMBERLAND NATIONAL PARK

Northumberland National Park is a kaleidoscope of dramatically changing scenery–from the round grassy hills of the Cheviots, the high boggy moors of the North Tyne area and the vast Wark Forest to the north-facing crags carrying Hadrian's Wall.

Left: Hadrian's Wall, shown here in snow just west of Housesteads, is of course the National Park's most famous monument.

The Pennine Way traverses the full length of the Park, starting at Greenhead in the south-west, partly following Hadrian's Roman Wall, then continuing north through Wark Forest, across the high moors on to the Cheviot Hills and ending at Kirk Yetholm in Scotland, just outside the northern boundary of the Park. This walk must be the perfect way to see the Park and most of its natural history. The National Park Department provides three visitor centres, and run a caravan and camp site in conjunction with the Caravan Club on the River Broamich in the Cheviot foothills.

Below: Dwarf cornel grows high up on Cheviot Hill.

One of the few parts of England to remain completely unspoilt, the Northumberland National Park was designated in 1956. Stretching from the Scottish Border on the north side of the Cheviot Hills southwards to the Roman Wall, a distance of 64km (40 miles) and covering an area of 1030 sq km (398 sq miles), most of the Park is upland over 300m (1000ft) high. It is an almost completely wild area with very few human settlements, but with a good network of roads and almost open access for the walker. One area owned by the Ministry of Defence between the Rivers Rede and Coquet is used as a training area and is closed when in use. Another large area owned by the Forestry Commission provides many trails, car parks, caravan and camp sites and picnic areas, as well as complete freedom for walkers throughout their forests. Although the Northumberland County Council do own some of the park, the majority of the land is still privately owned and farmed with normal access over rights of way.

Geology and vegetation The Cheviot Hills were probably built up as a result of volcanic activity in the Old Red Sandstone Period about 300 million years ago, with later deposits of sedimentary strata laid down

during the Carboniferous Period. These softer rocks surround the Cheviots and molten basalt was later introduced into them during a great upheaval which left the basalt exposed to form the cliffs of the Great Whin Sill. The last Ice Age and river erosion have formed today's landscape, cutting deep valleys into the softer rocks and leaving the harder volcanic rocks to form the hills. The purple-grey granite is exposed at a waterfall–Linhope Spout–and andesite, a lava rock, can be seen in every burn in the Cheviot area. The Great Whin Sill runs right across the southern boundary of the Park, its exposed north slope forming a craggy ridge that carries the Roman Wall along its crest.

There is a very wide range of habitat within the Park, supporting a diverse flora. As the area is mostly an upland one, upland grassland, heather moor and peat bog vegetation is well represented. In the past most of the upland area was afforested, carrying Scots pine, hazel, alder, elm, oak, rowan, ash and scrub birch, most of which was cleared by man during the spread of his early settlements. Any regeneration was prevented by cattle grazing. Only scraps of this original woodland have survived today, mainly on steep slopes where clearing is difficult.

The Cheviots Most of the tops of the higher hills are covered with a deposit of peat, with heather being the dominant plant on the drier parts and cotton sedges, deer sedge and

bilberry on the wetter parts, but in rocky ravines on the Cheviot Hill itself, where an altitude of 600m (2000ft) is reached, mountain plants occur. These include alpine scurvy-grass, chickweed willow-herb, alpine willow-herb, hairy stonecrop, mossy saxifrage, starry saxifrage, dwarf cornel, bog whortleberry, alpine clubmoss and roseroot. Moving down the steeper slopes on to the upland grassland where the soil is well drained, there are bent grasses and sheep's fescue, with smaller amounts of red fescue, moor mat-grass and wavy hair grass. Associated with this grassland are harebell, heath bedstraw, bitter vetch, field woodrush, tormentil and five species of bryophytes.

Within the steep Cheviot valleys the outcrops of andesite provide an interesting habitat for a wide variety of plants. This rock weathers into a rich brown soil with a high organic content and supports wild angelica,

woodruff, foxglove, marsh thistle, bluebell, wood crane's-bill, cow parsnip, greater wood-rush, dog's mercury, burnet saxifrage, golden rod, wood sage, greater stitchwort, valerian, the oat grasses, lady fern, male fern and the hard shield fern. Among the choicer plants found here are hairy rock-cress, maiden pink, the maidenhair spleenwort and the brittle bladder fern.

In the lower valleys there are areas of meadowland which are quite marshy, being fed continuously by drainage from higher ground. Here you can find marsh marigold, flea sedge, melancholy thistle, wood horsetail, globe flower, marsh valerian, spotted orchid, purple orchid and the beautiful grass of Parnassus. Another community of plants occurs on the gravel beds of the streams, where you may still find shepherd's cress, parsley piert, carline thistle, cudweed, purple

Above: One of the Park's more unusual mammals is the wild goat which grazes in small herds on the Cheviots.

Top right: A distant view of the Cheviot Hills, which rise to over 800m (2625ft).

Bottom right: The Cheviots have their own breed of sheep which graze the more fertile hillsides. Two Cheviot lambs are shown here.

Opposite left: The shy woodcock lives in the dense coniferous forests.

Below: Badgers breed on the high moors in the Park. This is a young individual.

willow, annual knapweed and monkey flower.

Coquetdale and North Tynedale Moving southwards where the Carboniferous grits, limestones and cement stones replace the granite and lavas of the Cheviots, the predominant fell sandstone forms the Simonside Hills and the sandy acid soils support vast expanses of heather moorland. Where this moorland is managed by burning off to provide a supply of young heather for the sheep and grouse, very little else is present but mosses and lichens. In undisturbed areas grow such plants as chickweed wintergreen, petty whin and stag's horn moss.

In this area there are numerous north-facing sandstone cliffs, exposed during the last Ice Age and all bearing the markings of glacial movement. It is here on the wetter ledges that you can find the lesser twayblade growing among the sphagnum moss. The woodland here is mainly birch with a few patches of juniper and upland oak; it supports a rich flora, especially on the more fertile soils, where you can find dog's mercury, bird's-nest orchid, enchanter's nightshade, wood sanicle, lesser skullcap, bearded couch-grass, garlic, wood anemone, pale sedge and cow wheat.

Moving west to Redesdale and the North Tyne region, large areas of blanket bog and grassland have been drained and planted with conifers. A good example of this blanket bog can be seen at Coom Rigg Moss, now a National Nature Reserve. This area has been

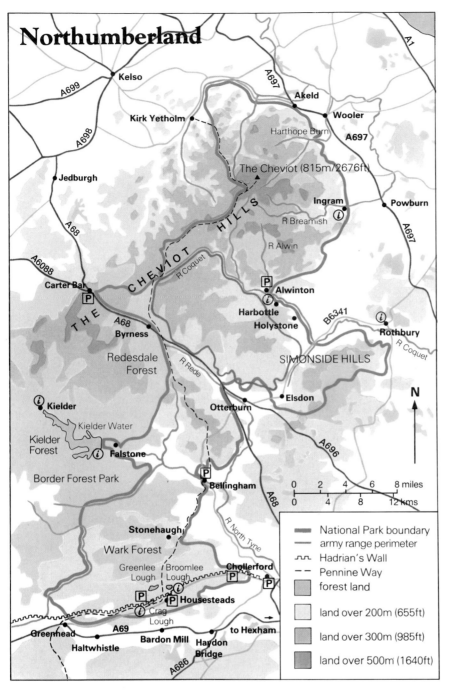

Northumberland

(map) The Cheviot (815m/2676ft)

SIMONSIDE HILLS

THE CHEVIOT HILLS

Redesdale Forest

Kielder Water

Kielder Forest

Border Forest Park

Wark Forest

Greenlee Lough / Broomlee Lough

Crag Lough

N

| | 0 2 4 6 8 miles |
| | 0 4 8 12 kms |

National Park boundary
army range perimeter
Hadrian's Wall
Pennine Way
forest land
land over 200m (655ft)
land over 300m (985ft)
land over 500m (1640ft)

undisturbed by man and provides a good selection of sphagnum and a few plants rare in Northumberland, such as long-leaved sundew, bog rosemary, bog asphodel and round-leaved sundew.

Upland loughs In the southern part of the Park, which is dominated by the intrusive Whin Sill carrying the Roman Wall, there are deep troughs gouged out by glaciation between the hard ridges of the whinstone. Here the Northumbrian Loughs have formed, providing an interesting aquatic vegetation. You can see the succession from open water to raised bog through the stages of reeds and fen. At Crag Lough you can find pondweeds and shoreweed, and in the reed fringes are white sedge, cotton sedge, mare's tail, bog bean, reed grass, marsh cinquefoil, marsh speedwell and various mosses. The dolerite rock weathers down well to provide an easily leached soil where cowberry and rosebay willowherb are common on the craggy slopes and heather and bilberry have helped to stabilise the scree slopes.

Northumberland's birds Most of the park is upland with streams and valleys, providing a diversity of habitats for a wide selection of birds. The hills and moors are dominated by the curlew during the breeding season–this bird has become the emblem of Northumberland National Park. The higher hills are the haunt of the golden plover, buzzard, raven and occasional breeding dunlin, with red

Above: A map of the Park. Most of Northumberland's rivers and streams have their sources within the Park. Indeed, four of the main rivers radiate from the Cheviot itself and, as this area is mainly very poorly drained peat and soil, it holds back the rainfall like a sponge, releasing the water gradually into the rivers.

Left: In the more fertile hillside soils of the Cheviots you can find the lovely mountain pansy.

Right: In one section around Alwinton grows the rare Jacob's ladder, usually only found in limestone regions.

grouse and ring ouzel on the hill slopes. The open moors are the home of the blackcock, short-eared owl and merlin, which nest in the deep heather.

It is, however, the river valleys that carry most species of birds, with heron, dipper, oystercatcher, ringed plover, common sandpiper, pied, grey and yellow wagtails, mallard and goosander using the streams as highways. Feeding and nesting in the trees lining the stream banks are the green woodpecker, pied and spotted flycatchers, redstart, chiffchaff, willow warbler, tree pipit, wood warbler and blue, great, willow, coal and long-tailed tits. The wheatear nests in the drystone walls or scree slopes and the yellowhammer and whinchat in the gorse.

Many mammals Rabbits and hares are the most common mammals to be seen by the visitor, the brown hare being as numerous as the rabbit in the rough upland pastures.

Badger and fox breed on the high moors as well as in the valleys and the fox is often seen on the hill slopes where there is less cover. The most elusive of the larger mammals is the otter, which uses the streams as highways, the spraints found on the dried river beds being evidence that it is still present in the Park.

Although there are no wild red deer within the Park, roe deer are everywhere and their numbers have increased dramatically in the last two decades, occupying the large stands of new coniferous forests. Fortunately the red squirrel does not have to compete here with the grey squirrel, which does not breed in Northumberland. The field vole is abundant, providing a food source for the predatory birds, and its relative the water vole is common along the river banks. Stoat and weasel are present, and during the last few years escaped mink have increased, becoming great pests in some areas.

Above: A view upstream of the River Rede in Redesdale Forest.
Guided walks are led by experts from various centres in the Park all year round. Full details are obtainable from: Information Officer, Northumberland National Park, Eastburn, South Park, Hexham, Northumberland (tel Hexham 605555). A number of small nature reserves are owned by the Northumberland Naturalists' Trust and are not open to the general public. Details of these sites and membership of the NT can be obtained from the Hancock Museum, Barras Bridge, Newcastle.

THE NORTH YORK MOORS

Moors, dales and rocky shores: these are the three basic elements of the North York Moors National Park, which abuts the North Sea and lies between industrialised Tees-side and productive arable country.

Once known as Black-a-more, because of the peat and heather, the name North York (not North Yorkshire) Moors came into use towards the end of the last century. Previously, there were 'black moors' (heather) and 'white moors' (grasses). The Park, designated in 1952, extends to 1432sq km (553sq miles), reaching its highest point on Urra Moor (455m/1489ft), part of the Cleveland Hills. An atmosphere of remoteness is still to be found – that remoteness which caused the raising of a great many moorland crosses to guide travellers. Over 30 of these crosses are named, and Ralph Cross – at the heart of the moors – became the emblem of the Park.

About 40% of the National Park is heather moorland. A profusion of heather, in fact, led to the Park's designation. The hills become, in the east, a range of imposing sea cliffs, with intervening valleys, and the Park has 40km (25 miles) of rocky coastline between Staithes and a point north of Scarborough. The boundary extends to Boulby Cliff, at 203m (666ft) the highest point on the east coast of England. Ravenscar, further south, rises to some 183m (600ft) from the sea. Within the Park are 1610km (1000 miles) of footpaths and bridleways.

The North York Moors National Park is surrounded on three sides by low country. To the north lies the Cleveland Plain and to the west and south are the Vales of York, Mowbray and Pickering, while the Park's western ramparts are the Hambleton and Cleveland Hills.

Geological aspects The basic rocks – Liassic, of the Jurassic Period are visible on the sides of the dales and by the sea, with some exceptional exposures at Ravenscar. The village of Robin Hoods Bay overlooks extensive scars of Lower Lias To the north there is a capping of sandstone, and in the south limestone is evident, forming the Hambleton and Tabular Hills. In and around the village of Coxwold, where the limestone has a higher proportion of sand and iron, the stone has a delicate honey tone.

The only volcanic rock evident in the Park – a band of whinstone or basalt – extends for 48km (30 miles) from Great Ayton to Ravenscar; the material was extensively quarried, much of it becoming roadstone. Thin beds of coal – 'fossil fuel' – were used for lime-burning, to improve the fields. Jet, a fossilised wood from coniferous trees, has been picked up around Whitby and, because it took a fine polish, became fashionable as jewellery. Much more significant, however, were the

93

Above: Robin Hoods Bay at low tide. A wide range of marine creatures can be found in the rock pools here when the waves retreat.

Left: The limestone soils of the southern part of the National Park encourage such species as this wood vetch to flourish.

Below: Fallow deer—a buck and a doe. The forests of the North York Moors National Park support red and roe deer as well as fallow deer.

deposits of alum, worked for nearly three centuries and used by the textile and tanning industries.

Features of special interest in the corallian limestone are the 'windy-pits' of Ryedale, and the caves in Kirkdale, near Helmsley, where archaeologists made interesting discoveries. From the Kirkdale caves were brought the bones of mammoth, rhinoceros and other subtropical fauna that lived before the onset of the last Ice Age.

The influence of man Life would have become tolerable on the Moors for man some 8000 years ago, when tundra conditions followed the retreat of glacial ice. Yet the earliest signs of man of which we are aware date back

only some 5000 years. The Bronze Age is significant because it was during this time that much of the natural forest on the hills was cleared, and barrows – the burial places known on the Moors as 'howes' – were made; they have been found in large numbers.

The natural regeneration of timber was not possible in later times because of extensive sheep-rearing. The sheep ate almost everything that grew. Rievaulx Abbey, in a deep valley near what is now Helmsley, grazed over 14,000 sheep on local moors.

Today, the moors are still grazed by sheep, and heather forms the staple diet of red grouse, which are preserved for sport. The moorland is strip-burned to ensure a continuation of young heather, which is at its peak as a food plant when it is about three years old.

The Moors These are not exceptionally high. The area occupied by moorland is shrinking fast as land is ploughed up for farming or forestry. Over a span of three decades a quarter of what was open moorland has been transformed in this way. The moors are intensively grazed. When the Bridestones Nature Reserve, near Low Dalby, was fenced off against sheep a rapid regeneration of timber began.

Heather moor is still widespread but bogland is limited. (The rainfall on the north-east moorlands is considerably less than that on the high Pennines some 40km/25 miles to the west). The heather, rooted on peat, has been the subject of special study, with attention paid to those areas severely damaged by moorland fires during a drought period a few years ago.

Flowering plants found on the moors include ling, bell heather, cross-leaved heath, bracken, bilberry and tormentil. Adders occur on some of the moors, and birds to be watched for include lapwing, curlew, golden plover and red grouse.

A visitor has easy access to a moorland habitat, for a number of good roads take to the hills. A recommended approach to the Park is through Thirsk and Sutton-under-Whitestonecliffe, followed by a steep climb up Sutton Bank, at the top of which is a large car park and an information centre. After a short walk a visitor can look along the plunging western escarpment of the Hambleton Hills and, if visibility is good, overlook the Plain. Away to the west is an uneven blue line the Pennines.

The Hambleton Hills crest at an elevation of some 305m (1000ft). The road eastwards from Sutton Bank includes views of moorland, but there is also newly created farmland and forestland. The road makes a steady descent to Helmsley, in the valley of the Rye. Here the main National Park offices are situated. Stokesley, just outside the Park's north-western boundary, has a road extending through Great Broughton and up Hasty Bank to cross a tract of moorland (the Cleve-

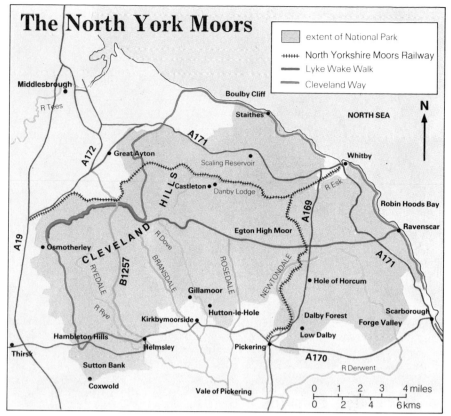

land Hills) to Chop Gate and Bilsdale.

A visitor who motors northwards from Kirkbymoorside to Gillamoor has the elation of a surprise view, where the Tabular Hills end abruptly, offering a vantage point for Farndale and the moors. Nearby Hutton-le-Hole has a remarkable folk museum, including reconstructed buildings of local style. A road from Hutton-le-Hole crosses the moors to the formidable 'bank' leading down to Rosedale.

Another surprise is afforded by the capacious Hole of Horcum, which is clearly to be seen from the Pickering-Whitby road. Extensive moorland views can be enjoyed until the road descends into the Esk valley

Above: The North York Moors National Park has two outstanding long-distance walks: the Cleveland Way, which follows the coast, and the famous 40-mile long Lyke Wake walk, which starts at Osmotherly and ends at Ravenscar.

Below: The nightjar is one bird to look for at night in the woodlands of the Park. Birds are not profuse on the moorlands but include red grouse, lapwing, golden plover and curlew.

Ling blooms on the moors from early August until late September, but long before its flowers are seen there are patches of purple from the bell heather (above), while cross-leaved heath may be found in the boggier places. A common plant is bilberry (in flower, left). Bracken is spreading in many places and another plentiful species of the uplands is tormentil.

It is estimated that about 15% of the Park holds coniferous plantations, and recreation and picnic areas are provided by the Forestry Commission. Low Dalby has a forest centre, and the Forestry Commission has camping and caravanning facilities and also accommodation for visitors in forest cabins.

Information about the Park

The **North York Moors National Park** has its headquarters at the Old Vicarage, Bondgate, Helmsley, York YO6 5BP. Write for a range of leaflets, booklets and posters which are indispensable guides to the area. The **Dalesman Publishing Company** at Clapham, via Lancaster has published a magazine, *The Dalesman*, for nearly 50 years and its 300 titles in print include books of interest to those visiting the Park. The main visitor centre for the Park is at the **Moors Centre** near Castleton in Eskdale. The **Sutton Bank Information Centre** is open from Easter to October and there is an **Information Centre** at Helmsley. At Ravenscar, near Scarborough, there is the start of the famous Geological Trail (a waymarked route). There are over 20 *Sites of Special Scientific Interest* in the Park, mostly at low elevations. Forge Valley, near Scarborough, is a **National Nature Reserve**, and in Farndale, where wild daffodils grow by the River Dove, there is a **Local Nature Reserve.**

near Whitby. You can also traverse high moorland by the main Scarborough-Whitby road.

The Dales Here and there on the sides of the dales, or on the lower slopes of the Hambleton and Tabular Hills, is a mixture of indigenous trees – a reminder of the type of woodland that once covered much of the area. To encourage the planting of hardwoods the Park authority provides farmers and landowners with trees to plant on unused ground. Extending from the south towards the heart of the moorland tract is a trio of little dales – Bransdale, Farndale and Rosedale; none of these has a motor road extending directly from its head.

Newtondale, between Pickering and Goathland, is an impressively deep valley, now well wooded with coniferous trees. A restored railway is used by a host of visitors each year, for the trains are hauled by steam locomotives. Eskdale, in the north, a long east/west valley, receives water from the other dales, including Commondale and Fryupdale. To the south of the Park lies verdant Ryedale.

The limestone countryside offers the most interest to botanists. Some notable species in the south of the Park are bird's-eye primrose, globeflower and white bogbean. Clay land in the valleys leading to the sea is botanically interesting, with primroses and drifts of bluebells in spring. Spotted and bee orchids flourish, and there is small scabious, salad burnet and wood vetch, as well as a host of commoner plants. There are a number of reserves within the Park, managed by the Yorkshire Naturalists' Trust.

Woods and forestland In the woods and plantations of the southern area are red, roe and fallow deer. The Forestry Commission began planting in the area in 1920 and today the Pickering Forest District (some 30,000 acres) is the largest forest tract of upland heath in England. A conifer forest is a relatively short-lived enterprise; the trees mature quickly and are felled, and then the cycle begins again.

Facilities granted to the public to visit the forests of the Forestry Commission are prominently indicated on the approach roads. Visitors are expected to explore the forests on foot, but deep penetration by car is possible at two forest drives – Hackness to Thornton-le-dale, and in Newtondale.

The coast The 40km (25 miles) of coastline within the National Park is generally of the high cliff type, with expanses of sand in the bays and, near Filey, a 'brig' or extension of rock into the sea. Filey Brig looks like a natural breakwater. The low-tide pools in places like Robin Hoods Bay are of great interest. In contrast to the big bird colonies on the chalk cliffs of Bempton and Flamborough to the south, there is comparatively little bird excitement along the dark cliffs although gulls nest here and the fulmar is a common sight as it patrols its breeding area

EXPLORING THE PEAK DISTRICT

The Peak District is a unique region of contrasts:
the sombre, peat-covered moors where golden plover
and grouse hold sway; the deep limestone dales with
their wealth of wild flowers; the clear, cold streams;
and the woodlands ringing with birdsong.

The unique character of the Peak District is a product both of natural features and the activities of man. Its location in the heart of Britain results in it being a meeting place of typically northern and southern species of plants and animals while the history of man's influence includes the reduction of tree cover, the introduction of sheep and cattle, the mining of lead and fluorspar, and the quarrying of limestone.

The landscape The name 'Peak' District is a misnomer since there are no peaks. Rather the area is composed of plateaux which are divided up by valleys and fringed with ridge-shaped hills. The highest hills are over 600m (2000ft): these are Kinder Scout and the

nels. These are known as groughs, and the peat mounds that separate them are known as haggs. It is on the haggs that plants are found –mostly bilberry and crowberry–on the drying peat.

Some people believe that the erosion of the blanket peat is due to natural causes stemming from a change in the climate; others argue that overgrazing by sheep, and regular burning, cause the destruction of the plant cover and permit the erosion of the exposed soft parts.

One of the most interesting of the plants of both intact and eroded peat is the cloudberry. This is the only true mountain species in the flora of the Peak District, for it grows only above 380m (1250ft). It is one of the northern species, along with crowberry, which reaches the south-east limit of its British distribution here.

Heather predominates on the shallower peats of the lower moors. Its regular, small-scale burning for grouse produces a patchwork pattern of dark, old heather interspersed with paler, recently-fired areas where

neighbouring Bleaklow, in the north of the district. These and their surrounding moors are on the hard gritstone which forms a swollen horseshoe shape round the north and the edges of the district. This area is known as the Dark Peak. Nearly encapsulated by the horseshoe is a limestone dome known as the White Peak: a plateau ranging from 240-300m (800-1000ft), which in turn is deeply dissected by the dales.

The Dark Peak The sombre-coloured heather moorland, dark brown peat, soot-blackened gritstone walls and the dull greens and browns of grassland and bracken merit the name Dark Peak. But although these gritstone hills are predominantly dark in colour, they are truly as splendid as any other uplands.

The tops of the higher hills, and some of the hollows caught within ancient landslides, are covered with peat. This accumulated mostly in periods of wetter climate beginning some 7000 years ago. The lower rainfall of the present climate is insufficient for its growth to continue, but 6-10m (20-30ft) of peat can be found in some areas. In the Peak District the deeper, wetter uneroded blanket peats are characterised by a uniform cover of the two common cottongrasses.

The wet blanket peat is the summer-time stronghold of the magnificent golden plover, whose haunting, piping call signals its territorial claims. Where peaty pools abound, a few dunlin come to breed. These are at the southern edge of their British breeding distribution. Both feed on the vast numbers of cranefly and their larvae which live on the wet peat.

In many parts of the highest plateau, the deep peat is being eroded by water forming networks of deep intercommunicating chan-

Above: Cottongrasses around a bog pool on Holme Moss, a typical sight on the Dark Peak. The range of plant species on the blanket bogs has been reduced by air pollution from the towns that surround the Peak District.

Right: The cloughs or moorland valleys have their own range of wetland plants. Here is ivy-leaved bellflower; other uncommon species of this habitat are the heath spotted orchid and sundew, an insect-catching plant.

Below: A male golden plover, settling down on its moorland nest; male and female take turns to incubate the eggs.

he colour is lightened by young shoots. The young plants provide nutritious feeding for grouse and mountain hare alike, while the older, taller bushes conceal the nests. The fact that heather recovers well after burning—and competes successfully with other colonizing species means that few other plants are abundant within these moorlands.

In contrast with the open blanket bogs and heather moors, a wealth of moorland plants is found in the narrow, often deeply incised valleys or cloughs. The abundance of crowberry, that evergreen relative of the bilberry, is renowned in the area. Most cloughs support a few specimens of it, but the banks in Derwentdale are covered with a mixture of crowberry, bilberry and heather. On the ungrazed rock ledges which occur in most cloughs, goldenrod, various ferns and small holly, rowan and oak trees are among the varied species able to grow in the absence of nibbling sheep.

Many of the cloughs have been invaded by sheets of bracken. Here the whinchats often find sufficient cover to raise their young. The bracken stops abruptly wherever the soil is moistened by spring, bog or flush. The latter results from water seepage just below the soil surface. The wealth of moorland flora occurs in these wet areas, but even these are impoverished compared to other moorlands—a product of collecting by naturalists, overgrazing and air pollution.

Woodlands Remnants of semi-natural oak woodland are found in the Peak District, but these consist mostly of scattered old trees which can hardly be recognised as woodland. Only the woodland managed by the Derbyshire Naturalists' Trust has its walls rebuilt to keep livestock from eating the seedlings. Woods on the gritstone areas are mainly of sessile oak, but silver and hairy birch as well as rowan are common associates.

The ground flora tends to be dominated by

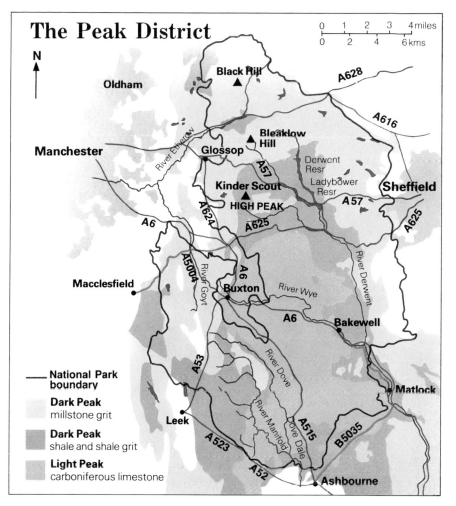

The Peak District

bracken in the more open sites, with bilberry and wavy hair-grass replacing it under denser canopies. The 30-year old enclosure at Padley Gorge illustrates superbly the difference between an enclosed wood and one open to grazing. Young trees, thigh-high bilberry and luxuriously growing cowberry with flowers and fruits, all vie for space.

The most noticeable creatures in some of the woods are the hairy ants, another

Above: The boundary on the map outlines the area described in this article. The Peak District National Park is a slightly smaller area as it excludes the quarrying districts round Buxton and some lowlands that fringe the moors.

Left: A view of the upper end of Lathkill Dale. This is a typical limestone dale, where shallow soils support a wealth of different plants, and with deeper soils and taller plants at the bottom. Lathkill Dale is part of the Derbyshire Dales National Nature Reserve; access is limited to the public footpaths, but much of the wildlife of the area can be seen in other dales in the district.

northern species. They build large dome-like nests of twigs, and forage everywhere in search of small insects. Their presence attracts green woodpeckers, but some of the thicker woods also support good numbers of other woodland birds such as tree creeper, greater spotted woodpecker and all the common titmice. The pied flycatcher is a special summer visitor which reaches its south-east limit in Britain in the Peak District. It shares a few woodland sites with the delightful redstarts, and occasionally with wood warblers.

Conifer plantations are more widespread in the Dark Peak than the old oak woods, but do not blanket the moors. Some harbour the last black grouse in the Peak District.

The White Peak The grey-stoned walls, light green pastures, old quarry faces and limestone outcrops convey the prevalent lighter colour of this area from which the name 'White Peak' is derived. On the whole this is the area of fossil-laden limestone rocks. That is not to say that all the soils, as might be expected, are rich in lime. Until the last century much of the limestone plateau was covered with limestone heaths where heather, mat grass and heath rush abounded. These developed on soils where the lime was washed out by percolating rain water. Sadly for naturalists, most have been reclaimed for farming.

However, the botanical gems are the limestone dales. Whether woodland, scrub or grasslands, the plant life is extremely diverse, and supports a great variety of invertebrates. Most of the woodlands are of ash, but wych elm is common. More rarely, pedunculate oak and small-leaved lime occur, and these are considered to represent the ancient wood of the area. Hazel is the commonest shrub, but the southern dogwood and spindle just penetrate the dales, where they grow with the

Above: The bullhead is a common fish of the White Peak streams—another is the brown trout. An abundant fish population is supported by plentiful supplies of mayfly larvae, shrimps and snails.

Right: Dark red helleborine, a rare and striking orchid, is sometimes found in the thin hazel scrub which occupies the limestone scree. Broadleaved helleborine is also found in this habitat, while rock rose, stone bramble and marjoram provide a common ground cover.

Below: The river Lathkill, like the few other White Peak rivers, supports an abundance of plant and animal life in its lime-rich waters.

northern bird cherry.

The ground flora is just as varied. Carpet of dog's mercury or, in damper areas, ram sons, are interspersed with nettle-leaved bell flower (a southern species), sweet woodruf lily-of-the-valley and primrose, to name but a few.

The dale-side grasslands, and those whic have developed in old quarries, are no les varied. Cowslips and early purple orchid ar the first to flower; the summer sees bird's foo trefoil and oxeye daisy blaze gold and white dotted with pink geraniums, thyme an orchids. Common blue, green hairstreak an brown Argus butterflies flit between flower competing with bees and hoverflies for necta

There is order in this colourful chaos Mossy saxifrage likes the cooler north-facin slopes, and stemless thistle maintains precarious hold on the warmest south-facin slopes in a climate which is really too we There are many small communities, each wit its own characteristic assemblage of plant occurring where conditions are suitable.

YORKSHIRE'S DALES COUNTRY

There is a wilderness character about much of the Dales country, created by the cloudy, rainy weather and the tracts of high, seldom-visited land that lie between the dales. The view (below) of West Stonesdale typifies the rugged grandeur of the area.

The Yorkshire Dales are set among the Pennines. Some 60 valleys lie within the Dales National Park area, and of them half a dozen are large and well-known. These are Swaledale, Wensleydale, Wharfedale, Dentdale, North Ribblesdale and Airedale. Between the dales themselves lie large areas of high country where, in a score of places, the fells overtop the 610m (2000ft) contour. The Pennines present a formidable north-south barrier to the westerly gales. As a result cloudy conditions prevail, and rainfall is heavy—1778mm (70in) of rain falls each year at Ribblehead, and 1473mm (58in) at Malham Tarn.

Though winter in the upper dales is long,

with a late spring and a cool and cloudy summer, there are clear, sunny days on which this area is revealed as one of the most attractive in England. A visitor to the high ground sees a succession of ridges, with the dales tucked between them. Upland plateaux are whitened by the downy heads of cotton-grass (actually a sedge); a cliff at Malham Cove, forming part of Britain's largest outcrop of limestone, gleams chalk-white against a blue-black storm cloud and, after evening rain, its damp surface glows a delicate pink as it catches the rays of the setting sun; and on dry ridges, and across half the landscape to the east, the heather blooms in late summer, to be followed in late autumn by the colourful tints of dying bracken fronds. With few trees in view on the top of the fells (apart from the new plantations of sitka spruce), the landscape can also often look stark and empty, however.

The geology of the dales For a ready guide to the local geology of the area, take a look at the drystone walls – thousands of miles of walls made without a dab of mortar. The

Above: A windswept hawthorn growing on limestone. The limestone terrain in the Yorkshire Dales is typified by cliffs and screes, dry valleys, pavements and potholes. Limestone soils are thin but sweet (rich in calcium). A rare flower, Jacob's ladder, grows in a few places, and at nearby Gordale Scar the high terraces at the approach to the gorge are decked with yew. Ferns, which root in the moist and sheltered grikes (fissures) also flourish on limestone.

Right: Purple saxifrage – an arctic-alpine plant – survives in the high, wild places of the Dales.

Below: Spring sandwort now grows where lead mines once poisoned the land.

builders of these walls did not believe in carrying rocks too far, and thus their wall faithfully reflect the underlying strata.

The dominant stratum is Carboniferous with the beds tilting towards the east and showing the succession of rocks: Carboniferous limestone (in places hundreds of feet thick); the Yoredale Series (bands of limestone, shales and sandstones, lying above the Great Scar Limestone); and Millstone Grit (coarse sandstones deposited in the delta of an ancient river which provides a virtually impervious cap to the isolated western hill and which are the dominant rocks to be seen in the east).

Drainage made the first cuts into the ancient plateau. The water-eroded valley were later subjected to the abrasive ice sheet of the Pleistocene period, when glacier moved down the valleys, broadening, deepening and polishing them, and also coating their sides with boulder clay.

Thus, about 10,000 years ago – a mere wink in the story of the rocks – the dales appeared in the form we recognise today.

Man – and his sheep The glacial lake occupying the floor of many of the dales did not last. The once-generous cover of tree was cleared as man made more grazing space for his domesticated animals.

The wide-open appearance of the dale landscape today is largely a result of grazing by domesticated animals, chiefly sheep. This was a pastoral landscape 1000 years ago. When native woodland was cleared for pasture, the sheep ensured, by their constant browsing, that little natural regeneration of timber would occur. If you see an isolated tree on a hillside, it is more than likely that it is growing from a pothole, or from the side of a cliff where it has rooted beyond the reach

of the ubiquitous sheep.

In quite recent times, over-stocking with sheep has debased many a fell, leading to the disappearance of heather from the drier ridges and to the formation of vistas dominated by mat grass.

The dales The best land is found in the dales, or valleys, themselves. Most of the old meadows and permanent pastures have been ploughed up and re-seeded with grass mixtures that include rye, and the result is a uniform green where years ago there were flower fields with a generous mixture of grasses, flowers and herbs. So few are the remaining old-style meadows that the Yorkshire Wildlife Trust has acquired some as nature reserves. A few upland meadows are still capable of producing such a huge crop of buttercups that there seems to be a yellow stain on the landscape.

At the road verges something of the old plant life endures. Many ancient thorn trees can be seen, and there is a seasonal profusion of such common plants as cow parsley and meadow cranesbill with, here and there, colonies or orchids.

The coming of the machines, which disrupted the nesting routine of a once-common bird, the corncrake, also means that waders (especially the curlew) are under assault from mowing machines when their young are but half-grown.

Most of the dales rivers today flow clear and cool, though they are frequently stained brown by peat. The gripping (mechanical drainage) of thousands of acres of hilly land means that rain runs off much more quickly than it once did. Also, an overspill of liquid from a silage pit can pollute the local beck and affect the main rivers.

Deciduous woodland A surprisingly large area of old deciduous woodland remains, most of it on steep fellsides, where it receives some protection from the weather and where the land is not of sufficiently good quality to be reclaimed for intensive farming. The fellside woods, which are generally on dry soils, grow an indigenous mixture of birch, hazel and ash. Lower down the dales, near Bolton Abbey in Wharfedale for instance, magnificent woods of oak, beech, sycamore and ash spring from the moist boulder clays.

If the sheep have ready access, there is little ground cover for other animals. But in high untended woodland trees rot where they fall and are colonized by insects. The insects attract nesting woodpeckers (both the great spotted and the green), and open glades encourage woodcock to nest. Badgers also live in these quiet old woods.

The absence of sheep leads to a lusty growth of native plants. Ling Gill, in North Ribblesdale, has a bountiful flora because many parts of it are inaccessible to sheep, and just across the valley is a fenced-off wood, Colt Park, which is a good example of an ashwood growing in a deeply dissected limestone pavement.

Crags and gills Steep-sided narrow gills (water-carved valleys) extend up to over 305m (1000ft) above sea level and, with their cliffs, are a favourite nesting haunt of the ring ouzel. The willow warbler is abundant, too, up to and above the heather line where there are no trees. The gills provide sheltered conditions for plants and wild creatures and greatly extend the moderating influence of the dales.

Industrial areas Some of the finest natural history habitats are in areas once devoted to industries that are now no longer in existence. The once-notable lead-mining industry poisoned the ground badly, but now patches of spring sandwort bloom on the arid land in spring. A former limestone quarry or a disused railway line, if neglected, soon burgeons into an outstanding area for plant life, and may have the added attraction of a pond or even a lake.

Old buildings themselves are quickly colonized by plants; elsewhere trees speedily

Above: The peregrine falcon (seen here with a chick) is an uncommon bird of the Yorkshire uplands, and the raven, too, is nearly as rare. The commonest bird is probably the humble meadow pipit, while the carrion crow appears everywhere. Dipper and grey wagtail can be seen on rivers and streams and the yellow wagtail haunts the moist lowland meadows. Wheatear and ring ouzel appear on the hills, along with nesting pairs of golden plover and dunlin. Lapwings are fairly common on marginal land, and everywhere—or so it seems—there are curlews nesting on hillside pastures or in lowland meadows.

Below: This map shows the location of some of the best-known Yorkshire dales.

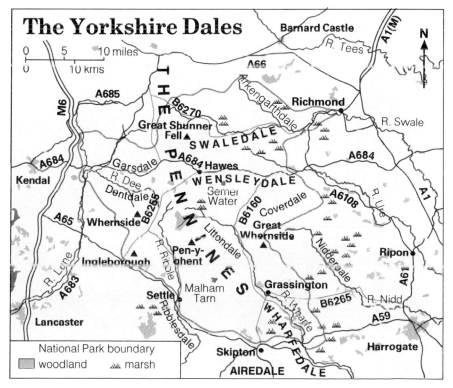

The Yorkshire Dales

In spite of these destructive forces, however, the remaining moors are among the finest in Britain, and the red grouse stays faithful to its open, windswept heather landscape. With a specialised diet that is almost entirely composed of heather, there is no option for the grouse but to cling to the 'tops'. On well-managed moors old heather is burned, or 'swiddened', to stimulate new growth of shoots for the grouse to eat.

Sheep, grouse and 'swiddening' preserve the moorland in its open, treeless state. The moorland zone is generally between 305m and 381m (1000-1250ft) high and lies between the high pastures of the farmlands and the even higher cottongrass mosses.

The high moss country is characterised by considerable deposits of peat.

Such rough grazings extend to the summits of the highest fells where few creatures live. Dotterel have been seen on Ingleborough in May, a pair of ravens may nest where there are crags and occasionally the soulful whistle of a golden plover can be heard in the solitude

establish themselves and, on banks of old debris where there is as yet little competition, a variety of orchids can be seen. One old quarry is noted for its bee orchids; another offers common, coral-root and frog orchids. There are also springtime drifts of bird's-eye primrose and clumps of globe flowers.

Heather moorland and mosses Over-grazing by sheep, and the colonization of areas of moorland by unpalatable grasses, have pushed back the heather line. In the North York Moors, too, vast areas of what was formerly heather moor have been reclaimed for farming.

A certain number of sheep pastured on the moors perform a useful task in keeping the heather to a reasonable height and encouraging new growth by their constant pruning; the problems begin when their numbers are excessive. Moorland fires, many of them started unintentionally by visitors, sterilise the peat, and afforestation with conifers not only changes the nature of the environment – it also provides an excellent refuge for such animals as foxes.

The high moors in the Dales country have fine populations of grouse. Here two male black grouse (above) confront each other. Gamekeepers burn old heather (below) to stimulate new shoots.

Left: Two notable examples of standing water in the dales are Malham Tarn (shown here) and Semerwater. Malham Tarn stands in a bed of impervious Silurian slate. The water covers 62 hectares (153 acres) and is 365m (1200ft) above sea level. With its limestone cliffs, extremely high-lying woodland and expanse of water fed by lime-rich streams Malham Tarn Estate is the nesting place of the great crested grebe (among many other birds).

Right: Limestone pavement at Southerscales Scar on Ingleborough (whose imposing 723m/2373ft summit is silhouetted in the distance). Note the plants growing in the grikes (crevices) of the limestone.

Wales

Pembroke's coast to Snowdon's peaks

Wild havens in Wales are dominated by soaring mountain scenery and by spectacular coastal views. It's no accident, therefore, that two of Wales' National Parks encompass mountain regions – while the third has been declared an important coastal site.

The magnificent seaward margin of the Pembrokeshire Coast National Park is best appreciated by walking the 168-mile Coast Path. Here the rock types are of absorbing interest – sandstones, granites, conglomerates, Carboniferous limestone and Old Red Sandstone, with blow-holes, caves and arches. The bird life here is rich, especially the seabird colonies on the offshore islands, while spring flowers and lichens create exquisite natural rock gardens.

Other coastal gems include the Gower Peninsula and the Dyfi Estuary. Even though the sand dunes are under increasing pressure from visitors, the saltmarshes and mud flats at Whiteford on the Gower provide a wonderful evocative atmosphere as the wild ponies canter among the yellow flags in June. The Dyfi Estuary is an important wildfowl refuge and there is a succession of plants flowering throughout the summer on the dunes.

Snowdonia National Park boasts much more than the highest peak in England and Wales; it has spectacular cwms, beautiful lakes, plunging waterfalls, lush forests and rolling sand dunes. Rare animals and plants abound – on the slopes grow mountain avens, moss campion and roseroot, while a glance skyward may reveal a glimpse of chough, peregrine falcon or buzzard; and the keen-sighted may spot a pine marten or elusive polecat in the woods.

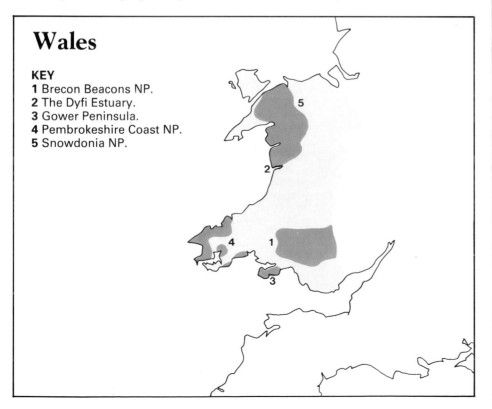

Wales

KEY
1 Brecon Beacons NP.
2 The Dyfi Estuary.
3 Gower Peninsula.
4 Pembrokeshire Coast NP.
5 Snowdonia NP.

Left: The Idwal Slabs at Cwm Idwal in Snowdonia. Though much of Wales' mountain landscape may seem harsh and inhospitable to wildlife, it is not barren. In particular, many species of arctic-alpine plants flourish on some of the lime-rich soils — these include moss campion, roseroot, starry saxifrage and the extremely rare Snowdon lily.

Below: The chough — instantly recognisable with red beak and legs — was once a widespread bird, occurring round much of the coastline of England, but now it is restricted to the remote western cliffs of Wales, Ireland and Scotland. Only in North Wales is its population on the increase.

THE BEAUTY OF THE BEACONS

The most southerly mountains in Britain are in the Brecon Beacons National Park in the counties of Powys, Dyfed, Gwent and Mid Glamorgan. Designated in 1957, the park provides high-level walking and pony-trekking over treeless moors and summits.

Below: The Black Mountain – whitened with snow! The Beacons Park is noted for its swallowholes – funnel-like pits in the surface of the moorland, looking from the air like bomb craters. The largest is 46m (150ft) across and many metres deep. Confined to the areas of Carboniferous limestone, many of them are the result of collapses in the roofs of underground caverns as acid water off the peat moors has dissolved the limestone below.

The Brecon Beacons National Park, covering 1344sq km (519sq miles), is made up of four upland blocks. In the east are the Black Mountains; in the west, to confuse things, is the Black Mountain; and between the two are the Beacons themselves and Fforest Fawr. There are many heights of about 610m (2000ft), while on Pen y Fan the Beacons reach 886m (2906ft).

The uplands To explore the higher ground you could begin with the Black Mountains, perhaps making your way up from Hay-on-Wye or Llanthony to the heathery heights of Hay Bluff and its close neighbour, the Twmpa, with their magnificent northwards views across mid-Wales. Turning south, you can travel for miles from summit to undulating summit, taking in the highest in this section of the Park – Waun Fach – and passing on south again to Pen Cerrig-calch, which is noteworthy as a peak of Carboniferous limestone outcropping amid a world of old red sandstone.

The craggy, triple-headed summits of the Beacons – Cribyn, Pen y Fan and Corn Dû – can be seen from across the wide valley of the Usk. Reaching nearly 900m (3000ft), these tough grits and conglomerates are the highest old red sandstone rocks in Britain.

West of the Beacons the land drops sharply to the Brecon-Merthyr road, but then rises just as quickly up the slopes of Fan Fawr, one of the summits of Fforest Fawr. Despite its name, Fforest Fawr (great forest) is not a forest but a treeless upland, the name 'forest' being a Middle Ages term for a royal hunting ground. West of Fan Fawr you can climb several other Fforest Fawr heights until you reach the loftiest of all – Fan Brycheiniog. This is a sister summit to Bannau Sir Gaer, which rises one mile to the west and is the highest point of the Park's westernmost section, the Black Mountain. From here there is an immense prospect all the way round from Cader Idris in the north to Exmoor in the south.

Streams and lakes Well blessed with rain, the uplands are the source of many sparkling streams, the longest and best-known of which

is the Usk, which crosses or skirts most of the Park, for it rises in the west on the north side of the Black Mountain and then heads east past Brecon to divide the Beacons from the Black Mountains before flowing out of the Park just south of Abergavenny. With its slopes climbing high above green farmlands and patches of woodland, the fertile vale of the Usk is beautiful from end to end.

Three parallel deep valleys have been cut close to each other into the southern flanks of the Black Mountains by the streams called Grwyne Fechan, Grwyne Fawr and Honddu. The first two are tributary to the Usk, but the Honddu escapes east to the Monnow, then the Wye. From the Beacons and Fforest Fawr flow many streams that make their way south or south-west down the coal valleys of Glamorgan, the most remarkable being those at the head of the Vale of Neath. Here four streams – Hepste, Pyrddin, Mellte and Nedd – have sliced deep ravines in the Carboniferous limestone and fall over high waterfalls where they reach the more resistant millstone grit. A few of the limestone streams disappear below ground, for the rocks here are honeycombed by some of the longest and deepest caves in the British Isles.

Of the Park's few natural lakes, by far the largest is at Llangorse below the western slopes of the Black Mountains. This is a fertile lowland water with large reed beds. Unfortunately, it is disturbed by power boats and water sports and has been polluted by detergents and agricultural fertilisers. There have been attempts to regulate the intrusions, but the problems of wildlife disturbance still persist.

On the Black Mountain are two fine neighbouring corrie lakes–Llyn y Fan Fach under the red sandstone crags of Bannau Sir Gaer, and Llyn y Fan Fawr under Fan Brycheiniog. Their rock-girt water is clear and pure but inevitably far less rich in life than that of Llangorse Lake which is 335m (1100ft) lower and set amid fertile soils.

The woodlands Although nearly all the original forest was cleared for farmland many centuries ago, there are still small tongues of broad-leaved woodland in most of the lowland valleys, mainly of oak with a scattering of birch, ash, alder and others. A few limestone slopes in the south are clothed with almost pure scrub-like ashwoods; and in the south-east there are relics of native beechwoods, the most westerly in Britain.

Here and there a quite alien type of woodland has been created by man, especially this

109

century—the extensive conifer plantations which cover large areas of the higher moorlands and also dominate some of the valleys, notably that of the Grwyne Fawr.

Wild flowers Most sandstones are limeless and have a mainly calcifuge (lime-hating) flora, but those of the Brecon Beacons Park are locally lime-rich and on the uplands they form soft, rotten crags with perennial water draining through them—perfect conditions for plants in great variety, including a number of mountain species which here are at or near their southern British limit. Purple saxifrage, mossy saxifrage and roseroot occur in profusion, and northern bedstraw, green spleenwort and the mountain form of lesser meadow rue can also be found.

Alongside the alpines is a luxuriance of lowland species which obviously enjoy the coolness, dampness and fertility of the often unless lime-rich rocks—primrose, cowslip, burnet saxifrage, rock stonecrop, lady's mantle, wood anemone and a host of others.

In the lowlands some of the best sites for wild flowers are the few pastures and meadows which have not yet been modernised by ploughing and re-seeding. Among the choicer species are meadow thistle, saw-wort, great burnet, dyer's greenweed, petty whin, whorled caraway, creeping willow, fen bedstraw, globe flower, wood bitter-vetch and various orchids and sedges.

In the oakwoods the most varied plant communities are those on the base-rich humus soils where there are plenty of ash trees among the oaks and alders in wetter places. Typical wild flowers are ramsons, wood sanicle, dog's-mercury, woodruff and yellow archangel, with toothwort and herb paris among the rarities. Most such woods flourish on well-watered ground in the valleys; but in the drier ashwoods of the limestone hillsides, such as those near Craig y Nos, the wild flowers are quite different. Among the characteristic species here are lily-of-the-valley, broad-leaved helleborine, shining crane's-bill, rockrose and green spleenwort. Besides the ash, the trees are mostly whitebeams and yews. The whitebeams are one of the most distinguished features of the flora of the Park. Some are very local or rare in Britain and two—*Sorbus minima* and *Sorbus leyana*—are found nowhere else in the world.

Water plants are at their best in Llangorse Lake where, despite the pollution that has reduced or exterminated some of the most sensitive rarities, there is still a fair range of resistant species, including three kinds of water-lily, common and lesser bulrush, greater spearwort, flowering rush, golden dock and arrow-leaved water-plantain.

The mammals of Brecon Besides the foxes, badgers, stoats and weasels found throughout the Park, two carnivores are worthy of special mention: the otter, which still thrives along the Usk, the Brecknock WT being a pioneer in the conservation of this now endangered

Above: On the heathery crags of Brecon the piping of ring ouzels is a persistent sound from April to July.

Opposite: A waterfall near Talybont in the Park—the scenery is typical of the area. Many of the Park's streams have brown trout, sea trout and salmon, the Usk in particular. The reservoirs are stocked mostly with brown and rainbow trout and locally with American brook trout. For coarse fish, the best locality is Llangorse Lake, where there are perch, carp and roach, along with large pike and eels.

Right: An appropriate member of the arctic-alpine plant community in Brecon—the Welsh poppy.

Brecon's geology and soils

In contrast with the Snowdonia National Park, where sedimentary rocks exist alongside huge quantities of igneous and metamorphic materials, the rocks of the Brecon Beacons are all sedimentary. The great bulk of them are reddish or purple sandstones, shales and conglomerates of the Devonian period and so are less ancient than those of Snowdonia. Many of them lie in horizontal strata which are clearly visible in the north-facing scarp faces. Older rocks are found only near Llandeilo and Llandovery, where there are Ordovician mudstones and flags, and also Silurian shales and mudstones full of fossils.

All along the southern flanks of the Park are rocks of the Carboniferous period—limestone and millstone grit which are neighbours of the coal measures that lie immediately outside the Park in industrial South Wales. Throughout the Park there is evidence of the great Ice Age and its after-effects—scratched rocks, glaciated pavements, moraines, cirques, corrie lakes, ice-smoothed valleys and deposits of clay and gravel.

The canal

A canal to serve industry and agriculture was built alongside the Usk between Brecon and Newport on the Usk estuary, and completed in 1812. Now restored as far as Pontypool after long neglect, it is used for pleasure boats and is a wholly delightful water-way that winds river-like through the Park for thirty-three miles. For much of its course it is lined with trees and bushes and is a valuable haven for wildlife, harbouring perch, dace and roach among the fishes, and a variety of aquatic plants.

Right: Parsley fern grows on the acid rocks of Brecon, along with viviparous fescue and cowberry.

Opposite page: Bank voles are common in the Park.

mammal; and the polecat which, as in the rest of mid Wales, has survived in reasonable numbers.

Small mammals–voles, mice and shrews–so crucial in the diet of many larger mammals and predatory birds, abound throughout the Park. The field vole is of special interest because of its occasional population explosions, as in 1956 when thousands of newly planted trees were ring-barked and killed by nibbling teeth. Bank voles and wood-mice are common, but the yellow-necked mouse is more local, and the harvest mouse has only been discovered in the Park in recent years.

Brecon birds Skylarks and meadow pipits are the only common breeding birds of high grassy places, but where there are screes or stone walls you will often see wheatears. The highest cliff ledges are nesting places for ravens, kestrels and (rarely) the peregrine falcon. On the heather moors there is a scattering of red grouse and here and there a merlin, while wet rushy hollows are the home of curlew, lapwing and snipe. Spring and autumn see a migratory trickle of a rare wader, the dotterel, but it is not seen every year.

In the broad-leaved woodland resident birds include nuthatch, treecreeper and all three woodpeckers. The buzzard–a bird of the mountains–is well-established, its mewing voice and graceful circling flight very noticeable in spring. Among abundant summer visitors are pied flycatcher, redstart, tree

pipit, blackcap, garden warbler, wood warbler, willow warbler and chiffchaff.

Where there are mature conifers you are likely to find goldcrest, coal tit and perhaps siskin, crossbill and sparrowhawk.

Characteristic water birds are dipper and grey wagtail on streams, and reed and sedge warblers and great crested grebe on Llangorse Lake. Migrants and waterfowl are specially watched for on Talybont Reservoir and Llangorse Lake.

Reserves and mountain peaks

The Park has five National Nature Reserves: **A** Craig Cerrig-gleisiad, 6 miles south-west of Brecon; **B** Craig y Cilau, 2 miles south-west of Crickhowell; **C** Cwm Clydach, 2 miles east of Brynmawr; **D** Ogof Ffynnon-ddu; **E** Cwm Coed-y-cerrig. There is also a Forest Reserve: **F** Penmoelallt, 3 miles north-west of Merthyr Tydfil. Full information about these reserves, and all other aspects of the Park, can be obtained at the excellent visitor centre on Mynydd Illtyd near Libanus, 4 miles south-west of Brecon. **Peaks: 1** Waun Fach 811m(2660ft); **2** Pen Cerrig-calch 701m (2300ft); **3** Cribyn 795m (2608ft); **4** Pen y Fan 886m (2906ft); **5** Corn Dû 873m (2864ft); **6** Fan Fawr 734m (2408ft); **7** Fan Brycheiniog 802m (2630ft); **8** Bannau Sir Gaer 750m (2460ft).

Brecon Beacons

Llandovery

BLACK MOUNTAIN
FFOREST FAWR
D
Llyn y Fan Fach 8 7 Llyn y Fan Fawr
R Nedd
R Mellte
R Hepste
R Pyrddin
A

R Usk
Brecon

BRECON BEACONS
5 4 3
6

Llangorse Lake

Talybont Reservoir
Monmouthshire & Brecon Canal

BLACK MOUNTAINS
2

E
B
C
Abergavenny

F
Tredegar
Ebbw Vale
Merthyr Tydfil

0   2   4 miles
0 2 4 6 kms
N

National Park boundary
nature reserves
land over 300m (1000ft)

THE DYFI ESTUARY NATURE RESERVES

The Afon Dyfi (River Dovey) flows out into Cardigan Bay just north of Aberystwyth. Where it meets the sea it forms, at high tide, an expanse resembling a huge lake nearly two miles wide and five miles long – the teeming Dyfi Estuary.

A typical fast-flowing west coast river, only 50km (31 miles) long from source to mouth, the Dyfi flows through some of the least spoilt countryside in mid-Wales. The waters of the Dyfi start their brief journey to the sea below the steep slopes of Aran Fawddwy near Dinas Mawddwy. The small glacial lake–Craiglyn Dyfi–which nestles below the mountain on its southern slopes overflows to form the young river.

The formation of the estuary The whole area has been fashioned by enormous natural forces. The striking ones are those of wind and

Above: A view of Dyfi Estuary, looking east, at low tide. There is a rich variety of habitats within the estuary, ranging from sand and mud flats to creeks and saltmarshes–all inhabited by a wealth of wildlife.

water, both of which exert incredible influences on the system, as winter storms prove regularly, for with the river in full flood and storm force winds giving the tides and currents even more energy, the main course of the river channel can change in just a few hours. Less obvious perhaps, but even more dramatic, has been the influence of ice. This area of mid-Wales was covered by ice sheets up to 800m (2600ft) thick until only 14,000 years ago. These sheets of ice moved gradually west and fashioned the landscapes of today. During the past 10,000 years, the coastline around the Dyfi has changed considerably, for at the end of the last Ice Age the sea level was about 60m (200ft) below that of today. This meant that the shore was about 12km (7 miles) west. The lowland area was gradually covered by forest. Some 10,000 years ago there was a sudden change in the climate which accelerated the melting of the remaining ice–the advancing sea level covered the low-lying land and drowned the trees.

By far the most significant changes have occurred in the past 150 years. Many of the remaining low-lying areas have been drained and the tidal influence of the sea has been restricted by the building of flood banks which form the boundary of the estuary as it is today. Perhaps the most recent, and maybe the most important, influence that man has had took place in 1922, when three specimens of cordgrass (*Spartina anglica*) were planted on the mudflats at the eastern end of the estuary. The plants flourished and today approximately one third of the estuary is covered by cordgrass. The plants can grow well below high water, withstanding long inundation by the sea. They act as a barrier to the flow of water and slow the current down, and this in turn reduces the carrying capacity of the current, which drops particles of clay and silt among the stems of the cordgrass. The gradual raising of the level of the ground forms islands, which merge to form a higher area of saltmarsh. This is why the grass was planted.

Ynyshir Reserve The Dyfi estuary forms the

Above: Biting stonecrop—one of the many plants found on the Ynyslas dune slacks.

Left: Brown butterflies can be seen in abundance at Ynyslas—including this gatekeeper (a female).

Below: The rabbit population at Ynyslas is high and attracts such hunters as this polecat to the dunes. Rabbits play an important part in the system for their grazing keeps down the taller vegetation, allowing smaller herbs to compete.

centrepiece of a kaleidoscope of fascinating and varied wildlife habitats—from sand and mudflats to creeks and saltmarshes. The first of them is the RSPB reserve at Ynyshir.

The name Ynyshir means 'long island' and from the air the long rocky outcrops are clearly visible. The low-lying land around the estuary was marsh and bog until much of it was reclaimed for agriculture during the last century. Today, the rocky outcrops are covered in fine stands of sessile oaks. These oak woodlands play host to a vast number of insects and numerous birds exploit this rich food source, perhaps the most typical being the pied flycatchers, many of which use the nestboxes on the reserve. Nearly 70 species of birds breed at Ynyshir and the area is a delight in the spring. However, the most impressive time of year for the birdwatcher comes during the spring and autumn migration. The RSPB has installed excellent hides with views over the saltmarshes.

Ynyshir also has a good selection of butterflies—the most typical is perhaps the speckled wood. Purple hairstreaks are common in the woodlands, where the caterpillars feed on the oak and the butterflies can often be seen during July and August around the tops of the trees.

Sandflats and mud banks Probably the most obvious features of any estuary are the extensive areas of sand and mud banks exposed twice a day at low tide.

At first glance, an estuary at low tide looks devoid of life, but a closer inspection of the ground will show a different picture. The most obvious sign is that of the lugworm which is often very abundant. Like this worm, all the animals must be able to escape from the surface—to avoid being swept away by the currents, preyed on and to protect themselves from drying out at low tide. Many animals build permanent burrows like the lugworm and most of them inhabit the first few centimetres of the surface. One of the most numerous is the small shrimp-like crustacean

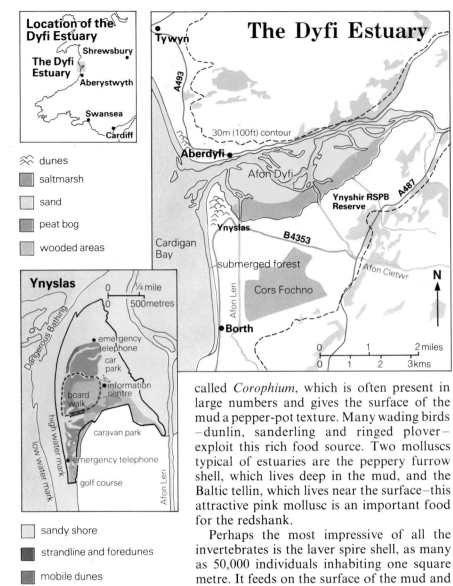

The Dyfi Estuary

Shrewsbury

The Dyfi Estuary

Aberystwyth

Swansea

Cardiff

≋ dunes

saltmarsh

sand

peat bog

wooded areas

Ynyslas

0   ¼ mile

0   500 metres

Dangerous Bathing

emergency telephone

car park

information centre

board walk

high water mark

low water mark

caravan park

emergency telephone

golf course

Afon Leri

sandy shore

strandline and foredunes

mobile dunes

fixed dunes

dune slacks

--- route of nature trail

— reserve boundary

Above: Maps of the Dyfi Estuary and the Ynyslas area. Because the Dyfi affords a classic example of a west coast estuary, with its mud and sand flats, creeks and saltmarshes, together with its attendant habitats—a shingle ridge and sand dune system and an estuarine raised mire — it was selected as a reserve by the NCC. Today, the 209ha (518 acres) of reserve adjoin the 250ha (618 acres) of the RSPB reserve of Ynyshir (with its saltmarshes, unspoilt woodland and fine heather-clad hill slopes overlooking the estuary), and provide a very fine example of coastal habitats.

The Dyfi Estuary

Tywyn

A493

30m (100ft) contour

Aberdyfi

Afon Dyfi

Ynyshir RSPB Reserve

A487

Ynyslas

B4353

Cardigan Bay

submerged forest

Afon Cletwr

Cors Fochno

Afon Leri

Borth

N

0   1   2 miles

0   1   2   3kms

and supports a large number of wading birds on migration to and from their breeding grounds in the north. The estuaries act as refuelling points along the west coast of Britain. The area is also important for its winter populations of wildfowl. The shelduck chiefly exploit the invertebrate food source but others, like the mallard, teal, pintail and wigeon, are mainly vegetarian. They feed on the abundant food washed in by the water and frequently dabble along the edge of the incoming tide. They also exploit the wet fields ditches and marshes adjacent to the estuary There is also a small wintering flock of Greenland white-fronted geese on the estuary –the only flock to be found in England and Wales.

Like the invertebrates, the plants too find it easier to colonize the more stable mud; the sand banks at the estuary mouth are devoid of any vegetation. The first colonizer is the long slimy alga *Enteromorpha*, but more typical is the glasswort (*Salicornia*) which is the first true colonizer of the bare mud. Cordgrass is

called *Corophium*, which is often present in large numbers and gives the surface of the mud a pepper-pot texture. Many wading birds –dunlin, sanderling and ringed plover– exploit this rich food source. Two molluscs typical of estuaries are the peppery furrow shell, which lives deep in the mud, and the Baltic tellin, which lives near the surface–this attractive pink mollusc is an important food for the redshank.

Perhaps the most impressive of all the invertebrates is the laver spire shell, as many as 50,000 individuals inhabiting one square metre. It feeds on the surface of the mud and leaves a tell-tale maze of minute tracks. The shelduck, our largest native duck, feeds on it.

It is not surprising that, with such vast food reserves, estuaries are so important for bird populations. The Dyfi estuary is no exception

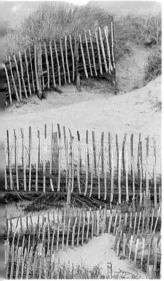

the most abundant plant, while further up the marsh thrift, sea aster and sea spurrey are more common. At the very top of the saltmarsh, where only the spring tides reach, grow other plants such as common reed and scurvy grass.

Ynyslas–shingle and sand dunes At the mouth of the estuary lies the last of the main habitat types–the shingle spit and sand dune system known as Ynyslas (a blue-green island). It gets its name from the distinctive colour of the marram grass and the fact that for many hundreds of years the dunes were an island at high tide.

The dunes form a rich wildlife habitat and are a botanist's delight. On the shore line only those plants adapted to the harsh environment of blowing sand, salt spray and even the occasional inundation by sea water

Top: Dyfi Estuary–the view from Borth Bog in the depths of winter.

Above: In order to prevent erosion some of the sand dunes are contained by fences, placed slanting across the slopes.

Left: The remains of a submerged forest can be seen on the beach just south of the estuary–stumps of Scots pine, birch and alder are exposed at low tide. They may be as much as 10,000 years old.

Right: The dune slacks are rich in plants, with eight species of orchids growing there in summer. This marsh helleborine is one of them.

can survive. Typically, they are annuals and have thick fleshy leaves to withstand the hot dry conditions. The plants, such as sea rocket and prickly saltwort, grow on the highest tide strand zone, where they take advantage of any organic material, such as seaweed, that has been washed up. Behind this strand zone, small hedgehog-like dunes appear, held together by marram.

Behind this protective wall of high dunes, the vegetation changes and becomes far more varied–this area is called the grey dunes because of the increased organic content of the sand that gives it a grey coloration. Typical plants of this area are carline thistle, germander speedwell, common stork's-bill and dove's-foot crane's-bill.

This increase in the variety of plants is echoed by the variety of butterflies. The commonest species are the browns–meadow brown, gatekeeper and grayling–but the small heath and common blue also appear, and the dark green fritillary is abundant.

The jewel of the dune habitats is the dune slacks, the damp hollows between the dunes. These fill up with fresh water in the winter and gradually dry out in the summer. They are very rich botanically and during June and July there are eight species of orchids to be found growing there. The most abundant is the marsh helleborine, with its beautiful cream flowers–these were first recorded in the 1960s and now there are well over 150,000 spikes.

There are no permits required to visit Ynyslas dunes or the Dyfi estuary, but you are advised to visit the Information Centre at Ynyslas before you go on to the reserve. The Countryside Council for Wales holds regular afternoon walks throughout the summer and you can obtain a list of these by writing to CCW, Plas Gogerddan, Aberystwyth, Dyfed SY23 3EE.

GOWER: CLIFFS, CAVES AND COASTS

Small though it is, the Gower Peninsula has great underlying geological diversity. The result of this on the land surface is impressive: so varied are the Gower soils and habitats that it is almost an entire ecological world in microcosm.

Mid-way along the south coast of Wales there is a relatively small promontory shaped roughly like a baby's bootee with the 'toe' pointing to the west. This is the Gower Peninsula, 'the Gower' or just 'Gower' to the locals. It is situated on the western boundary of the city of Swansea in West Glamorgan.

This is a climatically favoured area: in summer the inhabitants of the Gower are joined by people from Swansea and thousands of holidaymakers from further afield–all seeking sun, sea and scenery. Even in the average winter the climate is comparatively mild in temperature, though often windy or damp. Frosts are neither frequent nor usually severe, and snowfall (especially with the snow lying for some days) is so rare as to be something of an event. This mild winter climate has a particular impact on the agriculture of the Gower, allowing early crops, especially of potatoes–for which the Peninsula is famous.

The geology and consequently the soils and habitats–of the Gower are so diverse it is tempting to suggest that nowhere else in Britain could so much variety be found in so small a space (the Gower fits neatly into a rectangle of about 24 by 8km/15 by 5 miles). There can be few areas that offer so much ecologically, both to the general naturalist

Opposite page: A view of Worms Head at the western tip of Gower. This slender rocky promontory is connected to the mainland by a stony pavement for a few hours at low tide; its strange hump-backed appearance makes it easy to see how its name, 'worm', could have been derived from the Old Norse for a sea serpent. The foreground flowers are rock-roses.

Right: Spring squill–one of many flowers to be seen on Gower. Sadly, many species are threatened by improvements to the common grazing land at the top of the cliffs. Seeding with vigorous grasses and heavy applications of nitrogen undoubtedly improve the grazing quality, but at the cost of severely reducing the typical limestone flora.

Below: The vast numbers of shellfish on the sandflats of Gower attract such wading birds as the oystercatcher.

and to the specialist, coupled with great scenic beauty and rail networks.

Gower's cliffs The scenic splendour of the Gower is nowhere better seen than on the south coast. Here the spectacular Carboniferous limestone cliffs stretch for miles, their strata in some places running almost horizontally, in others contorted at all sorts of angles by upheavals in the earth's crust throughout geological time. These rock strata are, in essence, the different layers of a sea-bed formed from the chalky skeletons of minute marine organisms deposited over some 50 million years, starting 250 million or more years ago. The angles at which they lie govern the suitability of the rock to make ledges for nesting birds or plant colonies. The serried ranks of headlands and bays stretch from Mumbles, a Swansea suburb, to the Worms Head at the western tip of Gower.

Many of the cliffs along this coast exceed 30m (100ft) and offer good nesting sites for such birds as herring gulls and jackdaws. Perhaps because of the numbers of holiday-makers, other seabirds are harder to find. The occasional secluded bay holds a kittiwake colony–noisy and smelly and always a hive of activity with nests attached to improbably small out-jutting rocks, often under seemingly impossible overhangs. On the Worms itself there are more kittiwakes, with gulls, some shelduck and, on the tallest sheer north-facing cliffs, mixed colonies of razorbills and also

of guillemots.

The cliff plants are not quite so much influenced by people as are the birds, and the mild climate, linked with the limestone-based soil, gives rise to an excellent and colourful flora. Much of the colour comes from a spectacular profusion of relatively common plants–thrift, squill, thyme, daisy and rock-rose–but there are other attractions, including the multi-coloured basil-thyme and early purple and green-winged orchids. If you look closely at the rock-roses, you will see two types, one smaller and paler in flower than the other; this smaller one is the rare hoary rock-rose. Even more special, perhaps, is the yellow whitlowgrass, clinging like a yellow-flowered saxifrage to the shallow layer of soil in a crack halfway up a rock face. This is an isolated relic, cut off and somehow surviving on these cliffs during the Ice Ages: its nearest other colonies are in Portugal.

Caves, beaches and dunes The abundant sea caves along this coast also house some relics, although most are now in local museums. Some of the caves offered sufficient shelter to be used by wild animals in the past–as they are occasionally by sheep today–and because of the relics left when these ancient animals died they are called 'bone caves'. Among the animals found in them are elks, mammoths and woolly rhinoceros–clear indication that the climate of the Gower was once considerably less favourable than today.

Above: One of the many sights to be seen on the Gower Peninsula–Pennard Castle perched high on the hill, and Pennard Pill.

Below: Some extremely rare plants are known to grow on the Gower Peninsula. One such is the attractively named goldilocks (shown here), and another is the small rest harrow. These are two of Britain's rarest plants.

At the base of the cliffs, extensive sandy beaches attract holidaymakers. Biologically these beaches are rich in shellfish and, together with the many rock-pools, offer plenty of scope for the marine biologist. At low tide rocky reefs are exposed in some areas, the soft limestone deeply eroded and holed by the action of the water and offering a multitude of hiding places for lobsters and crabs. On the rock surface a plentiful covering of seaweeds provides concealment for the small shore animals on which turnstones and purple sandpipers feed.

Across some of the larger bays extensive sand dune systems have formed, clad in marram grass and with surprisingly pre-

cipitous slopes for so unstable a medium. Perhaps the most spectacular is Whiteford Burrows, best viewed from the raven's-eye view on top of Rhossili Down, but here the scenic impact is marred by a sprawl of caravans. Better known is Oxwich, a National Nature Reserve. Here a typical sand dune flora is enriched by an abundance of orchids, including marsh helleborine, while an excellent fresh water marsh has developed behind the dune system. The surrounding area is based on limestone and the marsh is rich in many forms of wildlife. Newts and dragonflies abound, and resident and migrant birds flourish, with the appearance, every so often, of a real rarity such as a little bittern.

Woods and uplands On its inland margins Oxwich is surrounded by one of the relatively few wooded areas of Gower. If any major habitat type is poorly represented in Gower, then it is woodland. Even conifer plantations are almost lacking, while deciduous trees are mostly to be found in narrow belts beside roads, along the courses of streams or in the deep and often dry valleys running down to the coast. Judging from the numbers of garden and scrubland birds, this lack of trees does not have a dramatic effect on the bird population, and larger species—crows, ravens, buzzards and sparrowhawks—seem to find nest sites without undue difficulty. Of the deciduous trees, it is the sycamore that impresses most. This tree is widespread, often with a carpet of arum and wild garlic beneath its branches; some have reached considerable stature and relative antiquity, to judge from their gnarled appearance and hoary fringes of lichens.

The Gower uplands are as acid as the south coast is alkaline with its limestone soils. Cefn Bryn and Rhossili Down are the highest points, each with an extended ridge running north-west/south-east. In some exposed parts near the old beacon sites the vegetation is almost alpine in appearance, with stunted heathers and ling predominating.

Birds here are few and far between: there are meadow pipits, wheatears and stone-chats in the gorse of sheltered spots, and overhead passing ravens and buzzards. To the

Above: Fulmars are on the increase in Gower (as elsewhere), and on windy days their flight prowess can be observed with ease, and at very close quarters, from a number of cliff-top vantage points, such as Thurba near Rhossili.

Above right: Basil-thyme in bloom—such plants as this flourish in the relatively mild climate prevalent on the Gower.

east of Cefn Bryn lies a huge high-level boggy area, the swampiest parts bright with the colours of sphagnum moss. Botanically this is a fascinating region, with such specialist plants as the insect-eating sundew, and attractive ones like the minute pink bog pimpernel, the striking golden spikes of bog asphodel and the feathery white plumes of bog cotton. This is meadow pipit country, too, with skylarks singing over the drier areas and the occasional curlew yodelling its breeding season song in the damper parts. In high summer cuckoos often abound, with plenty of pipits to foster their young and 'woolly bear' caterpillars for food.

The north coast The north coast of the

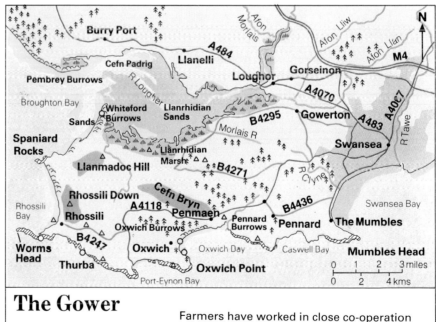

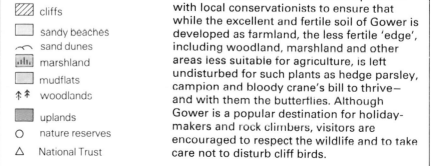

The Gower

cliffs	
sandy beaches	
sand dunes	
marshland	
mudflats	
woodlands	
uplands	
nature reserves	
National Trust	

Farmers have worked in close co-operation with local conservationists to ensure that while the excellent and fertile soil of Gower is developed as farmland, the less fertile 'edge', including woodland, marshland and other areas less suitable for agriculture, is left undisturbed for such plants as hedge parsley, campion and bloody crane's bill to thrive— and with them the butterflies. Although Gower is a popular destination for holiday-makers and rock climbers, visitors are encouraged to respect the wildlife and to take care not to disturb cliff birds.

Gower is vastly different from the south. The bulk of the Gower forms a gigantic break-water, protecting the Burry inlet from the wind and waves sweeping in from the south-west; in this shelter huge sandflats have formed, stretching away into the haze at low tide. The flats are dissected by deep cracks or runnels, making this a place to proceed with caution since the flooding tide sweeps in very smoothly but very rapidly. To be cut off as the

Above: Rest harrow—a plant to look for on the limestone grasslands of the Gower. It flowers from July to September.

Below: Spectacular cliff and sea scenery on the Gower coast. Such sites attract large numbers of seabirds.

tides comes in could prove to be dangerous.

The sandflats house uncountable millions of shellfish and at low tide, particularly during the winter months, they are dotted with gulls and waders seeking food. The cockle popu-lation is sufficiently high for a local industry to flourish. The cockle fishers rake the shellfish from the sand with special forks and often take their harvest back to the shore with the aid of a horse and cart. Not surprisingly, such a density of shellfish has also encouraged large numbers–often thousands, sometimes tens of thousands–of oystercatchers, giving rise to fears that the birds might deplete the shellfish stocks to such a degree that the industry would be put out of business. As all too often happens, sadly this situation periodically develops into one of direct conflict between the cockle fishers and conservationists op-posed to the view that the only solution to the problem is a wholesale slaughter of the oystercatchers.

The northern Gower coast is essentially a wild, remote and lonely place, characterised by the bubbling trill of the curlew or the soulful call of the grey plover. Usually only cattle and horses, grazing the nutritious grasslands washed by the highest tides disturb the waders on the flats, but occasion-ally a peregrine dashes through, sending redshanks into noisy hysteria and scattering the dunlin, which regroup away in the distance looking like wisps of smoke.

THE PEMBROKESHIRE COAST NATIONAL PARK

The Pembrokeshire Coast National Park is largely a border of land winding round a tortuous coastline, but there is also an upland region in the north-east, where the boundary turns inland to include the Preseli Hills which enjoy wide views over the sea to Devon, Snowdonia and occasionally even Ireland in the west.

The great cliffs and rocky islands of Pembrokeshire, thrusting out into the Atlantic, form the south-western peninsula of Wales. *Penfro* is its ancient Welsh name, meaning 'Land's End', and *Penfro* has long since been anglicised into Pembroke. In several ways the Pembrokeshire Coast is unique among our national parks. It is the smallest, at 580sq km (225 square miles), the most maritime and also the most lowland, much of it being below 60m (200ft). With 820mm (32in) on the west coast, it also has the least rainfall of any park. In addition it has the mildest climate and a greater proportion of arable land.

A look at geology Beginning at the Preseli Hills, you will find yourself in a peaty moorland world dominated by masses of heather and grassland. Some of the under-lying rocks are Ordovician slates and shales, but there is also much igneous rock standing up as huge isolated piles of mountain-top detritus and forming a very strange, almost moonscape type of scene. These hard igneous rocks continue from the Preseli Hills to the north coast to build up massive cliffs and promontories from Strumble Head west to St David's Head. Up the coast north-east of Strumble the headlands of Dinas and Cemaes are of Silurian sedimentary rocks.

In the far west the cathedral city of St David's—really only a village—is built on Pre-Cambrian rocks, but the purple stones of which the cathedral is largely built were quarried in the Middle Ages from Cambrian rocks near the sea cliffs to the south; these rocks form a rugged coastline from there for

Above: A view of Westdale Bay, on the Pembrokeshire Coast Path—you can see thrift growing along the top of the cliffs. The varied coastline of the Park, with its strong tides, is extremely irregular in shape and its many rock types and estuarine sands and muds provide a wide range of habitats for marine and shore life. The sea all around is rich in fish and the intertidal zone teems with invertebrates. Three bodies are directly involved with wildlife protection in the Park: the Countryside Council for Wales, the Dyfed Wildlife Trust and the RSPB. The CCW's reserves are at Skomer and Stackpole, the DWT has reserves at Skokholm, Dowrog Common (St David's), West Williamston (Cleddau Estuary), Gwaun Valley and elsewhere, and the RSPB owns Grassholm. For information apply to: CCW, Plas Gogerddan, Aberystwyth, Dyfed; DWT, 7 Market St, Haverfordwest, Dyfed; RSPB, The Bank, Newtown, Powys.

several miles to the deep sheltered inlet at Solva. There the Cambrian rocks end, where the ocean has carved St Bride's Bay out of the much softer Coal Measures to produce a shore of sands and cliffs that continues south for six miles to Little Haven.

The southern arm of St Bride's Bay is made up of Devonian rocks (Old Red Sandstone) which form most of the land on both sides of the deep inlet of Milford Haven, including the bold wind-swept promontory of St Ann's Head. But the Old Red Sandstone is interrupted around Marloes by a band of Silurian rocks which are volcanic at Wooltack Point and sedimentary along the back of Marloes Sands.

The south coast of the Park begins in the west with a magnificent line of Carboniferous Limestone cliffs, stretching eight miles from Linney Head to Stackpole Head. A famous feature here is the Green Bridge of Wales, a great column of limestone standing in the sea and connected with the main cliff by a natural arch that will one day collapse to leave an isolated pillar like the Stack Rocks nearby. From Stackpole the cliffs, which continue east to Tenby, are alternately limestone and sandstone. Then beyond Tenby, where the coast turns north, the cliffs are of less ancient rocks–first Millstone Grit, followed by Coal Measures. Many of the cliffs are extremely folded and crumpled, notably at Saundersfoot where the Ladies' Cave upfold (anticline) is a

Left: An adult slow-worm sun-bathing. The Park's other reptiles are the common lizard, the adder and the grass snake. Of these, the slow-worm is probably the commonest. The lizard reaches the highest ground (half-way up the slopes of Preseli), while adders are local on the heaths and sea slopes. The grass snake is restricted to sheltered inland places, usually near water. Frogs, toads and palmate newts are all widespread on the mainland. On the islands the distribution of reptiles and amphibians is patchy.

Right: The Park has a numerous and varied insect population, best-known among which are the butterflies and dragonflies. The flowery slopes above the sea are where the butterflies can be seen at their best. Among the residents are the large skipper, the small skipper (shown here on a clover head), the meadow brown, the gatekeeper, the grayling, the comma, the common blue and three fritillaries–the marsh, small pearl-bordered and dark green. Migrant red admirals and painted ladies are abundant in some years.

Below: A chough preening. This handsome but rare bird can be seen in the Park.

famous feature.

All the offshore islands are a continuation of the nearest mainland rocks. Off St David's there are Ramsey, the Bishops and the Clerks, which are mainly an extension of the Ordovician volcanic and sedimentary rocks of the Park's north coast. At the southern end of St Bride's Bay, Skomer is an outcrop of the Silurian volcanic rocks of Wooltack Point. Miles out into the sea lie Grassholm, the Hats, the Barrels and the Smalls–the most westerly fragments of Wales. They too poke up from underwater reefs of these Silurian volcanics. Skomer's close neighbour, to the south, is Skokholm whose pink cliffs proclaim that they are made of Old Red Sandstone. So do

and West Cleddau rivers at the head of Milford Haven. There are also woods alongside the lily ponds at Bosherston; and close to the sea are woods at Goultrop, at the south end of St Bride's Bay and near Saundersfoot. They all have a wealth of wild flowers, especially those at Bosherston, where ash trees, wood spurge, early purple orchids, black bryony and traveller's-joy all speak of a limestone soil. Up on the northern slopes of the Preseli Hills, near the famous chambered tomb of Pentre Ifan, is a very different kind of wood. Growing on acid rocky ground in a high rainfall area this ancient wood is known for the many lichens, mosses, liverworts and ferns flourishing in its deep, moist gullies.

Scattered along the north from the Preseli Hills to St David's are peat bogs large and small, some of them under the threat of drainage. They are home for many plants of acid wetlands–bogbean, bog asphodel, marsh St John's wort and various orchids and sedges. Among rarer species there are pillwort, wavy St John's wort, oblong-leaved sundew, bog orchids, marsh clubmoss and, uniquely in Wales, pale butterwort.

Sand dunes and saltmarshes add their specialities to the floral variety of the Park. On the dunes you'll find sea holly, burnet rose, sea bindweed and various orchids; and on the saltmarshes lax-flowered sea-lavender, a rarity elsewhere in Wales, spreads sheets of purple-blue. However, the outstandingly

hose of Gateholm, a half tide island near Marloes. Off Tenby in the far south, Caldey Island is half limestone, half sandstone.

Pembrokeshire plants One of the glories of his Park are the spring flowers which line the vaysides, especially along the banks of the southern lanes wherever the soil is lime-rich. There are long stretches white with scurvy grass or, in damper places, sheets of ramsons. Mingled with them are pink masses of campion and the pure blue of germander speedwell. Two tall umbellifers, cow parsley and alexanders, grow there with special luxuriance amid a profusion of extra-large hart's-tongues and soft shieldferns. Along south-eastern lanes in April you may come upon the Tenby daffodil, a plant of mystery because botanists are uncertain whether it is a product of gardens or is a genuine wild plant peculiar to this part of Wales.

Woodlands in this part of Wales are few and most are tucked away out of the prevailing south-west winds. They lie mainly along the sheltered Gwaun Valley near Fishguard and the equally quiet upper reaches of the East

Above: A view of Skokholm's cliffs; part of Skomer can be seen in the distance.

Right: A bedstraw hawkmoth –a speciality of the Park.

Below: Otters still frequent Pembrokeshire's streams.

beautiful wild habitats are the cliffs and slopes immediately above the sea where, in spring, you can find endless natural rock gardens colourful with the pink of thrift, the blue of squill and sheep's-bit, the yellow of gorse, kidney vetch, bird's-foot trefoil and cowslips, along with white patches of sea campion, scurvy-grass and ox-eye daisies. Summer brings the flowers of rock samphire, golden samphire and saw-wort. Among the rarer plants of the cliffs are yellow cicendia, hairy bird's-foot trefoil, spiked speedwell, hairy greenweed, perennial centaury and two kinds of rock sea-lavender.

The offshore islands, too, are a delight of spring wild flowers: Skomer, for instance, has

Above: A magnificent emperor dragonfly. Such dragonflies are widespread in the Park, but their favourite haunts are the boglands of the north and west and the lily ponds at Bosherton in the south.

Right: The very varied geology of Pembrokeshire is often impressive–as witnessed by these vertical rock strata, which can be seen on the coast near Marloes.

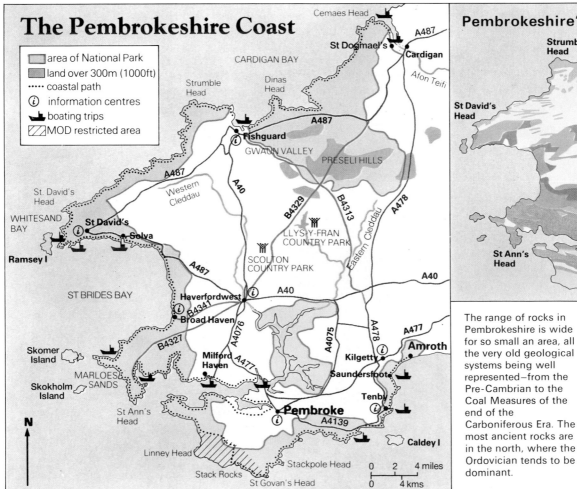

The Pembrokeshire Coast

- ▨ area of National Park
- ▨ land over 300m (1000ft)
- ····· coastal path
- ⓘ information centres
- ⚓ boating trips
- ▨ MOD restricted area

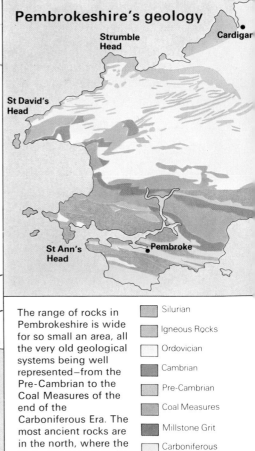

Pembrokeshire's geology

The range of rocks in Pembrokeshire is wide for so small an area, all the very old geological systems being well represented–from the Pre-Cambrian to the Coal Measures of the end of the Carboniferous Era. The most ancient rocks are in the north, where the Ordovician tends to be dominant.

- ▨ Silurian
- ▨ Igneous Rocks
- ▨ Ordovician
- ▨ Cambrian
- ▨ Pre-Cambrian
- ▨ Coal Measures
- ▨ Millstone Grit
- ▨ Carboniferous Limestone
- ▨ Old Red Sandstone

great sheets of bluebells and thrift, and red campion flourishes in abundance in a soil made nitrogen-rich by seabird droppings.

Mammal variety The most noteworthy wild mammals of this Park–and certainly the easiest to observe–are the grey seals. You will find most of them along the north and west coasts and very often all you see of them is their round heads sticking out of the water as they watch you with big-eyed curiosity. They breed in autumn, mainly on the islands of Ramsey (up to 300 pups each year) and Skomer (about 60-100 pups a year).

There is no shortage of foxes or badgers in Pembrokeshire. Foxes are found at all altitudes and badgers flourish in the lowlands, especially in woodlands and in the narrow little valleys going down to the shore. There are also ancient badger setts on the wild slopes near the sea cliffs, either hidden in bracken or wide open to the sky. They form deep, safe, roomy refuges not only for the badgers but also for stoats, weasels, polecats and rabbits. The ever-declining otter is still present along the streams but in its old haunts these days you are more likely to see American minks which, having escaped from fur farms, are now well-established in south-west Wales.

Hares are so few that they have even been introduced in a few localities, but rabbits more than make up for the scarcity of hares. Until myxomatosis decimated them in 1954-5, they were extremely abundant and trapping them for their meat was one of the local industries. Today they are again common in many places, but to see them in their former multitudes you need to visit such islands as Ramsey or Skokholm.

The red squirrel, once common in the woods, has now been almost entirely replaced by the grey. Of the smallest mammals, six are

Above: Kittiwake and chick on their cliff nest–the island of Skomer has large numbers of these seabirds.

Below: The lovely burnet rose flourishes on the sand dunes in the Park.

widespread: common, pygmy and water shrews and bank, field and water voles. The harvest mouse and dormouse are probably only very local. Bats found in the Park include the greater and the lesser horseshoes.

Seabird watching Birdwatchers come to the Park mainly to visit the cliffs and islands. Peregrines, ravens, buzzards and choughs can be seen anywhere, and there are fine congregations of breeding seabirds. Breezy Stackpole Head is one of the best mainland colonies, but an easier one to see (because you can take your car in close) is the great throng of guillemots, razorbills and kittiwakes on the twin Stack Rocks–two massive sea-girt limestone pillars just off the cliffs four miles west of Stackpole Head. (The Stack Rocks are usually visited on bank holidays or weekends, when the nearby military firing range is not in use. Please take great care to observe the notices that give details of when the firing ranges are being used.)

The best of the bird islands, from north to south are: Ramsey, which has small seabird stations but is most distinguished for around 10 pairs of choughs: Skomer, with huge numbers of shearwaters, kittiwakes, puffins, guillemots, razorbills and gulls; and Skokholm, which is famous not only for seabirds, including 6000 pairs of storm petrels, but also for its migrant land birds. Finally, far out to sea, is Grassholm, which has one of Britain's biggest gannetries at over 20,000 pairs.

THE SNOWDONIA NATIONAL PARK

The highest British mountains south of the Scottish Grampians occupy a region in north-west Wales whose ancient Welsh name is Eryri but which in English is called Snowdonia. Here, clustered compactly, are 14 peaks over 900km (3000ft).

Above: A view of snow-capped Snowdon (called Y Wyddfa in Welsh). It is an imposing 1085m (3560ft) high. The National Park, which takes in all the country from Conwy in the north to Aberdyfi in the south, was created in 1951.

The peaks of Snowdonia do not stand up as one solid massif; instead, they are divided into three blocks by deep, narrow valleys that became the trackways of early man and which our modern roads also follow. So, if you come into Snowdonia along the A5 from Shrewsbury you can see, from Llangollen onwards, how the land rises and strengthens all the way until, just after Capel Curig, you can look up at craggy summits whose steep flanks face you like a barrier. But the road skirting Ogwen lake, soon finds a way through and drops down Nant Ffrancon, which is a text-book example of a glacier-smoothed valley. Indeed, the whole Snowdonian uplands make the Great Ice Age seem quite a recent event. Everywhere you find evidence of the action of ice and frost: shattered cliff faces, scratched rocks, perched boulders, U-shaped valleys, hanging valleys and many glacier-scooped lakes.

When the National Park was designated in 1951 the name Snowdonia, which originally meant simply the mountain of Snowdon itself and its sister peaks and the valleys immediately around them, acquired a new dimension. The Park took in all the 80km (50 miles) of country from Conwy in the north to Aberdyfi in the south; and east-west it reached for 56km (35 miles) from Bala to Tremadog—an area many times greater than that of Snowdonia in its traditional meaning. Now, when we speak of the mountains of

places.

Birds are not abundant in the mountains. But almost every corrie has its pair of ravens, and some also have peregrines. Choughs feed in these high places in summer, and ring ouzels breed on the heathery rocks, while screes are the chosen home of wheatears. In many a gully, however, the only bird sound you will hear is the startlingly loud song of the wren.

Birds of moorlands are likewise few in species. The most obvious and widespread are buzzards and carrion crows, while skylarks and meadow pipits are the most numerous. There are local populations of snipe, lapwings, curlews, black-headed gulls, mallard and teal.

Lakes and streams Though a few of Snowdonia's many lakes have been turned into reservoirs, most have been little altered by man, except that some have had alien fishes put into them and others have long ago lost the woodlands that surrounded them. The upland streams, too, retain their pristine

Above: Over 300 million years of erosion have removed enormous quantities of Snowdonia's softer, sedimentary rocks and left the tough, volcanic rock of the summits, which look out across deep valleys. The soils formed from this erosion are generally lime-deficient, but here and there small pockets of sedimentary soils remain and are colonized by such lime-loving plants as this attractive moss campion. Elsewhere a moorland type of vegetation is common.

Below: The vegetation of Snowdonia's moorlands and summits is only semi-natural, being controlled by the grazing of sheep and, locally, by feral goats, as shown here.

Snowdonia, we mean not only Snowdon, Glyder, Carneddau, Hebog and Siabod, but also the many heights that lie further south— Moelwyn, Arennig, Aran, Cader Idris, Rhinog and the lesser ranges. In addition, the Park comes right down to the western coast of Wales and includes a complete range of lowland habitats—saltings, sea cliffs, sand dunes, farmland and broad-leaved woodland.

Mountain plants and birds The soils that formed from the erosion of Snowdonia's rocks are mostly deficient in lime and on them a moorland type of vegetation is common. But here and there are a few corries (circular hollows in mountainsides) and cliffs, some of sedimentary, some of igneous (volcanic) rocks, that are rich enough in lime to support a great variety of lime-loving plants, many of which are species better known in arctic or alpine regions of the world. Typical of these species are moss campion, purple saxifrage, starry saxifrage, mountain sorrel, roseroot, holly fern and green spleenwort, but there are many others. The Snowdon lily is one rarity that flourishes in just a few

populations of fauna and flora.

Characteristic of shallow lakes with gravelly beds are those underwater plants that grow as rosettes of green leaves – shoreweed, quillwort and lobelia. In a few lakes, such as Llyn Idwal, you may also find the little crucifer called awlwort and a minute unfernlike fern called pillwort. Muddier shallows are usually choked with bottle sedge and horsetail. Sheltered parts of the lakes may develop surface plants such as water lilies, crowfoots and floating water-plantain. On the squelchy margins of the lakes you may find bog bean, bog asphodel, bog mosses (Sphagna) and the insect-eating round-leaved sundew.

Practically all the lakes and streams have acid water and a few are so sour (some of those on peaty moorlands for instance) that they have no fish at all. Most other lakes have at least a limited invertebrate fauna supporting a population of brown trout.

Snowdonia's richest natural lake, and also its largest, is a lowland one – Llyn Tegid at Bala. This fine water, which looks towards the commanding peak of Aran Benllyn in the west, has long been renowned for its large and numerous perch, brown trout and pike. It also has a number of other fishes, including salmon, roach, grayling (not usually a lake species) and gwyniad, a silvery fish about 30cm (12in) long and found nowhere else in Wales. The gwyniad lives in shoals, usually in rather deep water and, feeding on plankton, is seldom attracted by any angler's lure.

Snowdonia's other rare fish is the charr, which inhabits deep cold water and comes into the shallows to breed at the end of autumn, when the males turn red on their undersides (hence the Welsh name *Torgoch*, meaning 'red belly'). For centuries the charr has been known in only three Welsh lakes – Cwellyn

Above: The cool, wet, windy climate of Snowdonia's uplands, and the rather infertile, badly drained podsols, do not encourage many wild flowers; nevertheless a few manage to survive, including this common tormentil, and also heath bedstraw and heath milkwort.

Below: A touch of distinction is given to Snowdonia by a rarity – the Snowdon lily. Merely a few centimetres tall, with small white flowers and grass-like leaves, this lily is found in Britain only on a few high cliffs of Snowdon, Glyder and Carneddau.

near Beddgelert and the twin lakes Padarn and Peris at Llanberis. But in the last few years Llyn Peris has become part of the Dinorwic pumped storage hydro-electric project. It was temporarily drained and its fish removed (via a hatchery) to a nearby deep mountain lake called Ffynnon Llugwy where, it is hoped, they will survive for ever.

Sand dunes and sea cliffs Snowdonia's extensive sand dunes – they are on the coast of Cardigan Bay – have long been used as playgrounds for holidaymakers, golf courses and, at Harlech, as a site for growing conifers. But despite these activities (and military occupation in war-time) there are areas of duneland that remain almost completely natural (or as natural as the rabbits introduced in the Middle Ages allow them to be). Their very varied flora is rich in lime-loving species (the lime comes from the crushed remains of sea shells that are blown up off the beach with the sand.) Some species keep strictly to the drier places, while others prefer the sandy hollows, called dune slacks, that are waterlogged or even water-covered all through winter.

In summer the dunes are fragrant and colourful with the flowers of thyme, lady's bedstraw, burnet rose, rest-harrow, hound's tongue, lady's fingers, sea holly, sea spurge, bee orchids, marsh orchids, marsh helleborines and a variety of lovely grasses that bend in the wind. Because of their abundance of wild flowers, these dunes are the home of many butterflies, moths and other insects. And among nesting birds on the sands are stock doves (they breed in rabbit holes), ringed plovers, redshanks, oystercatchers, lapwings, snipe and black-headed gulls.

South of the Mawddach Estuary stretch the Park's only sea cliffs. They are small, soft and eroding and of little attraction to nesting seabirds. The most distinguished seabird colony is actually 6.4km (4 miles) inland, where cormorants have bred for centuries on the high crags of Craig yr Aderyn. Owing to the presence of lime-rich boulder clay, the flora of the sea cliffs is of special interest and includes a few early purple orchids, rock samphire and sea spleenwort, as well as many

Right: A view of Nant Gwynant in the northern part of Snowdonia.

Below: Most reserves in Snowdonia are managed by the Countryside Council for Wales, and a few by the North Wales Naturalists' Trust and the National Trust. Their aim is to protect the habitats. Among them are the coastal dunelands of Morfa Harlech and Morfa Dyffryn; lowland dolerite cliffs and screes (Coed Tremadog); summits, crags, mountain slopes, lakes and streams (Snowdon, Cwm Idwal and Cader Idris); and high moorland (Rhinog). A permit is required for most reserves. Details from CCW, Plas Penrhos, Penrhos Rd, Bangor; NWNT, 376 High St, Bangor (enclose SAE).

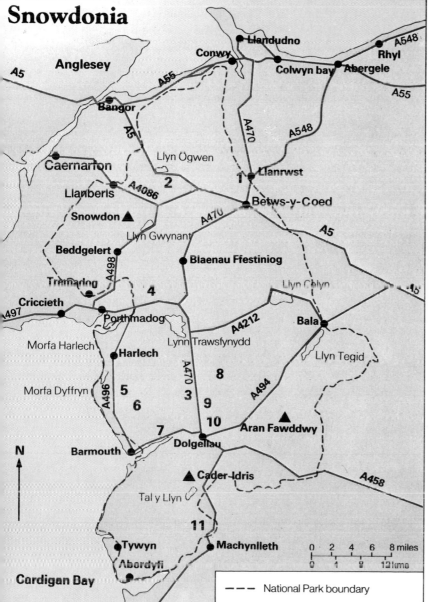

Snowdonia

Scale: 0 2 4 6 8 miles / 0 1 2 12 kms

- - - National Park boundary

Some nature trails in Snowdonia

1 **Lady Mary's Walk** (FC) Forestry exhibition above Gwydyr Castle, Llanrwst; 1.6km (1 mile) walk.

2 **Cwm Idwal** (CCW) 3.2km (2 mile) walk through the first National Nature Reserve established in Wales.

3 **Eden Valley Trail** (FC) 2.5km (1½ mile) forest trail from picnic site and car park near Ganllwyd.

4 **Coed Llyn Mair** (CCW) walk exploring the plant and animal life of an oakwood. 1.6km (1 mile).

5 **Cwm Nantcol Nature Trail** (NPIS) Picnic site on bank of Afon Cwm Nantcol, near Llanbedr. Short walk shows effect of glaciation on Nantcol Valley.

6 **Cefn Isa Farm Trail** (NPIS) 3.2km (2 mile) walk explaining the story of Welsh hill farming.

7 **Farchynys Woodlands** (NPIS) off Dolgellau/Barmouth road; typical Welsh oak wood; 1km (¾ mile) woodland path.

8 **Dolgefeiliau Forest Trail** (FC) picnic site off Dolgellau/Trawsfynydd road; walks showing plants and animals and explaining land use.

9 **Ty'n y Groes Forest Trail** (FC) picnic site off Dolgellau/Trawsfynydd road; 1.6km or 3.2km (1 or 2 mile) walk through 50-year old forest.

10 **Precipice Walk** (NPIS) off Dolgellau/Llanfachreth road, along high sheep walk 4.8km (2 miles).

11 **Tanycoed Forest Trail** (FC) picnic site off Dolgellau/Machynlleth road; walks through plantations of varying ages. 1.6km or 3.2km (1 or 2 miles).

NPIS = National Park Information Service.

plantations include the rarest of all – the dark and furry pine marten.

Broad-leaved woodland The mixed forest of oak, birch, alder and ash which are believed to have covered the lower slopes and valleys of Snowdonia in prehistoric times have long since been reduced to pathetic remnants. Even today the destruction of woodland goes on, with hardly any planting of broad-leaved trees ever taking place.

Ecologically this loss of trees is a great disaster, for no land habitat has more species of flora and fauna than oak woodland. Even in the bleak, high-level woods of Snowdonia, where undergrowth is suppressed by the grazing of sheep, there is sufficient insect life to support quite numerous communities of breeding birds: tits, nuthatches, woodpeckers and willow warblers, along with the redstarts, wood warblers and pied flycatchers that are a special feature of these western woods. It is in such woodland, too, that most of the moorland buzzards breed, and also those ravens unable to find a suitable crag. Fox, badger and polecat are the characteristic mammals of these woodlands, and also the grey squirrel which, in the last 30 years, has replaced the red squirrel almost completely. Growing on acid soils the oakwoods have a lime-hating flora, and wherever there is dampness and shade there is a green world of ferns, mosses, liverworts and lichens, including many rare kinds.

common shore species.

Moorlands and summits Though they may seem truly wild country, the uplands of Snowdonia are for the most part only semi-natural because their vegetation is controlled by the grazing of countless sheep, and locally by feral goats as well. This grazing has two main effects: it eliminates some of the taller flowering plants and encourages the spread of short grasslands; and it ensures that the semi-uplands are treeless, for without this grazing the hills would be largely covered with broad-leaved woodland or scrub up to about 500m (1500ft), and still higher on slopes sheltered from westerly gales.

Much of the upland vegetation, growing on rather infertile, ill-drained soils (podsols) in a cool, wet and windy climate, consists of a few dominant grasses such as sheep's fescue, common bent and mat grass, among which a few low-growing but attractive wild flowers manage to survive; typical of these are tormentil, heath bedstraw and heath milkwort. Moorlands with a blanket of peat may be covered by a mixture of heather, bilberry, crowberry and cowberry. Wetter places can be white with cottongrass, hummocky with purple moorgrass or thick with rushes. Some bare summits and screes are thickly matted with grey spreading woolly hair-moss. Clubmosses of three kinds – alpine, fir and stag's horn – are widely scattered about the mountain turf.

This century the moorlands have been invaded locally by the spruce plantations of the Forestry Commission. Although quite alien, and destructive of upland habitats, these dense woodlands have to some extent been colonized by native species of flora and fauna. Notable among the birds are black grouse, goldcrest, coal tit, siskin and crossbill. And mammals that seek the shelter of the

Above: The heathery rocks of Snowdonia's mountain heights are the breeding haunts of the ring ouzel.

Opposite page: A deserted cottage nestles under the looming mass of Snowdonia's mountains.

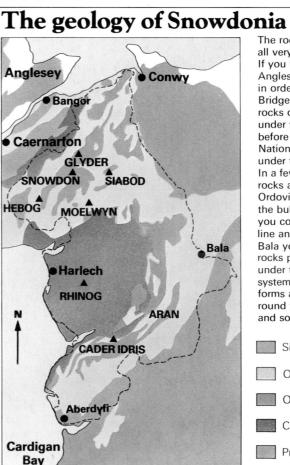

The geology of Snowdonia

The rocks of Snowdonia are all very old (Palaeozoic). If you travel south-east from Anglesey you can follow them in order of time. Near Menai Bridge the pre-Cambrian rocks of Anglesey cross under the strait, but just before they reach the National Park they vanish under the Cambrian rocks. In a few miles these Cambrian rocks are lost under the Ordovician rocks which form the bulk of Snowdonia. If you continue on a south-east line and leave the Park near Bala you find the Ordovician rocks plunging in their turn under those of the next system, the Silurian, which forms a broad perimeter all round the Park's eastern and southern flanks.

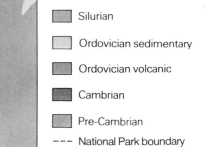

Silurian
Ordovician sedimentary
Ordovician volcanic
Cambrian
Pre-Cambrian
--- National Park boundary

Scotland

Solway Firth to the Highlands

Mountains, moorlands, lochs, coastlands and islands – these are
Scotland's wild havens in a nutshell. Because of the fairly low
population densities, much of this superb country remains
undeveloped and therefore retains a very special atmosphere.

At Caerlaverock on the Solway Firth the extensive mud flats and
saltmarshes provide ideal conditions for waders and wildfowl in
winter – wild skeins of barnacle geese flight in over the saltmarsh
or merse at dawn and dusk. And just across the border lies another
wetland reserve – Whitlaw Mosses. It's not a surprise in this land
of mires that fenland birds – sedge warbler, snipe and water rail –
are at home here.

A spectacular geological fault separates northern Scotland from
the rest of the country – this is the Great Glen, a narrow dip
infilled with water which has given birth to three long lochs,
including Loch Ness, which is now being explored by divers.

Loch Garten, near Aviemore, is the famous site where ospreys
returned to breed in 1959. These great birds of prey fly low over
water to snatch fish with their mighty talons. Craigellachie
Birchwood, also near Aviemore, has a fascinating nature trail to
follow, from which golden eagles may be sighted.

The Cairngorms rank high among Scotland's wildlife riches for
they are the nearest habitat we have to tundra. In winter the
summits are bleak and inhospitable, but when the snow melts in
spring, exquisite alpine plants burst into flower, mountain hares
shed their winter coats and snow buntings begin to nest.

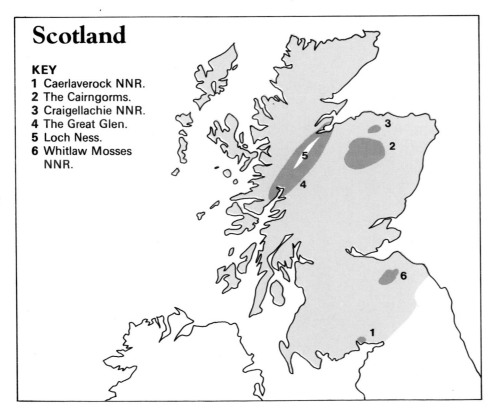

Scotland

KEY
1 Caerlaverock NNR.
2 The Cairngorms.
3 Craigellachie NNR.
4 The Great Glen.
5 Loch Ness.
6 Whitlaw Mosses
   NNR.

Left: The River Coe, with the peaks of the Three Sisters rising up behind Glen Coe. This famous Glen branches off from the Great Glen — the geological fault that divides northern Scotland from Central and Southern Scotland.

Below: Many of Scotland's pure upland streams and rivers are ideal spawning grounds for the salmon — that prince of fishes. This is an adult male in breeding colours.

135

CAERLAVEROCK–A WETLAND RESERVE

Caerlaverock National Nature Reserve is at its best in winter and should be visited between early October and the end of February for the best of the large flocks of wildfowl and waders. The reserve can be spectacular, with up to 30,000 birds of more than 60 species appearing on a single day.

The inner section of the Solway Firth has the third largest area of inter-tidal sand and mudflats in the British Isles and also some of the most extensive saltmarshes remaining in western Britain. The Solway is also one of the least developed and least polluted major estuaries in the country. The Caerlaverock National Nature Reserve was established in 1957 by the Nature Conservancy Council with the twin aims of protecting the largest and best saltmarsh within this complex and providing a sanctuary for the large numbers of Arctic-breeding wildfowl and waders which winter on the Solway–especially the Spitsbergen population of barnacle geese, whose numbers at that time were very low.

Caerlaverock is the largest wetland reserve in Britain and lies some 11km (7 miles) south-east of the town of Dumfries. It covers a total of 5501 hectares (13,594 acres) of coastal area, of which 600 hectares (1483 acres) is saltmarsh (known locally as merse) and 4901 hectares (12,111 acres) is inter-tidal sand and mud. The reserve is bounded on the north side by farmland but on the other three sides by water –the channel of the River Nith to the west; the smaller channel of the Lochar Water to the east; and the main channel of the Solway Firth to the south.

Many habitats The entire physiographic sequence from bare sand, through pioneer saltmarsh to neutral grassland is contained within the boundaries of the reserve. The huge expanse of foreshore, called Blackshaw Bank, is mainly composed of firm sand and provides both a feeding area for the wading birds and a

Below: At the landward edge of the merse at Caerlaverock is a 32ha (79 acre) marsh called the Flooders (shown here). It lies between an old sea wall and a raised beach and is largely fresh water, being inundated by the sea only when a high spring tide is pushed up by a south-westerly gale. It has a rich and varied flora. In the background you can see Criffel, rising to 569m (1869ft) just across the River Nith to the west and relieving the flatness of the marshes. The merse is owned by the Caerlaverock Estates, who have most generously leased the area as a nature reserve for the past 32 years; the foreshore is similarly leased from the Crown Estate Commissioners.

The eastern end of the reserve is maintained as a sanctuary area for the geese, but visitors to the Wildfowl Trust Refuge at Eastpark can use the hides developed by the Trust and also have access to the NCC for Scotland watchtower hide, which overlooks the huge expanse of eastern merse.

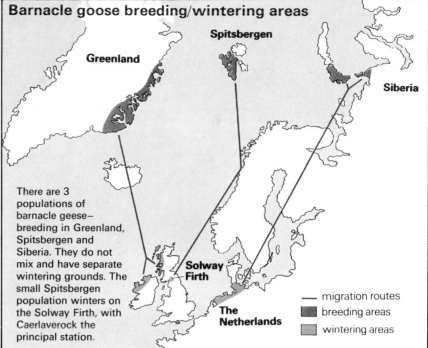

Barnacle goose breeding/wintering areas

Greenland
Spitsbergen
Siberia

There are 3 populations of barnacle geese—breeding in Greenland, Spitsbergen and Siberia. They do not mix and have separate wintering grounds. The small Spitsbergen population winters on the Solway Firth, with Caerlaverock the principal station.

Solway Firth

The Netherlands

— migration routes
■ breeding areas
■ wintering areas

safe night roost for the large flocks of geese. The merse neatly complements this by providing the feeding area for the geese, which graze its nutrient-rich grasses, and a high tide roost for the waders.

Along the accreting edge of the merse the principal sand-stabilising plant species is *Puccinellia maritima*. The main grass on the higher merse is *Festuca rubra*, but in the wetter areas *Agrostis stolonifera* becomes dominant in association with many sedges and rushes. The merse is inundated by the highest spring tides and is much intersected by creeks and channels, which quickly drain off the salt water. Most of the merse is grazed by the local farmers' cattle from May to September, this summer grazing benefiting the geese in that it encourages a close sward, which in turn gives better winter grazing for them. Another aspect of management on this large reserve is a wildfowling zone, strictly controlled by permit issue and wardening, over 186 hectares (460 acres) of the central merse.

Because of changes in the river channels from time to time, there is a cycle of erosion and accretion at the edges of the merse. For the last three decades the westernmost 5km (3 miles) of the merse edge have been eroding, while the 5km (3 miles) to the east have been accreting at a steady rate. Overall the inner part of the Solway Firth is slowly silting up.

Barnacle goose success story Barnacle geese have wintered at Caerlaverock for at least 200 years and probably far longer than that. At the turn of this century they were described as very abundant and their numbers probably exceeded 10,000, although they were never counted. In the early 1930s Peter Scott estimated about 5000 but by 1948/49, when a survey was undertaken, only 300-400 could be found. The reasons for the decline are not fully understood, but three factors are likely

Above left: The delicate blooms of ragged robin can be seen on the Flooders from May to August or even later.

Below: Barnacle geese bathing at Caerlaverock. After breeding on the island of Spitsbergen some 1130km (700 miles) from the North Pole, the barnacle geese accomplish the return to Caerlaverock, where they overwinter, in a single flight of about 2896km (1800 miles).

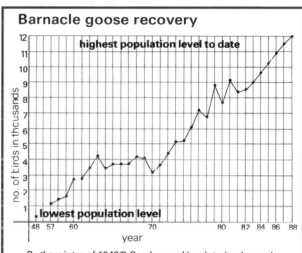

Barnacle goose recovery

highest population level to date

no. of birds in thousands

lowest population level

year

By the winter of 1948/9 Caerlaverock's wintering barnacle geese were reduced to about 300 birds. Following legal protection and the establishment of Caerlaverock NNR the population recovered.

to have contributed to it: a series of poor breeding seasons in the 1930s due to bad weather on their Arctic breeding grounds; excessive disturbance on the wintering grounds during World War II, when the Caerlaverock foreshore was used as a practice bombing range; and the increasing popularity of wildfowling as a sport at a time when the population was low.

From this nadir of near-extinction the corner was slowly turned. Barnacle geese received legal protection from shooting in Britain in 1954, and in Spitsbergen in 1955, and the establishment of a Refuge by the Wildfowl Trust in 1970, adjoining the eastern end of the NNR, increased the protected wintering area, and the geese received protection from shooting in Norway in 1971. A series of good breeding seasons in the 1970s, due to good summer weather, increased the population again and by October 1980 it had reached 9050. In the winter of 1987-88, there were 12,000 barnacles wintering. Thus 30 years of conservation work and measures have restored a viable population of barnacle geese to the Solway. It is a conservation success story of which Britain and Norway can be proud.

The barnacles have a very regular annual cycle. The first birds invariably reappear at Caerlaverock in the last few days of September, while the main flock arrives during the first week of October. From then until the end of February they graze the saltmarsh grasses and nearby pasture and barley stubbles. With the cessation of disturbance from shooting, the majority of the flock moves to Rockcliffe Marsh in Cumbria, at the head of the Solway, to feed during March and April. At the end of April or early in May, the whole flock moves to a group of islands off the west coast of

Above: Greylag geese in flight. Up to 1000 or more roost on the foreshore from November until March.

Right: A bonus for the reserve in the early years was the discovery of a colony of natterjack toads, right at the north-west limit of this attractive amphibian's European range. The colony is at present in a very healthy state, having enjoyed two good breeding years in 1981 and 1982.

Below: Up to 2000 wigeon arrive at Caerlaverock from their breeding grounds in Iceland and Scandinavia.

Norway, just inside the Arctic Circle. After feeding there for three or four weeks the birds return to their breeding grounds on Spitsbergen.

Other geese at Caerlaverock Two species of grey geese, the pink-footed and greylag, also winter on the Solway. The huge sandflats of Blackshaw and Priestside Banks offshore provide one of the best estuarine roosts in Britain for the Icelandic-breeding pink-footed goose. The first birds return by late September and quickly build up to two or three thousand in number. Twenty years ago as many as 10,000 were present in some winters by the end of the year, but nowadays the large numbers come later. Increasingly the pink-feet have taken to remaining in eastern and central Scotland during the early winter, often moving down to the Solway when a hard spell of weather sets in further north. In early February 1983, after a hitherto mild winter, a heavy snowfall over much of Scotland moved large numbers of pink-feet to the south. On 14th February a total of 12,200 pink-feet were counted flighting off the reserve foreshore at

dawn to feed on farmland a few miles inland. This number remained for several weeks, providing a magnificent spectacle as they flighted over the reserve each dawn and dusk in large skeins and V formations.

Fifty years ago greylag geese were more common than pink-feet in winter, but in recent years the larger flocks of greylag have moved inland and further west into Galloway, where they roost on freshwater lochs. However, up to 1000 or more still roost on the foreshore from November until March. White-fronted, brent, bean, Canada and even snow geese are all seen occasionally on the reserve, usually mixed in with the barnacle or pink-feet flocks. Whooper swans from Iceland arrive in October and stay until March.

Yet more birds While almost every species of duck on the British list has been recorded at Caerlaverlock, four species are numerous in winter. Most of the mallard are likely to be of British stock, but the big flocks of teal (up to 1000) which build up each autumn appear to come mainly from eastern Europe. If there is a plentiful spillage on the local barley stubbles, as many as 2500 pintail may stay in the area during October and November, roosting on the reserve foreshore by day and flighting to the fields at dusk.

Each autumn there is a big build-up of waders as the birds return from their breeding quarters on the hills and coasts of Scotland, Iceland, Scandinavia, Greenland and Siberia. Some, such as the greenshank, pass on south after a few weeks, but the generally mild climate of south-west Scotland induces many to stay through till the spring. As many as 15,000 oystercatchers have been counted at the high tide roosts, while curlew, lapwing, golden plover and dunlin are all present in thousands at times. Black-tailed godwits are

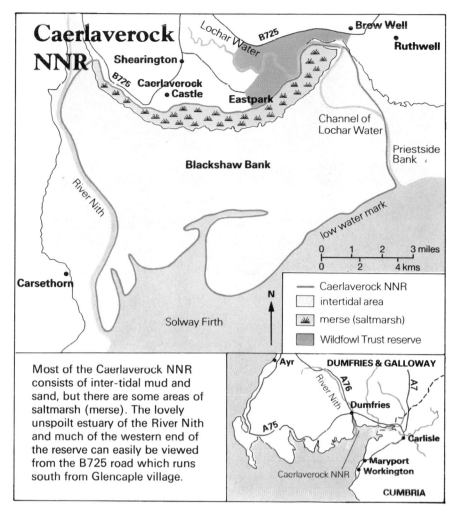

Caerlaverock NNR

Most of the Caerlaverock NNR consists of inter-tidal mud and sand, but there are some areas of saltmarsh (merse). The lovely unspoilt estuary of the River Nith and much of the western end of the reserve can easily be viewed from the B725 road which runs south from Glencaple village.

Below: A few Bewick's swans arrive at Caerlaverock from Siberia in November and disappear at the end of February. The 60 or 70 to have come in the past few years are Scotland's only regular wintering flock.

frequently seen and a spring passage of one to two hundred Icelandic birds is noted annually.

The large numbers of waders and wildfowl attract a following of predators – peregrine, merlin, sparrowhawk and hen harrier hunt over the merse daily in winter. Peregrines have even been seen to tackle barnacle geese on a number of occasions, although their more usual prey is a teal or a golden plover. Kestrels and short-eared and barn owls quarter the marshes for mice, voles or smaller birds, the kestrels hunting by day and the owls flitting silently about by night.

Caerlaverock's flora The flora of the reserve is of considerable interest in its own right and about 250 species of higher plants, representing over 60 families, have been recorded. The plants growing on the merse are all tolerant of occasional inundation by salt water. Grasses, sedges and rushes are well represented, and of particular interest on the merse is the chestnut sedge *Blysmus rufus*, a local northern species. Sea milkwort, sea aster and thrift are typical flowering plants of the merse.

The 32 hectares (79 acres) of the brackish marsh known as the Flooders has a rich vegetation, with the water parts dominated by large areas of horsetail. Here in June thousands of spikes of northern marsh orchid flower, and other common plants include yellow iris, ragged robin, yellow rattle and various watermints.

THE CAIRNGORMS—A MOUNTAIN WILDERNESS

Travel by road or rail between Perth and Inverness and you pass the finest tract of wild country left in Britain. At first sight the Cairngorms look no more than massive, rounded hills, but closer inspection reveals a spectacular and unspoilt environment, with many different kinds of habitat.

From the valley floor at 220m (700ft), where the River Spey meanders through a rich mosaic of forest and farmland, a journey into the Cairngorms leads through moorlands and natural forests of Scots pine towards a summit plateau at over 1000m (3500ft). Biting into this plateau are corries (massive bowl-shaped hollows) and glacial troughs where the red granite of the Cairngorms is exposed in huge cliffs, some over 300m (1000ft) high.

Unspoilt scenery Two special qualities distinguish the Cairngorms from all other British mountains–their size and their natural, unspoilt scenery. The summit plateau covers an area of nearly 26sq km (10sq miles) and contains an arctic environment virtually unaffected by man's activities – a place where wind, snow and frost dominate the scene.

On the lower slopes of the massif are the largest remnants of natural forest left in Britain. In the heart of this great tract of native pinewood, stretching from Abernethy in the north to Glen Feshie in the west, are areas that have never been subject to the effects of axe, fire or plough, and in these places you can still sense the true atmosphere of the ancient forests of northern Europe.

Moorland and forest A large part of the Cairngorms is a National Nature Reserve. On entering the reserve, for example from Aviemore, you pass through an extensive tract of Scots pinewood and come out into an area of moorland and bogs. The moorland occupies land from which the forest cover has been removed in the past by felling and burning. The dominant species is heather (also known as ling) which, when in flower in August, creates great purple vistas that inspire the imagination of every onlooker.

The moorland is, however, relatively poor in species, apart from mosses which usually carpet the ground beneath the heather. Where the heather is low in height–on windy spurs and steep banks subject to erosion–other species such as bell heather, cowberry and bearberry become abundant, while in the wetter hollows cross leaved heath, deer sedge and cotton grass are prominent.

In places, especially on the northern side of the Cairngorms, the moorland zone is being invaded by young birch, pine and rowan trees. In the pinewoods which grow on these slopes, the trees show a superb range of different ages–from prolific seedlings and saplings, through young trees, to towering specimens 300 years old.

Elsewhere in the reserve, regeneration of the forest (the re-establishment of new trees to replace old ones as they die) is prevented by browsing herds of red deer, which eat new seedlings as soon as they appear. The deer seek food and shelter in the winter in the areas of natural woodland, but these are now too small to cater for the numbers of deer that are present. As a result, the woodlands have taken on a 'park-like' appearance –a high forest of old Scots pines, intermixed here and there with birch and rowan, but with almost no young trees. Along the stream sides alder and willow are common.

Besides red deer, the forest fauna includes fairly large numbers of roe deer, but these are usually seen singly or in family groups, rather than in herds. Unlike red deer, the roe bucks hold territories for the whole year,

Above: The massive, rounded outline of the Cairngorms plateau, seen from the banks of Loch Morlich in winter. The habitat has more in common with the mountain ranges of the Arctic Circle – for example those in northern Scandinavia – than it has with those in the temperate parts of Europe such as the Alps.

Left: Cloudberry, with its orange fruit and soft foliage, is a truly northern species–it grows on peat-covered mountains in Scotland and North Wales, but is absent from England south of the Peak District.

and remain in these with their own family groups.

Chewed pine cones on the forest floor are a sign of red squirrel activity. The old pine forests now form a stronghold for this species, which has been replaced by the grey squirrel in so many other British forests.

The forests also support bird species of special interest, of which the crested tit and the crossbill are among the best known. Although both have now spread to some of the recently planted forests, their main breeding areas are in the native pinewoods. The crested tit with its black and white 'vest', white cheeks and black 'bib' attracts attention easily. It makes a trilling, spluttering call as it feeds on insects in the leaves, twigs or dead wood of the pine. Old pine stumps are favoured nesting places for the crested tit: it excavates a cavity in the soft wood, and builds a nest of moss and grass inside.

Along one hill slope in the Cairngorms, the pinewood reaches its altitudinal limit of 640m (2100ft). This is a natural tree line,

and is the only example in Britain. The woodland is a fragment that has escaped centuries of burning and felling, and was probably too remote to have been worth cutting down. The bent and twisted Scots pine trees, many of which are over 100 years old, reach a maximum height of only 3m (10ft). Walking

Below: A bog pine, exposed in an area of eroded peat. These jagged remnants can be thousands of years old, and bear witness to the fact that this open moor was once a pinewood.

up through the woodland you can see that the trees become more and more stunted, until a pine and juniper scrub gives way to open moorlands, which lead up to the Cairngorms plateau.

The plateau More snow falls in the Cairngorms than in any other British mountain area, and this is indicated by the pattern of vegetation. Strong winds blow the snow from exposed ridges and spurs, piling it up in sheltered hollows, often to great depths. Heather cannot survive prolonged periods of snow, so at the higher altitudes it is confined to areas exposed to the wind. Where snow lies in the hollows, bilberry, crowberry and species such as rigid sedge (*Carex bigelowii*) and dwarf cornel become common. Where snow lasts still longer, these communities in turn give way to those dominated by mat grass.

The increasing severity of the climate as you climb higher into the mountains is also reflected in the appearance of the heather. On windswept ridges above about 760m (2500ft) it forms a dense mat 2-5cm (1-2in) high, growing in strips at right angles to the prevailing wind, with loose bare gravel showing between the strips. The heather dies back along the exposed face of the mat, and the strip grows slowly forward along its lee face.

Heather growth is poor above 1000m (3500ft), and the most exposed areas of the plateau are covered with loose, gravelly soils in which little grows except tussocks of three-leaved rush. A common community of the slightly less exposed slopes is one in which the dominant species is the woolly fringe moss (*Rhacomitrium lanuginosum*). This forms dark green carpets, sometimes mixed with bilberry and cowberry or with rigid sedge. Here also you may find Britain's smallest willow–the dwarf or least willow (*Salix herbacea*) whose bent and stunted stems rise to no more than 8cm (3in) high but bear beautiful ovate leaves of a bright green colour, and tufts of fluffy seed heads. Where the snow lies deepest and longest of all–often lasting until August or September–much of the ground is bare or, in the wetter parts, covered by a patchwork of mosses and lichens.

Above: A ptarmigan on the high plateau. During winter these birds are pure white with black tail tips, but from spring to autumn their plumage is patterned in grey, yellow, black and white, providing an excellent camouflage.

Opposite page: Reindeer – a recent re-introduction to the Cairngorms. Quite a large herd now roams freely over the mountainsides.

Below: The Scottish wildcat is another predator that inhabits the pinewoods and moors of the Cairngorms. This rather elusive animal makes its den in holes among rocks, under trees or even in disused rabbit burrows.

Alpine grassland, areas of frost-shattered rock and boulders, and pools and streams complete the range of habitats on the plateau and provide nesting and feeding areas for the birds. These include dotterel and snow bunting, which are the summer inhabitants of this arctic landscape. But a visit to the plateau would be incomplete without the sight and the sound of the ptarmigan, a bird which lives for the whole year on the high slopes surrounding the plateau. Usually nesting on boulder-strewn heaths between 880m (2900ft) and 1150m (3800ft), the ptarmigan feeds on crowberry, bilberry, dwarf willow and heather tips. A sudden croak, or a brief flutter of wings, will quickly draw your attention to a small flock creeping away among nearby rocks.

A journey in winter across the Cairngorms can be a most arduous undertaking, amid wind, mist and blizzard. In summer, on the other hand, the relatively flat surface of the plateau, gently undulating and covered with low vegetation, provides easy walking and a magnificent view into the cliffs, screes, lochs and rivers in the corries below. In clear weather you can enjoy a superb panorama over the whole of the Scottish Highlands. Here are some of the finest, most unspoilt mountains in Europe, and for both their solitude and their wildlife, the Cairngorms stand supreme.

Looking ahead The beauty of this landscape depends on our care and respect. Too many hotels, roads, skiing facilities or even forestry plantations in the wrong place will destroy the very qualities for which the Cairngorms are famous. Enjoy the view, but also think about the future of these magnificent mountains.

CRAIGELLACHIE BIRCHWOOD

Craigellachie Birchwood, a National Nature Reserve near Aviemore in Scotland, is of great interest for the valuable contrast it provides to the mainly pine woodland of the Cairngorms. There is no pure birch woodland to equal it in the area.

Craigellachie birchwood lies immediately to the west of the village of Aviemore, some 45km (28 miles) south of Inverness, and covers an area of 260ha (642 acres), of which 101ha (250 acres) are birch, the remainder being open moorland on higher ground above 380m (1250ft). The whole area is of exceptional biological interest, particularly because

Above: Silver birches in spring leaf on the slopes of Craigellachie. This species is the most common in the wood, but downy or hairy birch is also found.

Right: Globeflowers — look for them by the nature trail.

the northern end of the loch, attempting to re-establish themselves. Here, where the stream runs into the loch, a fan of vegetation spreads outwards on the silty bottom. The thickest part is a large mass of bottle sedge, an erect plant which bears conspicuous fruiting spikes in July and August. Near the deeper water grows bog bean, with trifoliate leaves and whitish fringed flowers. The lesser spearwort, a straggling plant with yellow flowers and lance shaped leaves, grows where the stream enters the loch.

Craigellachie Rock This name, derived from Gaelic, means 'rock of the stony place'. Rising vertically to a height of 91m (300ft), the rock mass towers above the loch slightly to the west, and is home to hundreds of nesting jackdaws. During sunrise the air is vibrant with wingbeats and raucous calls as these

of its insect fauna, especially the moths, which include such species as the Kentish glory, the Rannoch sprawler and the great brocade.

The Nature Trail Because of major road improvements in 1980, the entrance to the reserve is now by tunnel. The points of entry are from either the Aviemore Castle Centre Complex or by a track from the main road which bypasses the youth hostel. The nature trail starts from the tunnel.

One of the first major points of interest is Loch Puladdern. This attractive tree-fringed loch, one of three areas of open water on the reserve, is fairly shallow, with a maximum depth of 3m (10ft). During road construction in 1980, the remains of an old oak tree were dredged up: carbon dating claims the age to be 2000 years. This raises the question, was Craigellachie at one time an oakwood? Before road construction, alder trees lined the east bank. Now only small saplings can be seen at

Above: The common sandpiper has been known to nest on the shores of the loch.

Right: A Scotch argus butterfly–this species can be seen in large numbers on sunny days in July and August. Widespread in Scotland, it has a distinct preference for birchwoods. The caterpillars hatch in September and feed during the day; they hibernate throughout the winter, then resume feeding in spring, pupating in July and emerging two weeks later.

Below: Craigellachie's first red squirrel was recorded near the reservoir in August 1983.

birds go in search of food. At first sight, the visitor might believe that jackdaws are the only inhabitants of the rock, but a few minutes spent here may reveal a peregrine falcon, a rare bird that was at one time persecuted and shot but is now protected by law.

The trail now starts to ascend slowly on boulder steps towards the first observation platform, on either side of which both species of birch can be seen. Silver birch, sometimes called pendulous or weeping birch (*Betula pendula*), is the most common. It is easily recognisable by the pendulous habit of its branches and its warty twigs; it grows fast and is relatively short-lived. It helps to improve conditions for the succession of plants and trees which eventually follow. The downy or hairy birch (*Betula pubescens*) is more bushy and its twigs are covered in small hairs. Neither species casts a heavy shade, hence ground vegetation flourishes, providing important habitats for many birds, mammals and plants. It is here that chaffinches, wrens, coal tits, long-tailed tits, blue tits and great tits can be seen among the branches of the trees.

The visitor may catch glimpses of the willow warbler which is a summer visitor to these parts, but it is more likely to be heard than seen. A small, quiet but abundant visitor, its plumage is olive-brown and the call, a plaintive 'too-eet', is similar to that of the chaffinch, but is softer and carries further.

The observation platforms From the observation platform, which faces east, panoramic views of the Spey Valley can be seen. The eye can follow the River Spey for several miles as it meanders in a north-easterly direction towards the sea.

At this point, the visitor has the choice of either a short trail or a long trail. The long trail takes in the higher contours of the hill, and duck-boarding is used to ford the wetter areas. On both sides of the boarding bog asphodel blooms in profusion in summer–a small but charming plant with deep orange flowers. Another attractive plant is the globe flower, which is about 2.5cm (1in) across and resembles a full moon. May and June are the best times for seeing these plants. Orchids abound, notably the heath spotted and the northern marsh orchids. The common sundew and the butterwort, both insectivorous plants, also grow here, favouring the wetter ground. On a damp day the visitor may be aware of a strong, sweet smell which comes from an aromatic shrub called bog myrtle.

Leaving the wetter areas, the trail now runs level on stony ground until it reaches the next

platform. It is on these dry areas before the platform that the chanterelle fungus can be found. In a good year the ground is covered with these funnel-shaped fungi. Large numbers of edible boletus species share the same habitat. This is a large fungus, 5-10cm (2-4in) across the dome-shaped cap and generally yellowish-brown in colour.

On arriving at the second observation platform and looking south-east, the vista can

Above: A golden eagle and its chick. The golden eagle is a spectacular sight over the Reserve, soaring as it uses the updraught from the ridge and constantly gaining height.

Below: The grass beneath the birches is dotted with ferns and heathers.

Opposite right: A roe buck in velvet, prior to fraying. Where the duckboarding passes through arches of overhanging birch, stand quietly and scan the hillside– you may spot roe deer. A sharp barking noise means you have been detected. The roe deer's ability to scent danger is phenomenal, as its sense of smell is one hundred times greater than that of man. Small birch saplings standing alone are favoured by the bucks as fraying or scent posts.

During winter, when grazing on the high ground is scarce, red deer descend to feed on the lush herbage around the boarding. In late evening or early morning, 15 or 20 red deer are not uncommon.

only be described as breathtaking. Beyond the village of Aviemore the wide valley provides fertile farmland for sheep and beef cattle. On slightly higher ground are extensive forests, managed both privately and by the Forestry Commission. Most of these forests are of Scots pine, and individual trees reach ages of 250 to 300 years. The whole Cairngorm mountain range can be seen at a glance. The visitor can look up into the famous Lairig Ghru pass which runs from Spey-side to Braemar, a distance of 40km (25 miles), and is used extensively by hill-walkers throughout the year. It is from this point that the osprey may occasionally be seen, keeping a watchful eye on the Spey below. As it glides along, at times only 30m (100ft) above the water, the bird will suddenly dive out of sight and reappear further downstream carrying its catch, probably a sea trout. Below the platform the ground dips downhill and is grass-covered, interspersed with bracken and

Craigellachie Birchwood

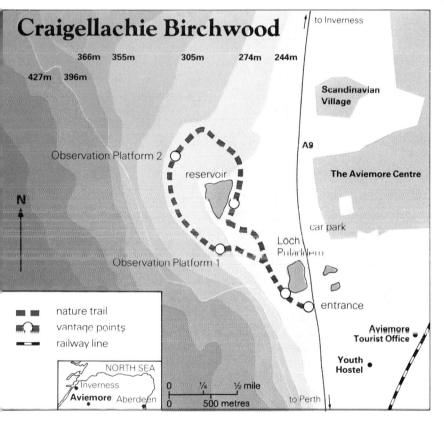

to Inverness

366m 355m   305m   274m 244m
427m 396m

Scandinavian Village

A9

Observation Platform 2

reservoir

The Aviemore Centre

N

car park

Loch Puladdern

Observation Platform 1

entrance

nature trail
vantage points
railway line

NORTH SEA
Inverness
Aviemore Aberdeen

Aviemore Tourist Office

Youth Hostel

0   ¼   ½ mile
0   500 metres

to Perth

Above: A map of Craigellachie Nature Reserve, showing the path of the nature trail and some places of interest along the route.

Right: The chanterelle fungus can be found near observation platform 2. Yellow in colour and with a smell akin to that of apricots, this fungus measures from 2.5cm to 8cm (1-3in) across. When it is properly cooked, the chanterelle is second to none in flavour.

heather. On a sunny day during July or August the Scotch argus butterfly can be seen here in large numbers.

There is an experimental enclosure near the platform which, through lack of visitor pressure, is relatively undisturbed. The great spotted woodpecker makes full use of this and has been known to nest in one of the decaying trees.

The old reservoir Leaving the last platform behind, the trail now begins to descend along a very stony road which is used occasionally by the water company for access to the reservoir. As the road levels off, the trail takes a turn to the right, passing the old reservoir. On the northern side a small burn feeds the reservoir, continually depositing a fine layer of silt which forms a spongy bed on which grows the common rush. A great variety of plant life occurs in and around the shore. The water horsetail is easily recognisable by its erect, jointed stem. The large, golden-ringed dragonfly can be seen as it hawks along in a predetermined flight path, vigorously threatening any intruders. Another dragonfly is the four-spotted libellula, brownish in colour, with a black tip to its body. This species, too, is a strong flier and is on the wing from mid-May to August.

Most of the water surface is covered with two species of pondweed, the broad-leaved pondweed and the bog pondweed. Various water birds frequent the reservoir, including mallard, wigeon, goldeneye and occasionally teal. A regular visitor to the reservoir is the heron. This large wader can be seen standing in the shallower water while looking for the small trout or frogs which form its staple diet. From the reservoir, looking west towards the skyline, the early morning visitor may see a buzzard working its way along the ridge. Finally, just below the old reservoir, the nature trail rejoins the start, and the exit is via the same tunnel.

THE GREAT GLEN OF SCOTLAND

Look on any map of Scotland and one of the most noticeable features you see is the straight diagonal line that divides the Highlands, running from Fort William in the south-west up to Inverness in the north-east. This line is the Great Glen.

For most of its 88km (55 mile) length, the Great Glen is extremely narrow–less than 1.5km (1 mile) wide–with the ground rising steeply on each side to the mountain massifs of the Monadhliath to the south and the north-west Highlands to the north. More than half the length of the glen is occupied by three lochs: Loch Lochy in the south-west, Loch Oich in the middle, and Loch Ness in the north-east. At its highest point the glen is only 45m (150ft) above sea level; consequently it provides a 'through route' between the two halves of Scotland for the dispersal of lowland plants and animals (including man!) while acting as a barrier to high-altitude species.

Birth of the glen The Great Glen lies along the line of a major geological fault, and the land on the two sides of the fault has, at some time in the past, moved relative to each other. This can be seen in the rocks on either side of the glen: those on one side are different from those directly opposite. The land mass to the north of the fault is composed of metamorphic rocks of the Moine series, formed during

Above: The Caledonian Canal leading into Loch Lochy.

Below: Bugle is an important source of nectar for the chequered skipper butterfly, a species unique in Britain to the glen.

the Precambrian period more than 570 million years ago. These very hard, ancient rocks weather slowly to give poor acidic soils. At the northern end of the glen, from the Moray Firth inland to Drumnadrochit, the Moine rocks are overlaid with more recent sedimentary deposits of Old Red Sandstone, laid down between 350 and 390 million years ago. Although acidic in composition, these softer rocks weather more readily and produce some fertile soils.

On the southern side of the Great Glen Fault the rocks are also predominantly of the Moine series, though in places they are more calcareous than those to the north. There are also deposits of Old Red Sandstone, but they extend further inland–as far as Foyers, which is some 10km (6 miles) south-west of Drumnadrochit. There is also an isolated outcrop on the southern shore of Loch Oich. Two granite intrusions occur along the glen, one on the north side on the shore of Loch Linnhe and the other on the south side at Foyers.

Geologists have attempted to correlate the

Man's influence The twin effects of geology and the coming and going of the Ice Age, along with the present climate of the area, have done much to determine the distribution of the different types of vegetation. But on top of this natural pattern, man and his domestic animals have superimposed their own influence.

In the Highlands, flat land is at a premium and the valley floor of the Great Glen provides one of the few areas suitable for arable cultivation and improved pasture. The size of the farms varies from small crofts to large estates. Land unsuitable for cultivation has long been used for grazing, both by domestic stock (mainly sheep) and red deer. Since the 1920s large areas, particularly the steep sides of the glen, have been given over to Forestry Commission plantations, usually of exotic conifers.

The lochs, too, have not escaped man's attention. The Caledonian Canal, opened in 1822, links the three lochs of Loch Lochy, Loch Oich and Loch Ness, thereby linking the east coast of Scotland to the west.

Four woodlands Around the southern end of the Great Glen and along the northern shore of Loch Linnhe grow woods dominated by sessile oak, the only native species of oak in north and west Britain. Growing on acid soils, these woods have only a limited range of plants in the ground layer, with just a few herbs, such as bluebell, pignut and bugle, present as well as some grasses and mosses. The shrub layer is also sparse, hazel being the commonest species.

One species unique to this area is the chequered skipper butterfly. Formerly thought to occur only in the East Midlands of England and East Anglia, it was discovered in the southern half of the glen in 1939—it has since become extinct in England. This species

different rock exposures on either side of the fault, and thus to determine the direction of movement along the fault and when the major activity occurred. But the results are conflicting and the debate continues. It is currently thought that the Old Red Sandstones could have been deposited after the main movement along the fault had taken place.

The modern glen is very much a creation of the last Ice Age. It shows the classic features of a glaciated valley: a steep-sided U-shaped cross-section; overdeepening where the valley floor, now occupied by lochs, has been gouged out by glaciers; and hanging tributaries where streams show an abrupt increase in gradient where they drop into the glen.

Above: In the woods of native Scots pine and the plantations of Sitka spruce, the crossbill (this is a female) feeds on the cones, using its hooked bill to extract the seeds.

Below left: Melancholy thistle grows beneath the stands of alder.

Below: Pine martens live among the conifers. They are rarely seen, though the number of droppings they leave suggests there is a good-sized population.

has very precise requirements, needing sheltered but sunny glades in which to fly, wood false-brome grass for its larval foodplant and early-flowering herbs to provide nectar for the adults.

On the cold, north-facing slopes of the tributary glens, such as Moriston, Garry, Mallie and Loy, remnants of Scots pine woodland still occur. Elsewhere the main conifer woods are those planted by the Forestry Commission. Some species of mammals and birds native to pinewoods have been able to move into the maturing forestry plantations–red squirrels and crossbills, for example, which are both capable of feeding on Sitka spruce cones as well as those of Scots pine. Pine martens, too, live in both types of forest, where they prey on small mammals and birds.

A third type of woodland growing in the Great Glen is alder. Here it occurs in two quite different habitats: low-lying waterlogged ground, as at Urquhart Bay on Loch Ness and islands on the River Lochy at Fort William, and flushed hill slopes (those with some movement of water through the soil). Ash, wych elm and, at Urquhart Bay, several species of willow, are found in the alder woods, The ground flora includes meadowsweet, dog's mercury and melancholy thistle.

The fourth type of wood found in the glen is birchwood, which predominates towards the northern end of the glen. The ground flora

Right: Most of the steep hillsides of the Great Glen are covered with sessile oaks or forests of exotic conifers planted by the Forestry Commission, but along the cold north-facing slopes of the tributary glens there are remnants of Scots pine. Some mammals and birds have been able to spread from these native pines into the conifer plantations, but the specialised insects of pinewoods have been unable to do so. Many of them are beetles–such as the timberman longhorn beetle– whose larvae inhabit dead wood, and they are specific to Scots pine.

Below: A view across the Moray Firth at the north-eastern end of the Great Glen. The geological fault, of which the Great Glen is a part, meets the sea at the Moray Firth and runs up the north-east coast of Scotland towards Wick.

The Great Glen

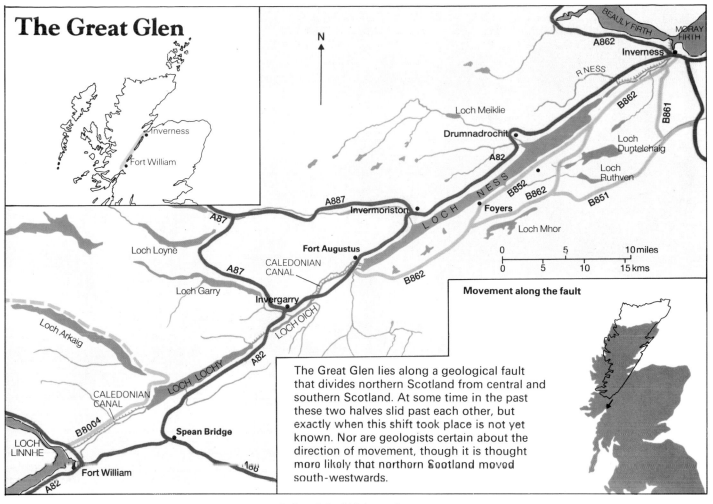

Inverness

Fort William

The Great Glen lies along a geological fault that divides northern Scotland from central and southern Scotland. At some time in the past these two halves slid past each other, but exactly when this shift took place is not yet known. Nor are geologists certain about the direction of movement, though it is thought more likely that northern Scotland moved south-westwards.

Movement along the fault

under the birches is similar to that of pinewoods, with heather, blaeberry (also known as bilberry) and wavy hair-grass.

The lochs The three lochs occupying much of the Great Glen range in size from Loch Oich, at only 5km (3 miles) long, to Loch Ness, at 39km (24 miles) long, with Loch Lochy at 16km (10 miles). All have steeply sloping sides and extremely oligotrophic (nutrient-poor) water. The presence of peat suspended in the water blocks out the light from all but the top 6m (20ft) or so of the water. This, along with the steep sides of the lochs and the often severe waves that break along the shores, means the scope for plants to grow along the loch sides is limited. In the

Below left: Chickweed wintergreen, a member of the primrose family, grows beneath the Scots pines in the tributary glens.

Below: In the hills on either side of Loch Ness are numerous small shallow lakes called lochans, which are the British breeding stronghold of the Slavonian grebe, the most spectacular of our breeding grebes.

more sheltered shallow bays—such as Urquhart Bay and Inchnacardoch on Loch Ness, Bunarkaig on Loch Lochy and the southern end of Loch Oich—a few plants grow, mainly common reed, bogbean, amphibious bistort and marsh cinquefoil. These areas provide the only feeding grounds for mallard, teal and redshank.

All three lochs contain trout, salmon and eel, and Loch Ness has in addition brook lamprey, three-spined stickleback and charr. Both lochs Lochy and Ness have pike. Salmon fishing on the lochs and the rivers Ness, Lochy, Garry and Moriston is an important source of revenue to the owners of the fishing rights.

THE DEPTHS OF LOCH NESS

The Loch Ness & Morar Project, set up in response to reports of a Loch Ness monster, has discovered many surprising creatures living in the great depths of this loch, but no monster—yet!

Loch Ness is by far the greatest volume of fresh water in the British Isles and, with a maximum depth of 230m (754ft), is second only to Loch Morar (310m/1017ft). It is up to 1.6km (1 mile) wide and stretches for 35km (25 miles) along the Great Glen south-westwards from its outlet at Inverness.

Loch Ness was created 300 million years ago when a tear in the earth's crust caused the northern part of what is now Scotland to slide past the southern part. As the two halves moved they separated slightly from each other and the land between them sank. The result was the formation of a steep-sided flat-bottomed valley, which was later to become Loch Ness.

With the coming of the Ice Ages, the rift valley was subjected to successive glaciations, and many of the species now present in Loch Ness are relicts from these colder times. At each glaciation, the weight of ice over Scotland forced the earth's crust downwards. When the ice later melted it raised the level of the sea sufficiently to flood some of the Scottish valleys, including the Great Glen, before the crust, relieved of its burden of ice, recovered some of its former altitude, raising the level of the area again. It seems unlikely that the sea has entered the Loch since the ice last retreated about 10,000 years ago.

An unproductive lake The biology of Loch Ness is governed by its great volume and depth. The productivity of any lake—the amount of life it can sustain—depends upon the quantity of nutrients washed into it from the surrounding soil and the amount of sunlight striking the lake and being available for photosynthesis. Loch Ness fares badly on both counts. The hard rocks of its steep catchment area yield few nutrients to the rivers and streams feeding the loch, and there is little arable farming in the area to increase the supply artificially by fertiliser run-off. The amount of sunlight is limited by the growing season being so short, since the Loch is so far north, and is restricted even further by the frequent cloud cover.

Loch Ness is, therefore, classified as being an oligotrophic lake—one that is poor in nutrients and incapable of sustaining very much life. By contrast, a eutrophic lake is one that has a high level of nutrients and a high productivity.

The shape of Loch Ness also has a bearing on its productivity. During the winter the water temperature is more or less uniform at 5.6°C (42.1°F), and it seldom falls below this. In June, however, the temperature at the surface of the water may be as high as 11°C (52°F), while 40m (130ft) below the temperature is around 7°C (45°F). The result is a layer of relatively warm water (called the epilimnion) floating on colder, denser water (the hypolimnion). Between the two there is often a zone where the temperature drops sharply. This is called the thermocline and it acts as a barrier, separating the two masses of water and preventing nutrients utilised in the upper layer being replaced by those from lower down. Come the winter, as the temperatures of the two layers equalise the thermocline layer disappears, and the nutrients in the different layers can mix.

Microscopic plants The lack of nutrients and sunlight places a severe restriction on the quantity of microscopic plants (the phytoplankton) present. Photosynthesis is limited to about the top 6m (20ft) of the water since below this depth the sunlight is too weak for photosynthesis to occur, due to suspensions of peat in the water. The peat also causes the water to be acid, which discourages the presence of blue-green algae. Among the green algae found in the loch are single-celled diatoms and desmids. Diatoms are much more common in a eutrophic lake; the desmids are more typical of nutrient-poor lakes.

Microscopic animals Dependent upon the phytoplankton are the zooplankton—microscopic animals. At Loch Ness the zooplankton are almost all crustaceans. There are two orders: the Cladocera and the Copepoda. The Cladocera can be further divided into two groups, Calypterma and Gymnomera. Calyptera have their body and limbs enclosed within a hingeless shell and swim with their antennae. They use their legs to draw water inside the shell, where they filter out food particles. In the Gymnomera the

Profile of Loch Ness

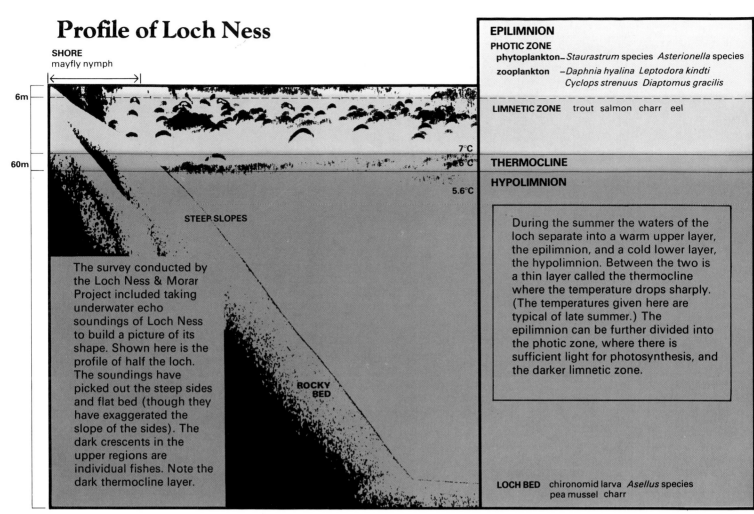

SHORE
mayfly nymph

6m

60m

7°C

6°C

5.6°C

STEEP SLOPES

ROCKY BED

The survey conducted by the Loch Ness & Morar Project included taking underwater echo soundings of Loch Ness to build a picture of its shape. Shown here is the profile of half the loch. The soundings have picked out the steep sides and flat bed (though they have exaggerated the slope of the sides). The dark crescents in the upper regions are individual fishes. Note the dark thermocline layer.

EPILIMNION
PHOTIC ZONE
phytoplankton– *Staurastrum* species *Asterionella* species
zooplankton –*Daphnia hyalina* *Leptodora kindti*
Cyclops strenuus *Diaptomus gracilis*

LIMNETIC ZONE trout salmon charr eel

THERMOCLINE

HYPOLIMNION

During the summer the waters of the loch separate into a warm upper layer, the epilimnion, and a cold lower layer, the hypolimnion. Between the two is a thin layer called the thermocline where the temperature drops sharply. (The temperatures given here are typical of late summer.) The epilimnion can be further divided into the photic zone, where there is sufficient light for photosynthesis, and the darker limnetic zone.

LOCH BED chironomid larva *Asellus* species
pea mussel charr

shell covers only the brood pouch. They feed upon the herbivorous zooplankton.

Copepods are pear-shaped creatures without shells. They use their antennae and their legs as swimming limbs. There are two groups: the cyclopids and the calanoids. The former carry their eggs in two sacs at the tail; fertilisation occurs via a spermatophore attached by the male. They feed on food particles in the water, though larger ones than those eaten by filter feeders. The calanoids carry a single egg sac and are filter feeders.

In general, the zooplankton of Loch Ness are transparent to avoid predators. They cope with the low nutrient levels of the lake by remaining relatively small and by producing fewer but larger eggs than their counterparts in more productive waters. Some species produce resting eggs that survive the winter and then hatch in the spring.

Shore life The steepness of the shore, and the waves breaking along it, create problems for animals living there similar to those encountered in fast-flowing streams. The nymphs of mayflies and stoneflies, which both live among shingle stones, overcome this problem by having grasping claws to hold on to the stones, and by having flattened bodies to reduce the impact of the water flow. These nymphs are very similar to each other except that stonefly nymphs have two tail filaments and mayfly nymphs three.

Fishes in the loch Most fishes in Loch Ness

Below: Salmon spawn in the feeder streams of the loch. After 2-3 years the young head for the sea, returning up to five years later to spawn and complete the cycle. Thus the largest fishes in the loch owe their size to the sea, not the loch–a fact highly pertinent to the possibility of a monster.

belong to the salmon group. Some are resident throughout most of their lives, while others are migratory, spending their adult lives at sea and entering the loch only to breed. Among the coarse fishes, only pike and sticklebacks occur in the loch.

The dominant fish of the shallow water is the brown trout. Small specimens feed on the zooplankton and on shoreline creatures, though in the summer a large proportion of

1 *Asterionella* is a diatom—a single-celled green alga. It floats near the surface where it can obtain enough light for photosynthesis. Individual plants sometimes pack together in rafts, and sometimes (as shown) form radiating groups. Length: microscopic.

2 *Mayfly nymph* lives under gravel on the shore, near the water's edge, slowly developing into an adult. Length: 10mm.

3 *Holopedium* is a member of the zooplankton found in the upper levels of the water. Its body is embedded in a mass of transparent jelly, which it secretes itself. Length: microscopic.

4 *Daphnia hyalina*, another member of the zooplankton, belongs to the order Cladocera. Its body and legs are encased in a rigid shell and it swims with its two long antennae. Length: 1-2mm.

5 *Cyclops strenuus abyssorum* is a copepod, one of the groups of animals found in the zooplankton. Copepods have distinctive pear-shaped bodies and their legs are free for swimming. Length: 1-1.5mm.

6 *Leptodora kindti* is the largest member of the zooplankton. It belongs to the order Cladocera and is a predator, feeding on herbivorous zooplankton. Length: up to 10mm.

7 *Ostracods* are crustaceans which look like tiny silver beans. Their body and limbs are enclosed in a hinged shell, which can open allowing the limbs to protrude. Ostracods are found on the surface of the loch bed. Length: microscopic.

8 *Procladius* is a predatory chironomid, the larvae and pupae of which live on the loch bed. Shown here is the adult emerging from the pupal case. Length: 10mm.

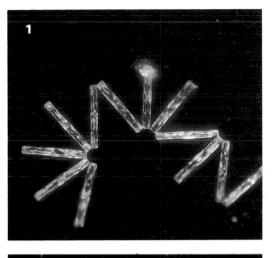

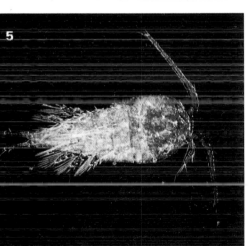

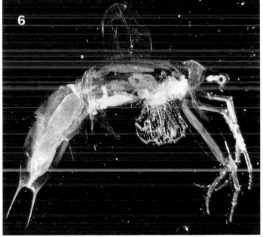

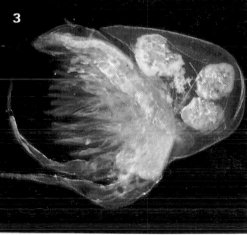

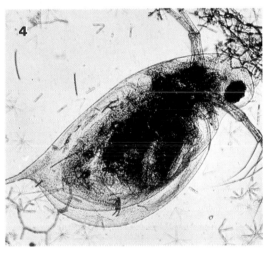

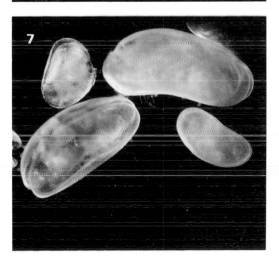

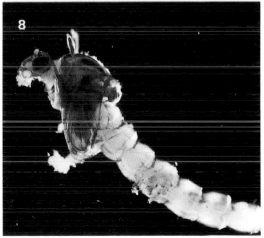

their food comes from insects falling into the water. Larger trout (they may run to more than 5kg/11lb) take smaller fishes and are known as cannibal trout. The deeper water is the domain of the alpine charr.

Creatures of the deep Although the upper layers of an oligotrophic lake such as Loch Ness are poorer than the upper layers of a eutrophic lake, in the lower layers the reverse is often the case. In a eutrophic lake the high levels of nutrients in the water, combined with plenty of sunlight, can cause the plankton population to expand dramatically. When the plankton die the resulting organic matter falls to the bottom of the lake and decays, a process that consumes oxygen, which means there is less oxygen available for the animals living at the bottom. In an oligotrophic lake, on the other hand, the lack of nutrients in the upper levels prevents any build-up of plankton, and therefore any subsequent possibility of the oxygen level being reduced in the lower layers. Equally important, the sheer volume of water in the hypolimnion means it would take a great deal to deoxygenate it.

The Loch Ness & Morar Project was set up in the 1970s to investigate Scotland's two deepest lochs. By sampling the life present in the deep water of Loch Ness it has discovered that high oxygen levels have allowed life to extend down to the silt of the loch bed at depths of 200m (650ft) and more. Here is a community of animals in a stable world of great pressure (20 times atmospheric pressure), unchanging low temperature (5.6°C/42.1°F) and constant darkness. Many animals down here are relicts from the last Ice Age. An example is a species of pea mussel, *Pisidium convectus*, a tiny bivalve mollusc that feeds by filtering out particles from water.

The insect world has also penetrated to

Above: The pike is one of only two coarse fish species found in Loch Ness. The other is the stickleback.

Opposite: A view of Loch Ness — the hard rocks surrounding the loch yield few nutrients and the vegetation is sparse.

Below: A young charr. The charr population of the loch is a relict from the last Ice Age and occurs at depths down to 30m (100ft) or more. Exceptionally strong sonar contacts by the Loch Ness & Morar Project seem to indicate predators, probably fishes, moving within the lower levels of the charr population. The Project is seeking to establish whether these fishes are larger than the cannibal trout.

these depths. Larvae of chironomid midges have been found—some, called bloodworms, contain haemoglobin to store oxygen in times of deficiency. This ability is not required, however, in the reasonably oxygen-rich waters at the bottom of Loch Ness. How the midge pupae succeed in reaching the surface of the loch to emerge as adults through a water column greater than the height of the Telecom Tower in London remains a mystery.

Fishes have also been observed on the loch bed. The Loch Ness & Morar Project first achieved this in 1981 by using an underwater camera, though it was not until a year later that three charr were actually taken, at a depth of 220m (720ft). Charr are known to feed on bottom-dwelling creatures when their usual food, zooplankton, becomes scarce so, bearing in mind the level of oxygen at the bottom, their presence is not surprising. It is of interest, however, that the fishes contained zooplankton in their intestines, indicating that they had made a fairly rapid descent from the upper waters.

WHITLAW MOSSES NATURE RESERVE

The Borders Region of south-east Scotland contains one of the highest concentrations of mires in the country. Lying amid the smooth, rounded hills of the central Borders are four mires of national importance, together known as Whitlaw Mosses.

Whitlaw Mosses National Nature Reserve consists of four separate mosses (the word moss being a regional name for a small confined mire). The four are Murder Moss, Blackpool Moss, Beanrig Moss and Nether Whitlaw Moss. They all lie within a mile of each other, and together their total area is no greater than 20ha (50 acres).

The high density of mires in the Borders region of Scotland is due to the geology of the area, helped by the activities of ice sheets during the Ice Ages. Huge forces on the rocks caused the landscape to buckle and fold, in places creating rock strata that were close to being vertical. Then, during the Ice Ages, a succession of ice sheets covered the area,

wider term than bog. Most, if not all, peatlands are mires, but if they are to be called bogs as well, then they have to satisfy other conditions.)

Two important types of mire are valley mire and basin mire. In valley mires there is a slight movement of water down the valley slope, usually via a central channel, whereas true basin mires have a level, generally stagnant, water table. This is the condition at its simplest. Quite often, so-called basin mires have drainage channels at the surface, and an inflow and an outflow stream. Such a mire can only be described as a 'basin-valley' mire, of which the Whitlaw Mosses are good examples.

Rich fen and poor fen The kinds of vegetation found in basin and valley mires are determined partly by the height of the water table and partly by the nutrients in the water. Water flowing over rocks such as limestone, which is rich in minerals, gives rise to a much more diverse range of plants in the mire than does water flowing over rocks poor in minerals. The former mire–rich in minerals and usually alkaline–is called rich fen while the latter is known as poor fen, or more commonly a bog. A poor fen is lacking in minerals and is usually acidic.

In the case of Whitlaw mosses, the land consists of bands of limestone shale among more acidic rocks. These bands enrich the waters entering the mires with lime, which has

roding the softer exposed rock strata more than they did the harder layers, thus creating a series of ridges and hollows.

All the Whitlaw Mosses lie in hollows carved out by the ice sheets. With the passing of the last Ice Age, the sea rose to its present level and the hollows were flooded to become lochs. Then, as they silted up and vegetation moved in, they gradually developed into mires.

Types of mire A mire is formed when a gently sloping valley or a hollow becomes waterlogged. The result is that the oxygen level in the water drops and so plant remains decompose only very slowly, the material building up as peat. (Mire, by the way, is a

Above: Murder Moss, one of the four Whitlaw Mosses. The apparently uniform, even uninteresting, look of this mire, which is typical of Border Region mires, is deceptive. A close inspection would reveal a great diversity of rich-fen species and a profusion of invertebrate life.

Right: As its name suggests, the northern marsh orchid is a distinctly northern species common in fairly nutrient-rich fens and damp meadows.

encouraged the development of rich fen. In many mires a clear gradation can be seen from rich-fen plants in one part to poor-fen plants in another. In valley mires with a central channel rich in nutrients, the rich fen tends to form along this, decreasing as you move away from the channel to become poor fen at the outer margins. A basin mire, however, if fed by enriched waters at the mire's edge, has rich fen at the edge and poor fen in the middle. In Whitlaw Mosses, only Beanrig Moss shows any clear zonation of the plant communities, though all four mosses have poor fen as well as rich.

The plant communities The most obvious feature of the Mosses' vegetation is the willow carr. This is best seen in the large carr of Blackpool Moss, dominated by common sallow with tea-leaved willow, goat willow and the bay willow, with its glossy leaves. On all the Mosses the carr is surrounded by extensive areas of sedge swamp and moss fen. Beneath the willows the ground flora consists of fairly uniform stands of horsetail and meadowsweet, with a carpet of mosses including the spear-tipped *Acrocladium cuspidatum*, leafy species of *Mnium*, and *Climacium dendroides* looking rather like a miniature tree about an inch or so high.

A careful search through the undergrowth of the carr may reveal the rare and inconspicuous coral-root orchid. Another northern species, the northern marsh orchid, occurs outside the carr in the rich sedge swamps. The robust purple flower heads of this orchid are easily seen among the sedges, of which the bottle and slender sedges are the most common. Horsetails are also to be seen here, and there are pockets of greater spearwort with its yellow flowers—a close relative of the buttercups. In places the sedges share their dominance of the swamps with the marsh cinquefoil—a striking plant with purple flower heads—and the tough-rooted but highly attractive bogbean. The pink-flowered marsh lousewort and the marsh hawk's-beard also grow in the sedge swamp.

In slightly drier swamps, still in areas of rich fen, the vegetation changes to plants such as round-leaved wintergreen, water avens,

Above: Found only in the north of England and throughout Scotland, the Scotch argus is a common butterfly on Border Region mires such as Whitlaw. In late summer they become the most numerous butterflies in a habitat not noted for such insects.

Right: The rare coral-root orchid grows in the dense shade of the willow carr on two of the Whitlaw Mosses. Growing to a height of 25cm (10in), pale yellow-green flowers are borne from May to July (above right). This plant relies for growth more on the association between its coral-like rhizome (below right) and a fungus than it does on photosynthesis— hence its pale green stem.

Below: An insectivorous plant, round-leaved sundew grows in the acid, poor fen conditions found in parts of Beanrig Moss.

angelica and grass of Parnassus.

From Moss to Moss The vegetation varie[s] somewhat from one Moss to another. O[n] Blackpool and Murder Mosses common ree[d] grows in dense stands about 2.5m (8ft) tal[l] usually on sites that were once open pools. I[n] the centre of Murder Moss are rectangula[r] pools, the remnants of former peat cuttin[g] long disused. Here can be found marestai[l] common and small bur-reed, floating broad[

Glasgow • Edinburgh

Whitlaw Mosses NNR

Borders Region

Whitlaw Mosses National Nature Reserve is private land managed and protected by the Nature Conservancy Council for Scotland in agreement with and with the co-operation of the land's several owners and tenants. The Mosses are dangerous and easily damaged. To protect them and the public, permission has to be obtained from both the owners and the NCCS before visiting.

leaved pondweed and the insectivorous plant, bladderwort. Next to the pools are carpets of brown mosses and flea and glaucous sedges, all species that thrive in the lime-rich conditions found there.

Beanrig Moss has some good examples of poor or acid fen. These are interspersed between areas of rich fen and contain hummocks of a wine-red species of *Sphagnum* moss, with cranberry, sundew and cross-leaved heath—all plants requiring an acidic environment. Beanrig Moss, therefore, has hummocks of acidic poor fen surrounded by hollows of rich fen where the water is neutral.

Nether Whitlaw Moss is the most uniform mire of the four, with extensive *Sphagnum* lawns in the poor fen, and some localised pockets of rich fen. This Moss is a good example of a floating mire, where plants such as bogbean have grown over the surface of the water. The result can be very dangerous to the unsuspecting walker.

Above: The most common and evident dragonfly on the Reserve is the black darter, so-called because of its restlessness, alighting on plants after just short bursts of flight. Only the male, shown here, is truly black. The female is mainly yellow and brown.

Below: A secretive bird, but highly amusing to watch and extremely noisy, is the water rail, which breeds on all four of the Whitlaw Mosses. Often heard grunting, squealing and whistling among the reeds, it occasionally approaches quite closely before scurrying away, its red beak adding a splash of colour to the undergrowth.

Whitlaw's animals The Mosses provide an ideal breeding ground for a small range of fenland birds. In early summer the reeds and sedges come alive with the raucous chatter of sedge warblers, offset by the sweeter notes of the willow warbler in the trees. Reed bunting, redpoll and several more common woodland birds breed on the Mosses, or are frequent visitors to them. Occasionally the reeling song of the grasshopper warbler can be heard as this shy bird flits back and forth between tall reeds and low cover. Another shy bird, the water rail, is present on all four of Whitlaw's Mosses, while the more evident snipe is always present in the swamps in large numbers. Herons wait motionless by the sides of pools for unwary frogs, sticklebacks and small pike to pass by.

Invertebrates abound in the fens, the less conspicuous among them being the most interesting. In recent years three species previously unrecorded in Britain—a true fly, a sawfly and a water beetle—were first found at Whitlaw. Several other rare species occur here, including a flightless water beetle, which indicates that the habitat is relatively undisturbed.

The fens are not well known for their butterflies, but there is a large colony of Scotch argus due to the presence of their larval foodplants, purple moor grass and meadow grass. This species is the last butterfly on the Mosses to emerge, having only one brood in the later summer. A sun loving species, it often vanishes suddenly during cloudy spells, only to reappear when the sun comes out.

The open water pools attract several species of damselfly and dragonfly. The most common of these is the black darter; more colourful are the common blue, large red and emerald damselflies.

Ireland

Killarney to Strangford Lough

The profile of Ireland – The Emerald Isle – is like a saucer, with a marginal fringe of mountains surrounding bogs on a low lying central plain; in addition to these habitats there are magnificent coastlines and some important inland loughs. Early isolation from the Continent of Europe has meant that many quite common animals – the adder, common toad, common shrew, mole and weasel – failed to reach Ireland. However, it has specialities not found elsewhere, notably six fish species, a saxifrage unique to the Isle of Aran and the Irish hare.

There are also several plants originating from the Mediterranean region which are found in Ireland but not in Britain. The largest of these, the strange strawberry tree, grows in the rich, damp woodlands bordering the beautiful Killarney Lakes.

One part of the west coast, the Burren, has a landscape for which Ireland is justly famous. At first sight it is bleak and inhospitable, but this apparently barren limestone terrain is a botanist's paradise – the cool, humid climate compensating for the rapid water loss through the fissures in the limestone. Among the plants found here are the Burren orchid and the spring gentian.

Notable wildfowl sites occur at Strangford Lough and Wexford. Strangford, a sea water lough, is almost completely land-locked, so the tidal waters move back and forth through a narrow sea inlet providing shelter for seabirds and marine life. Seals and porpoises move into the Lough via the narrows and each autumn a great influx of waders and wildfowl congregate there.

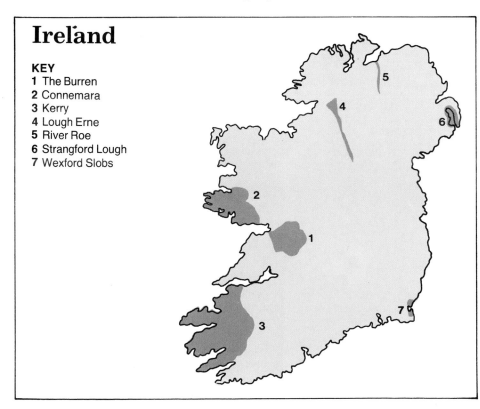

Ireland

KEY
1 The Burren
2 Connemara
3 Kerry
4 Lough Erne
5 River Roe
6 Strangford Lough
7 Wexford Slobs

Left: The lakes and oakwoods of Killarney in Kerry are renowned for their lush, unspoilt beauty and their unusual wildlife. The mildness of the climate has much to do with this — the welcome warmth of the North Atlantic Drift current bringing mild, benign weather for most of the year.

Below: Flowers, fruits and leaves of Kerry's best known rarity — the strawberry tree. The leaves are evergreen and the species exhibits the unusual habit of bearing flowers and fruit at the same time.

THE BURREN: A PLANT PARADISE

The name 'Burren' comes from the Irish word 'boireann', meaning a great rock, and is most appropriate for, from a great distance, the landscape of the Burren is dominated by mountains of bare, grey stone. These hills rise to about 300m (1000ft) above sea level and are separated by dry valleys. The great limestone monoliths have been rounded by the action of glaciers, and over hundreds of thousands of years water has dissolved the limestone so that now caves penetrate deep into the hills. On the surface of the hills the water has carved out of the limestone deep crevices which criss-cross the countryside.

Vast areas of the Burren are utterly devoid of soil, so that plants grow only where little pockets of soil have accumulated, such as in the bottoms of crevices and between small rocks. In general, however, the bare limestone has a smooth, level surface; hence the term 'limestone pavement' given to this formation.

Mild climate The climate of the Burren is mild and moist. Rainfall varies with altitude and situation but can range between 1200mm and 1700mm (about 50-70in) a year. The annual temperature range is remarkably small and the average winter temperature is a mild 6°C (43°F). While frosts do occur, they are

Above: The limestone pavement of the Burren, with a profusion of plants growing in the crevices. In the foreground is the bloody crane's-bill, with its bright purple-pink flowers. This plant is abundant here, but occurs nowhere else in Ireland. It can be seen in detail in the picture opposite left. Other species to be seen growing in the crevices include burnet rose (to the left of the picture) and bird's-foot trefoil (in the centre).

Above right: The Burren rock-rose is found nowhere else in Ireland except on the Aran islands.

Right: Mountain avens clinging to a rock in the Burren. In late June and July the flowers are replaced by elegant, fluffy seed heads.

seldom severe and snow rarely lies on the ground.

The Burren is, nevertheless, a windy place. The Irish naturalist Robert Praeger described its winter climate as a succession of westerly gales with westerly winds in between! There are no trees, shrubs or hedges on the limestone pavements, as the Atlantic gales act like pruning shears, cutting all plants down to the level of the pavement. (In this, the wind is assisted by goats, which graze throughout the Burren.) Blackthorn, ash, juniper and hawthorn all grow here in the pavement cracks but are cut back near to ground level by the gale-force winds.

Ecological puzzle The fascination of the Burren lies in the intermingling of plants from very different regions and habitats. Plants from the Arctic tundra and high mountains mingle with orchids and ferns more frequently found in warm climates. This perplexing mixture is made more interesting by the rampant carpets of montane and Arctic plants

in a mild climate at low altitudes – almost at sea level, indeed.

While these ecological puzzles exercise the discussions of learned botanists, any keen naturalist can find great delight in the brilliant colours and delicate forms of the plants dotted among bare rocks.

Beauty of the Burren The Burren's symbol is the spring gentian, a plant with startlingly blue flowers that stand about 4cm (1½in) tall above a rosette of small, bright green leaves. From early May until mid-June its five-petalled blossoms are sprinkled through the pavement, grassy areas and stable dunes. Very occasionally, plants with the palest blue, almost white, flowers can be found.

Another of the Burren's gems is the mountain avens, whose prostrate stems give rise to pure white, eight-petalled flowers. Both the spring gentian and mountain avens are plants of cold habitats. The gentian is common in alpine pastures throughout southern Europe and occurs in one small area of the

Pennines. The mountain avens grows within the Arctic Circle.

There are two perennial saxifrages growing in the Burren. Along the west coast almost at sea level is the Irish saxifrage, a plant with white flowers and often red leaves. Inland, a very similar species, the mossy saxifrage, forms cushions of green leaves on the pavement and rocky grasslands.

Plants from the south By contrast, some of the Burren's plants come from much warmer habitats. One of these 'southern' plants is the Irish orchid, which is abundant around the Mediterranean but restricted in the British Isles to the Burren and a few other places in Ireland, though it has recently been discovered on the Isle of Man. Its flower spikes are composed of numerous small, greenish-cream flowers and the leaves are sometimes blotched with purple.

Several warmth-loving ferns are also found here. The maidenhair fern grows at the bottom of crevices where there is plenty of shelter and a moist environment. Many other ferns inhabit the crevices, including hart's tongue, the sea spleenwort and the rustyback, which is often seen growing on mortared walls.

The wild flowers of the Burren are usually in fullest bloom in late May and early June. Gentians and mountain avens mingle with rock roses and cat's foot, and there are many grasses and sedges, of which the most beautiful is a grass called *Sesleria albicans*, with steel-blue flower spikes.

Heat stores The factors that allow such a remarkable flora to inhabit a landscape as desolate as the Burren's are complicated. Essentially, however, the bare rock seems to act like a great storage radiator, absorbing heat in the summer and slowly releasing it through the winter to keep the climate of the area mild. The warm winds from the Atlantic also help to keep frost at bay, so that southern plants like the maidenhair fern can flourish.

Above: Underground streams breaking to the surface of a Burren hillside.

Below: Spring gentian— perhaps the Burren's most beautiful flower.

The alpine plants, on the other hand, grow well there because there is no competition from larger, more vigorous herbs, which are ruthlessly cut back by the wind.

Another important feature of the Burren is the rapid drainage through fractures in the rock. As water percolates through these, the rock slowly dissolves and the cracks become larger until crevices and even caves are formed. The good drainage produces another remarkable feature of the Burren—the vanishing lakes known as turloughs. In winter when the rainfall is highest the water lies in these hollows, but in summer the rainfall is insufficient to overcome the steady seepage underground and the turlough becomes a lush, grassy sward, rich in herbs such as shrubby cinquefoil.

An officer in Oliver Cromwell's army recorded that the Burren was a treeless, waterless place, bare of soil. He did not pause long enough to look at the plants lurking in the crevices or lying snug to the ground over thin soil. From a distance, the hills are nothing more than grey rock, often glinting in the sun after a fall of rain. A close inspection reveals a dazzling array of plants, a real botanical wonderland.

THE UNIQUE FLORA OF CONNEMARA

On the west coast of Ireland lies a small region of County Galway called Connemara, an area justly famed for its unique collection of plants–some of them are extremely rare and a few are to be found nowhere else in the British Isles.

Below: The northern part of Connemara is dominated by the Twelve Bens, a series of peaks, the tallest of which–Benbaun–is 730m (2395ft) above sea level. Much of the surrounding lowland is moorland studded with outcrops of rock. In the summer these moors are lit up with a brilliant display of flowers–here the yellow of dwarf gorse (*Ulex gallii*) intermingling with the purple spikes of bell heather (*Erica cinerea*), a common species in the area.

Connemara is the name given to the western-most part of County Galway on the west coast of Ireland. It is a botanical paradise, the home of plants from as far apart as the Arctic region and Spain. The climate is mild; the prevailing westerly winds are laden with moisture and the rainfall is high–as much as 2500mm (100in) a year in the mountains. This is about four times the rainfall in parts of eastern England, which is the driest region of the British Isles.

Mountains and moorland Much of the northern part of Connemara is occupied by the pyramidal peaks of the Twelve Bens. These mountains are composed of schists and quartzite, and rise to more than 600m (2000ft)

above sea level. Their steep slopes, glistening with water, provide a spectacular backcloth to the undulating moorlands of southern Connemara.

The Bens have an interesting Alpine flora, although none of the species is restricted to the area. Purple saxifrage can be found on the highest peaks, along with Alpine meadow-rue. In sheltered places lower down, other saxifrages and a number of uncommon ferns, such as the holly fern, grow.

Most of the low-lying southern part of Connemara is covered with a blanket of peat, with outcrops of schist and quartzite. Hundreds of small loughs are scattered throughout the area. The moorlands themselves are devoid of trees and seem desolate, but in sheltered valleys oak woodland survives. In a few places forestry plantations are now established, but only where there is shelter. The moors are dominated by heathers, including ling, sedges and moor-grasses, such as purple moor-grass. In the dampest hollows are 'quaking' bogs, their surfaces consisting of little more than thin rafts of sphagnum moss.

Heaths and heathers Connemara is unsurpassed in the British Isles for its heaths and heathers. In March on Errisbeg Mountain (which lies west of the village of Roundstone) the Irish heath comes into bloom. This plant has pale pink flowers and grows in the beds of streams on the western side of the mountain. This colony is the most southern in Ireland,

for the main habitat of the Irish heath is in County Mayo, just to the north. It is not native to Britain, however, the nearest European colonies being in northern Spain.

In July and August, Mackay's heath comes into blossom, carpeting the ground between Roundstone and Clifden in the south-west. This heath is similar to the cross-leaved heath –which is found in both Britain and Ireland– except that it has clear pink flowers and a hairless ovary. Mackay's heath does not grow in Britain and its only other location is in northern Spain. Irish specimens do not set seed but reproduce vegetatively, even small fragments of root being capable of regenerating to produce new plants.

Despite its sterility, Mackay's heath can hybridise with the cross-leaved heath, and the hybrid is abundant in areas where both parents grow. Strangely, however, the two species do not hybridise in Spain.

Connemara is the only region in Ireland to boast the Dorset heath, a plant found locally in parts of southern England. About six plants are known in Connemara, all in one small area, which makes this one of Ireland's rarest native species.

The gem of Connemara's flora, however, is undoubtedly St Dabeoc's heath. This plant has elegant urn-shaped flowers, which are bright purple and up to 1.5cm ($\frac{5}{8}$in) long– much larger than those of other native heaths. Very occasionally, albino plants with pure white flowers are found, and a form with reddish-pink flowers is also known but extremely rare.

New discoveries The unique flora of Connemara has long drawn botanists and plant collectors. For example, the Welsh antiquarian, Edward Lhuyd, visited the area in 1700 and collected both the Irish heath and St Dabeoc's heath. Yet, despite almost three centuries of

Above: A view of the village of Roundstone from Errisbeg Mountain. The yellow flowers in the foreground are of dwarf gorse.

Right: Errisbeg Mountain is the only site in Connemara for the Irish heath. This is the tallest of the heaths, growing to a height of 2m (6ft). It flowers in March, producing long spikes of pale pink, tubular blooms with protruding reddish anthers.

Left: The finest of Connemara's many species of heath is St Dabeoc's heath (*Daboecia cantabrica*), a summer-flowering plant producing large pale purple –occasionally white or reddish-pink– flowers.

botanical exploration in Connemara, new plants are still sometimes discovered there. In 1965, for instance, the forked spleenwort, a small fern known from a few places in western Britain, was discovered on Errisbeg Mountain, where it grows in the cracks of one massive boulder – occurring nowhere else in Ireland. The following year, slender cotton-grass, which is well known in the bogs of southern England, was discovered in Connemara. It has since been found elsewhere in Ireland.

Strangest of all was the discovery near Carna, in 1971, of a rush with grass-like leaves (British rushes have a distinctly different leaf structure from that of grasses). At first botanists were puzzled, but the plant was soon identified as *Juncus planifolius*, a native of South America and Australasia. It is certainly not native to the area but was introduced accidentally by man. It thrives in roadside ditches in Connemara and is spreading.

This species is one of a small number from the Southern Hemisphere that enjoy the equable climate of Connemara and have become naturalised there. The New Zealand flax is another. It forms huge clumps of sword-like leaves and is widely planted as a windbreak. Fuchsia grows in the hedgerows of Connemara, flowering profusely from May until Christmas. In its native Chile, the scarlet and purple hanging blossoms are pollinated by hummingbirds, but in Ireland this role is eagerly performed by bees.

Lough plants The Connemara loughs contain many fascinating plants, some of which are found in few other parts of the British Isles. One such is the pipewort, which grows either submerged or in damp peaty soil at the edges of loughs. Its grass-like leaves are a transparent pale green, and in summer the flower heads emerge above water looking rather like large hat-pins. Each head is formed from numerous tiny bluish-white flowers. It is native to eastern North America and, in Europe, is restricted to western Ireland and the isles of Skye and Coll.

One Connemara lough, near Renvyle, is the only site in the British Isles for *Hydrilla verticillata*, a pondweed rather like Canadian pondweed, except that it has narrower leaves which are usually arranged in whorls of four.

Coastal plants The coastal dunes provide a quite different habitat from other parts of Connemara. The soil contains lime, so lime-loving species abound, some of which are common in the Burren, 75km (45 miles) south-east across Galway Bay.

The spring gentian and the pyramidal bugle are among the flowers found on stable dunes, and a form of sorrel with hairy leaf stalks and veins found there is considered by some botanists to be a distinct species. Babington's leek, a species of wild onion, is a rare inhabitant of these sands. It may be a relict of ancient Celtic agriculture brought to Ireland from Spain thousands of years ago.

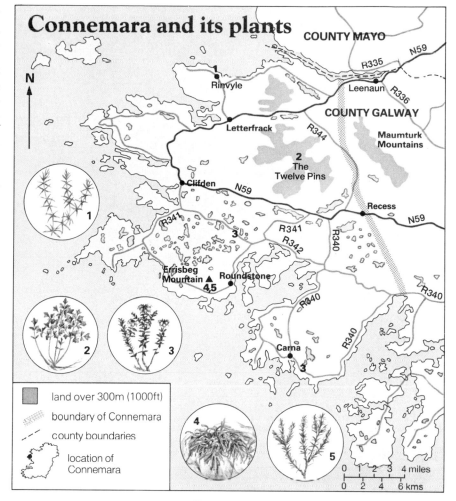

Connemara and its plants

land over 300m (1000ft)

boundary of Connemara

county boundaries

location of Connemara

Above: Some of the more localised plants of Connemara: (**1**) *Hydrilla verticillata*; (**2**) Alpine meadow-rue (*Thalictrum alpinum*); (**3**) Mackay's heath (*Erica mackaiana*); (**4**) forked spleenwort (*Asplenium septentrionale*); (**5**) Irish heath (*E. erigena*).

Right: Mountain avens – a Burren outlier – is found on one mountain in Connemara, near Recess.

Below: The rare white-flowered St Dabeoc's heath.

KERRY: GIFT OF THE GULF STREAM

Kerry has been described as 'a world on its own' – an apt description when it comes to the wildlife inhabiting this unique corner of Ireland, since the mild, wet climate supports an unusual collection of plants and some strange animals as well.

Above: Killarney's famous and beautiful lakes. Among the oaks fringing the lakes can be found stands of the rare strawberry tree, as well as the more common yew and holly – all the gift of the mild climate created by the North Atlantic Drift.

Kerry, sited in the south-west corner of Ireland, is a land of great purple mountains (the highest in Ireland), glittering lakes, tiny tarns and three massive shoulders of rugged old red sandstone that thrust themselves deep into the Atlantic Ocean. The sea surrounding the coast of Kerry brings the welcome warmth of the Gulf Stream or North Atlantic Drift to the area, producing a mild, benign climate in which very hot summers, like cold winters, are exceptional and in which a soft, warm rain can be expected to fall every week of the year. With this climate there is a lushness in the flora of Kerry found nowhere else in Ireland, and some of the introduced species of plants have even spilled over into the wild country-side – New Zealand flax, balsam, fuchsia and many others mixing freely with the native flora.

Kerry's wild flowers The most interesting of Kerry's wild flora are the several native species peculiar, in the British Isles, to the south-west corner of Ireland. The flora of Kerry is based on two different geographical groups or elements. The slender naiad, pipewort and Canadian blue-eyed grass all belong to the North American element. The pipewort is a truly North American species, being unknown in the rest of Europe, except for small colonies in the west of Scotland, but some naturalists doubt that the blue-eyed grass is a native of Ireland, saying that it was probably introduced in 1847 along with American

known as St Patrick's cabbage or, elsewhere, as wild London Pride.

There is also the Kerry lily, whose white flowers do not appear before the middle of June and are gone by the end of July, the lovely lady's tresses orchid, the frog, spider, butterfly and fragrant orchids, the Irish spurge, the lush royal fern which grows tall enough to act as a hedge between fields, and the bog cotton which grows in the wetlands bordering the famous Ring of Kerry. But perhaps the most attractive aspect of Kerry's flora is the series of moss-covered oak woods that have persisted almost unchanged for up to 200 years.

Some of the currents in the North Atlantic Drift bring more than just warm water to the coasts of Kerry. The seeds and fruits of tropical American plants are carried in the ocean currents from the Caribbean and can float buoyantly on the water surface for up to two years. These seeds, known as 'sea beans', are sometimes washed ashore on the Kerry coast, especially after a gale from the south-west.

Cold-blooded animals A number of animals are peculiar to Kerry, including several species of spiders and insects that are known only to specialists, and also the unique spotted slug of Kerry; in the British Isles this slug is found only in Kerry and Cork, and in Continental Europe it is confined to the Iberian Peninsula.

grain during times of famine. Be that as it may, the North American element of Kerry's flora is generally regarded as of great antiquity, showing a pre-glacial arrival in Ireland.

The other important part of Kerry's flora is the Lusitanian element, which is even older than the North American, probably reaching Kerry long before the Ice Ages, when there was a continuous coastline between Kerry and the Iberian Peninsula. These plants include the arbutus or strawberry tree, the large-flowered butterwort or bog violet which bears a massive, intensely blue flower at the top of a delicate, thin stalk and has light green, insect-catching leaves, and a saxifrage

Above: There is no difficulty in identifying the famous strawberry trees of Killarney when they are in fruit. When there is no tell-tale strawberry-shaped fruit, however, you can still recognise the tree by its shiny, dark green, serrated leaves, its white bell-shaped flowers and its flaking, fibrous, dull reddish brown bark. The leaves are evergreen, and the flowers, rather unusually for a tree, appear in October. The tree rarely grows more than 10m (33ft) tall.

Right: Tomies Wood, near Killarney—the mild climate and heavy rainfall create exceptionally humid conditions which are ideal for the abundant growth of mosses seen here. Some of these mossy oak woods in Kerry are old, but today they are threatened—in particular by the all-engulfing spread of the introduced *Rhododendron ponticum* which thrives in woodland habitats at the expense of the native plant species. The mildness of Kerry's climate means that many tropical shrubs from South America and Australia can be grown in the open. Examples of this are the glade of Australian tree-ferns established at Glanleam on Valencia Island, the biggest Embothrium (a South-American tree), growing on the same island, and a Chilean myrtle known as 'Glanleam Gold'.

The only Irish species of toad is the natterjack, which is confined to small areas at the head of Dingle Bay around Rosbegh, Castlemaine and Lough Caragh, although an attempt was made to give it a wider distribution – unfortunately without success. It is a matter of some dispute as to whether the natterjack, with its isolated and limited distribution, is a native or introduced species.

Irish mammals There is, however, little doubt about the discovery in 1964 at Listowel in Kerry of a mammal new to the Irish fauna – the bank vole. The rate of its recent spread into such counties as Cork and Limerick would suggest a fairly recent introduction, but whether it was done deliberately, or occurred by accident, is impossible to say.

Ireland is well-known for its own forms of two species of mammals found on the British mainland – the mountain hare and the stoat. Both animals are plentiful in Kerry. The Irish hare is a dark, russet red, while the Irish stoat differs from the British species in being almost a third smaller, darker and with less white markings on its underparts. The pine marten, too, is more common in the west of Ireland than elsewhere in the British Isles, and tales of pine martens removing bin lids to get at the contents are frequent.

Perhaps the most important mammal in Kerry, however, is the red deer. Ireland's ancient species of wild red deer once roamed the whole of the Irish countryside, but down

Above: A red deer stag in Killarney's mountains – just a remnant of the large herds of wild red deer that once roamed throughout Ireland. Hunting and harassment have accounted for many of the deer.

Right: The spotted slug of Kerry – found only in Cork and Kerry.

Below: The blue-eyed grass belongs to Kerry's 'North American' group of plants, the others shown here to the 'Lusitanian' element.

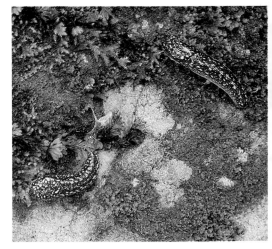

Some of Kerry's plants

St Patrick's cabbage (London Pride)   **Blue-eyed grass**   **Irish spurge**   **Kerry lily**

which feed on eel grass in Tralee Bay, to the American waders which seem to make Akeagh Lough their first port of call, Kerry is rich in winter birds. And, though the handsome chough, with its red beak and legs, is only just holding its own in Ireland as a whole, you do not need to go far in Kerry without hearing its distinctive screaming call.

But it is the vast multitudes of seabirds, their breeding colonies sited on the many famous islands off the south coast, which make Kerry a bird-watcher's paradise. The most important sites for the seabirds are the cluster of islands around Great Blasket Island, the Skelligs and Puffin Island. Here great colonies of Manx shearwaters, storm petrels, fulmars and auks breed in huge numbers.

Perhaps the most famous of all the Kerry islands is the cathedral-topped island of Skellig Michael. It has a long history of monastic settlement; the monks' old cells, which crowd the cushions of sea pink 600m (nearly 2000ft) above the wild waters of the Atlantic, can be reached only by a stone stairway made 1600 years ago. As you walk up this old stairway, the sound of each footstep produces soft crooning noises from the storm petrels that have chosen to breed beneath each step.

Rabbits, reputedly descended from Belgian hares introduced to the island a century or more ago to provide meat for the lighthouse men in hard winter gales, have built extensive warrens on the island and caused some of the old beehive-shaped cells to collapse. This is unfortunate since the storm petrels breed between the walls of these beehive cells. It is estimated that 40,000 pairs of storm petrels breed on this one island alone; in fact, it is believed that the Kerry Islands hold the largest colonies of this species in the world.

Above: Choughs roosting on a cliff ledge. The sea cliffs and mountain ledges of Kerry are much favoured by these birds which, in other parts of Ireland, are just holding their own.

Left: One rarity to grace south-western Ireland is the large-flowered butterwort, or bog violet.

Below: The three great peninsulas of Kerry are the westernmost parts of Europe. The high mountains are bare and windswept, and much of the lower land is acid peat, but the valleys are lush with vegetation.

the centuries it was hunted and harassed until today only a very few remnants can be found in the mountains above Killarney. Stags from Windsor Great Park and from Scottish deer forests have been introduced into this herd, no doubt improving the size of the deer, but decreasing the purity of the old line somewhat. Today the purity of the blood of these ancient wild deer is threatened even more, for the herd shares the same mountains with feral herds of Japanese sika deer.

The lakes and rivers of Kerry are full of fish, but they are also the habitat of American mink, which have escaped from fur farms and become established in feral populations that persist round the edges of such lakes as Lough Currane near Waterville. On one of the islands in this Lough, terns have bred for many years, but have now deserted the site because of the presence of the mink.

The birds of the air The site and situation of Kerry, and the abundance of reed-fringed lakes, marshes and mudflats, means that it is a great wintering area for wildfowl and waders. From the light-bellied Brent geese

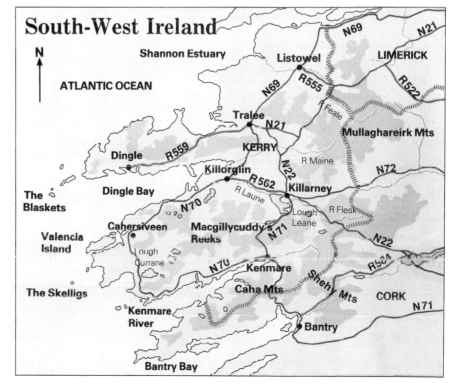

South-West Ireland

N

ATLANTIC OCEAN

Shannon Estuary

Listowel

LIMERICK

N69

N21

R555

N69

R522

Tralee

N21

R Feale

Dingle

R559

KERRY

Mullaghareirk Mts

Killorglin

R562

R Maine

N72

Killarney

N22

The Blaskets

Dingle Bay

R Laune

Lough Leane

R Flesk

N70

Valencia Island

Cahersiveen

Macgillycuddy's Reeks

N71

N22

Lough Currane

N70

Kenmare

Shehy Mts

R584

The Skelligs

Kenmare River

Caha Mts

CORK

Bantry

N71

Bantry Bay

Above: Lough Macnean, in Fermanagh, is one of the many loughs in the Erne river basin. The rare Cornish heath grows on the slopes to the north of this lough.

Below: A snipe sitting on its nest. The wetland meadows in the Erne basin are ideal for such birds, which probe the mud along the lough margins with their long beaks for prey.

THE WINDING BANKS OF THE RIVER ERNE

The maze of water, the small rounded hills known locally as drumlins, and the natural broad-leaved woodland give the region drained by the River Erne–some 4000sq km (1500sq miles) in north-west Ireland–a special character which has impressed naturalists and visitors for centuries.

The rivers and loughs of the Erne drain a large area in the north of Ireland, their catchment extending through as many as six counties. The largest loughs–Upper and Lower Loughs Erne–lie in County Fermanagh with Lower Lough Erne, an almost triangular lough, being the deepest in Ireland at 64m (210ft).

Watery landscape Water is the essence of this land. The ancient seas and lakes that once covered the area deposited the sediments which formed the limestone and sandstone of the mountains that straddle the River Erne. The highest point is Cuilcagh (670m/2200ft high), a flat-topped limestone mountain, capped with harder millstone grit. Over many millions of years, more water, seeping through cracks in the limestone, has dissolved the rock, leaving a network of caves tunnelling through the mountain. In places, the caves have collapsed, creating gaping holes that have their own fascinating flora and fauna.

In more recent epochs, great sheets of ice covered this land and, as they melted, small hills of clay and gravel were left behind. These hills are called drumlins; they swarm across the Erne basin and impart to the area the characteristic 'basket of eggs' landscape.

Now, water lies in the poorly drained hollows between the drumlins, or flows sluggishly in streams around the hillocks. Partly drowned drumlins form islands in the larger loughs. The clay of the drumlins supports good pasture, so the main landuse in the Erne basin is dairy and beef farming.

Although the most distant parts of the Erne catchment are as far from the ocean as it is possible to be in Ireland, the climate is generally moist and mild. Warm, westerly winds keep severe frost and snow at bay, and bring plenty of rain—the annual rainfall is about 1300mm (50in).

Island woods Folklore says that there are 365 islands in Upper and Lower Loughs Erne, but in reality there are only about 250. Like the surrounding mainland, many of the large islands are farmed, but the smaller more inaccessible ones retain natural woodlands, some of which are now preserved as nature reserves. The dominant tree is sessile oak, but ash is also common and hazel, holly and yew are frequent in the understorey.

In the spring, the woodland floors are carpeted with bluebells, wood anemones, primroses, wild garlic and strawberries. Watermint and grass of Parnassus are also common along the lough shores.

Mainland woods On the mainland, most of the natural woods were cut down centuries ago and replaced by grassland. Here, in the drier pastures, cowslips are still abundant. In a few places, on steep rock-strewn hillsides and in sheltered river valleys, natural forest has survived. One of the best examples is in the Correl Glen Nature Reserve. This lies in a sandstone area, so the soil is peaty, without lime. Exposed, heather-covered moorland gives way to birch scrub and then, in the most sheltered parts of the valley, to oak woodland. Holly and rowan are common, too.

The ground flora includes wood sorrel, bilberry, woodrush and ferns. The moist habitat is excellent for mosses and liverworts; they clothe the trunks and branches of the oaks and in turn provide root-holds for other plants. The trees themselves become gardens, festooned with ivy, polypody ferns, wood sorrel and the occasional bluebell.

Mysterious Cornish heath On the high hills, where the underlying rock is not limestone but there are extensive moors, the blanket peat is dominated by ling and cross-leaved heath, and sedges, bog cotton and purple moorgrass also abound.

One of the most perplexing plants in this region is the Cornish heath; a small colony of

about 500 plants grows on the south-western slope of Belmore Mountain. There is no other wild population of this heather in Ireland, and its nearest station is on the Lizard in Cornwall. In Ireland all the plants have white flowers, while in Cornwall the colour ranges from deep pink to white. As yet, no satisfactory explanation has been offered for why Cornish heath grows on this isolated hillside, so far from its southern haunts.

Flora of water meadows It is said that for half of the year Lough Erne is in Fermanagh and for the other half, Fermanagh is in Lough Erne! Until modern drainage works, including a hydro-electric dam at Ballyshannon, were constructed, the Erne did flood every winter, inundating the low lying fens and marshy meadows. Even with modern flood controls, some areas are still flooded.

These wetland habitats contain numerous plants, typical of lake margins and fens. Bulrushes and reeds grow in the shallow water, while yellow water-lilies thrive in the deeper water of the sluggish streams and small loughs. The rushes and reeds also invade the water meadows, where they grow with purple loosestrife, meadowsweet and ragged robin, as well as marsh marigolds and wild iris. The Erne basin is an excellent habitat for horse-

Above: The pastures of the Erne basin are bordered with hedgerows where honeysuckle grows, climbing and twisting itself around other hedgerow shrubs, such as blackthorn and hawthorn. Its flowers come out in the summer, their sweet aroma filling the country air on warm evenings.

Below: In spring the less attractive smell of wild garlic (known as ramsons in parts of England) pervades the woods on some of the islands. You may come across bluebells, wood anemones, and primroses flowering among the garlic at this time of year.

tails—all the horsetails recorded in Ireland grow here.

Wetland and water birds The rushy meadows are important habitats for birds, especially those which probe for their food—curlews, lapwings and snipe. Until recent years, one of the joys of summer was the constant chorus of corncrakes. But this bird has become so rare in the past decade that its creaking song no longer echoes over the Erne. It does nest in one or two places but is not abundant. Even rarer is the bittern, which is now just an occasional winter visitor though its relative, the grey heron, is thankfully not on the decline.

Lower Lough Erne supports a breeding colony of the scoter, a small, dull brown duck which usually breeds in coastal habitats. About 60 pairs live on the lough, and their nesting areas are protected in several nature reserves. Three species of tern, the most abundant being the Sandwich tern, also nest here on gravel islands. Mute swans nest within the town of Enniskillen and Bewick and whooper swans are regular winter visitors.

The Irish subspecies of the dipper lives by the fast-flowing mountain streams. It plunges below the water to catch insects and then bobs out again, tripping from stone to stone.

Fishes of the Erne The herons, terns and cormorants that fish in the Erne have an abundant supply of food. Another folktale says that Lough Erne is only half full of water —the other half is fish. Eel, pike, rudd, perch and bream are native and abundant. Pike can grow very large—a 27kg (60lb) fish is the largest recorded. Another plentiful fish is the native brown trout, and individuals weighing 6kg (14lb) are not uncommon.

Perhaps the most interesting fishes in the Erne are charr and pollan, for they both differ from the British fishes sufficiently for some zoologists to consider them distinct species. But most now regard them as isolated local races.

Mammal life The Erne basin is still inhabited by otters. They are not as common as they used to be, but in quiet backwaters these marvellous creatures can be glimpsed. Another mammal with a refuge here is the red

Above and above right: Along the banks of the loughs the sight of a heron catching prey with its sharp beak is still a common one.

Opposite page: Bewick's swans are regular winter visitors to the banks of Lower Lough Erne. This pair are busy preening their feathers.

Below: The Erne loughs lie just within the border of Northern Ireland, though the whole river system includes parts of the Republic.

squirrel—although the grey does occur, it has not ousted the native red. As the red squirrel will eat a wide range of plant seeds, including those of exotic conifers, its survival in Fermanagh seems assured.

Conflicting interests The Erne basin contains many fine wetland habitats. It is an area of outstanding beauty, but like so many beautiful places it is being exploited as a tourist playground. Years ago only wooden rowing boats plied the waterway, but now numerous powerful cruisers sail on the loughs. Sadly, this leads to a clash of interests between those who wish to promote the tourist potential of the loughs and those who wish to protect the lakeland wildlife.

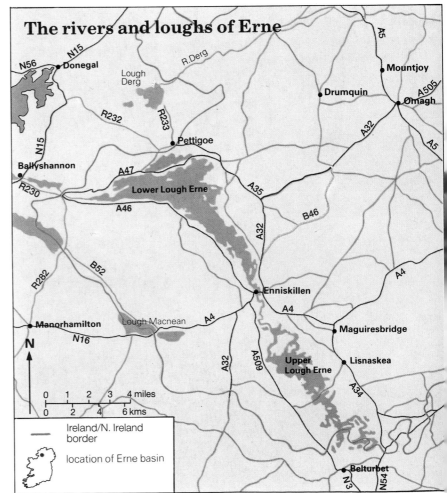

The rivers and loughs of Erne

Ireland/N. Ireland border

location of Erne basin

A WALK ALONG THE RIVER ROE

Roe Valley Country Park in Northern Ireland, with its wild beauty, its legends, history and wildlife, is a rewarding haunt at all seasons of the year. A walk through its woods and by the river reveals a host of rich and varied animals and plants.

Above: A view along the River Roe–the 'red' river. In times gone by the river attracted men who built mills and cut water courses to drive great wooden water wheels for grinding corn and processing flax. The men also cut down trees to provide space to bleach their strips of linen. But today only the racing, rushing River Roe is the same; the mill races are overgrown and heavy with still water, and along the edges of the river are silent, empty buildings.

The River Roe–the 'red' river–is born on the cold slopes of the Sperrin Mountains, fills with peaty water from heather covered hills and gathers enough strength on the journey to cut its way deep into a gleaming gorge of mica schist, before slowing down in sight of the sea and then slipping quietly away into Lough Foyle. It falls 30ft for every mile of its 39-mile course and, down the centuries, has carved out of the rock the Roe Valley Country Park in County Derry, the finest country park in the whole of Ireland.

The walk In September 1976 the Visitors Centre was opened in the Park and filled with displays illustrating the life and times of the Roe Valley. There is also a café and informa-

tion room on the site. Your walk through the Park begins at this Centre.

Even as you leave the Centre to start the walk you are in the midst of the mills and machinery that once made the valley a hive of activity. And framed by an arch in the Largy Bridge is the legendary Dogleap, where a faithful hound of an O'Cahan jumped across the river and brought help from the Castle at Dungiven, a feat impossible for a mere modern hound.

After passing the Dogleap, take the pleasant woodland and riverside path in the deep gorge down to O'Cahan's Rock. The path follows the river for a mile or more, sometimes rising to the rim of the valley and sometimes skirting the edge of the river where your face will be wet with spray, then return by the new bridge at O'Cahan's Rock. Here, where a horse and its legendary rider leapt across the wide river, you can still see the mark of a hoof in the rock.

Down the centuries this fine river has gouged out a great gorge, exposing laddered sections of rocks deposited in past ages. These rocks range from recent glacial gravel deposits, through red triassic and carboniferous sandstones, to the Dalriadan mica schist. If you listen to the river you can hear that it is still cutting its way deeper by the rumbling sound of great boulders in potholes on the river bed. It is, perhaps, not surprising that the energy of the river was harnessed by men for centuries, not only to drive the great water wheels of the mills but, towards the end of the 19th century, to generate electricity in the turbines of a power house sited close to the bridge, one of the earliest hydro-electric generating stations in Ireland.

Plants in the Valley The woodland trees lining this lovely gorge date from the late 17th century. Undoubtedly this area was originally a natural association of broad-leaved trees, but through time, denudation and clearance of the land during the Ulster Plantation by the London Companies for fuel, timber, linen and agriculture, the present, rather different, woodland association has grown. It is partly the result of regeneration, but also of the planting of hardwoods by landowners as people became established in the area. Today the woodland consists of oak, ash and holly, with introduced beech, sweet chestnut and sycamore, and a fringe of softwoods such as Scots pine, larch and specimen trees of silver fir, Douglas fir and Sitka spruce. The area is free of rhododendron and laurel, plants regarded by some as the scourges of planted woodlands.

Because of the damp conditions, the Park is rich in bryophytes. Along the Wet Walk some eight species of ferns flourish, including the lovely lady fern and the hart's tongue fern and, on moss-covered branches of old oak trees stretching out over the river, jungles of polypody ferns. In season, too, there is a rich crop of fungi—red agaric, puff-ball and many more, including the poisonous death cap and destroying angel.

Before the canopy of new spring leaves shuts out the sun, such plants as lesser celandine, wood anemone and wood sorrel flourish and set seed, followed by those with some tolerance of shade—bluebell, red campion and the beautiful enchanter's night-shade, which covers the floor of the woodland like a spell.

Other species have a more protracted flowering period, the various violets for instance, which have several blooming per-

Above: The painted lady is one of the many butterflies to be found in the Roe Valley Country Park. One of the most interesting is the speckled wood; it is one of the few species which is more common in Ireland than in Britain, where it has a lower density and is more thinly spread. There is the usual selection of whites, and of vanessids such as the red admiral and the fritillaries, although the silver-washed fritillary is rare in the Park in spite of being common just a few miles away.

Left: Navelwort, also known as wall pennywort, can be found clinging to rocks and walls throughout the Park. It is named for its round, dimpled leaves.

Following the River Roe

The Roe Valley combines both historical and wildlife interest.

 1 Car Park.
 2 Dogleap Centre.
 3 Power House.
 4 Largy Bridge.
 5 Corn Mill.
 6 Caravan Site.
 7 Traditional Gate.
 8 Great Tree.
 9 Site of O'Cahan's Castle.
10 Lookout point.
11 Larch trees.
12 Sir Thomas Phillip's lade.
13 Boardwalk.
14 Summer House.
15 O'Cahan's Rock.

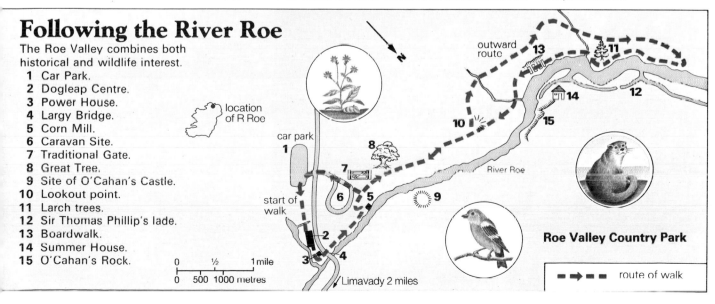

location of R Roe

Roe Valley Country Park

- - ➤ - - route of walk

iods throughout the year, and self-heal and bugle, together with such plants as the superb woodruff, which is an indicator of the long continuity of woodland in the flora.

There is also toothwort, saprophytic on birch and abundant in some years, while aquatic species like water avens and marsh marigold flourish in the old mill races. Orchids are plentiful in the proper season, though there is no species which is of exceptional merit. There are good spikes of early purple and spotted orchids, with an abundance in some seasons of the bird's-nest orchid. Introduced species, like the monkey flower and balsam, grow along the edge of the river in quiet spots, and the North American fringe cup was first reported in the Park about ten years ago; it has become abundant with the help of the flooding river.

Bird bounty Roe Valley has a variety of species of woodland birds, including jays, tits and magpies, but notable absentees are the nuthatch and the woodpeckers. A survey carried out in spring between Dogleap and O'Cahan's Rock, a distance of about a mile, showed that the most prevalent species was the chaffinch, which occupied 26 territories, followed by the robin (more abundant in Irish woodland than in British), with 23 pairs, followed by 20 pairs of blackbirds. Other passerines, such as the wren, various tits and the tree creeper, appeared in descending order of numbers, with one pair each of dipper and grey wagtail at the water's edge. In the tall tree canopy, sparrow hawks, wood pigeons and magpies were found to be the commonest species.

The winter population of birds frequenting the Roe Valley is enhanced by berry feeders such as the redwing and fieldfare, and seed eaters such as the siskin, bullfinch and green-

Above: In the damp woodlands of the Park such species as the lesser celandine flourish. This species flowers early, before the woodland floor is shaded by the canopy of new spring leaves.

Right: Although it does not breed within the Park, you may well spot a hen harrier winging its way through the trees. This magnificent hawk hunts small mammals, reptiles and birds.

Below: You do not necessarily need good eyesight to find the stinkhorn fungus in the Roe Valley. The disgusting smell it gives out may well be the first sign you get of its presence. The smell is designed to attract flies which distribute the spores.

finch; and a visit at this time of year is often made memorable by the sight of a troupe of tiny pink, white and black long-tailed tits.

Mammals and other animals Ireland has a rather sparse fauna of mammals and many species present in Britain are missing, if not from Ireland, then from the Roe Valley.

However, three badger setts are sited high over the river, one of which is shared with a fox, which changes its abode frequently during the breeding season. Where the river slows down and the rock gives way to small sand-filled coves, you will find the prints of otter feet in the wet sand, and a spraint (dropping) or two. The otter prints sometimes last for weeks, until obscured by the pin-prick footprints of brown rats.

The first feral mink appeared in the Park in 1979, but instead of building up a viable population as was expected in this desirable habitat, it disappeared again without trace. Of the red squirrel little is known; although it occurs in woodland just a few miles away it has not yet been reported from the Roe Valley.

STRANGFORD: AN IRISH SEA LOUGH

Strangford Lough, on the north-east coast of Northern Ireland, is a sea lough–an almost totally land-locked body of salt water which, because of its sheltered position, harbours a unique range of seabirds and marine animals.

At first sight from the roadside at Greyabbey or Kircubbin you might be mistaken into thinking that Strangford Lough is a large freshwater lake like many of the other Irish loughs. Looking out in every direction you are completely surrounded by land, with many hump-backed islands to the west, the Mourne Mountains in the distant south-west and Scrabo Hill with its conspicuous tower to the north. If you taste the water, however, you will find that it is salt, and many more islands will appear on the east side of the Lough as the tide falls. Strangford Lough is in fact a sea lough, connected to the Irish sea by a very narrow channel.

Bird life The islands provide breeding

Above: Whooper swans roosting at sunset on Strangford Lough. The present-day character of this Lough is largely a result of the last Ice Age, when the area lay beneath a slow-moving ice sheet. The ice transported rocks and soil into the area and then retreated, leaving behind characteristic rounded hills or drumlins. The Irish Sea then inundated the area, turning some of the drumlins into islands and submerging others completely.

grounds for many birds in the summer, while the extensive intertidal mudflats to the north provide rich feeding grounds for visiting birds during the winter. Four species of tern breed on the islands in the summer–sandwich, common, arctic and roseate–together with ringed plovers, oystercatchers, lapwings and snipe. The islands with more ground cover provide breeding grounds for mallard, shelduck and some eider ducks.

The autumn sees a massive influx of birds from the north–waders, ducks and geese. The most important of these are the brent geese, and the 10-12,000 of these which arrive in Strangford represent 40% of the pale-bellied race of this species. They feed on the eel-grass beds which are exposed at low tide, and disperse later in the winter to other sites along the east coast of Ireland. Other winter visitors are thousands of ducks, predominantly wigeon, whooper swans and 30-40,000 waders–curlew, redshank, dunlin and many others.

Life on the sea-bed The Lough has a wide variety of sublittoral communities, mainly due to the range of water movement within it. This results in a range of sediments from boulders, through gravel where the tidal currents are strong, to the finest mud in areas of little water movement. The water is never very clear, due to suspended mud in the winter and a rich growth of plankton in the summer. As a result, seaweeds grow mostly in relatively shallow water, few living below 12m (about

40ft). In deeper water the sea-bed is dominated by animals feeding on the abundant plankton and detritus suspended in the water.

The sea-bed in the Narrows area consists mostly of boulders with some areas of bedrock. The strong tidal streams provide abundant food for the animals that can survive in these currents, and the entire sea-bed is covered with a dense carpet of hydroids, deadmen's fingers, sponges and mussels. Some active animals live in crevices among the boulders, including edible crabs, velvet swimming crabs, butterfish and Yarrell's blennies.

In the southern part of the Lough itself, where the water movement is not quite so strong, the sea-bed is covered with a dense carpet of brittle stars living on coarse gravel and boulders. Other animals often live among the brittle stars, for instance the sea anemone *Urticina eques* and the great scallop *Pecten maximus*.

The horse mussel beds Where the water is quieter, among the islands and along the edges of the main channel, there are often dense beds of horse mussels (*Modiolus modiolus*). These are very rich areas as the mussels lie on the surface of the mud in clumps, cemented together with byssus threads secreted by the mussels themselves. The shells of the mussels provide firm attachment for many other filter-feeding animals, including the variegated scallop *Chlamys varia* and a range of sponges, hydroids and sea squirts. Many

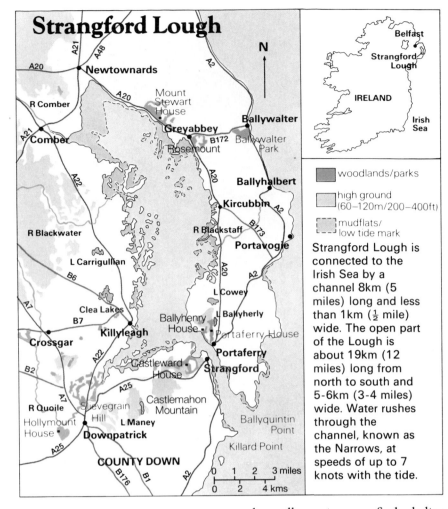

Strangford Lough

N

woodlands/parks

high ground
(60–120m/200–400ft)

mudflats/
low tide mark

Strangford Lough is connected to the Irish Sea by a channel 8km (5 miles) long and less than 1km (½ mile) wide. The open part of the Lough is about 19km (12 miles) long from north to south and 5-6km (3-4 miles) wide. Water rushes through the channel, known as the Narrows, at speeds of up to 7 knots with the tide.

Above left: A sea anemone, *Urticina eques*, surrounded by a gathering of common brittle stars (*Ophiothrix fragilis*) on the bottom of Strangford Lough.

Below: A queen scallop (*Chlamys opercularis*) with brittle stars. The pinkish body in the bottom left of the picture is a species of starfish called sun star (*Crossaster papposus*). In Strangford Lough the sun star comes close to its southern limit, for it is primarily a creature of colder northern waters.

worms and small crustaceans find shelter within the mussel clumps and the whole community can be very diverse, with 50 species living together in 1 sq m (10 sq ft) of sea-bed. This community is the one most vulnerable to dredging as it is entirely based on the mussel clumps; if these are removed nothing but mud remains.

Large areas of pure mud do exist, probably where conditions are not quite right for the mussels. This mud is very soft and sticky, and is the home of the Dublin Bay prawn or scampi (*Nephrops norvegicus*). These prawns, which are really more like small lobsters, live in tunnels which they construct in the mud. The usual burrow is V-shaped, sometimes with an additional side-entrance, and may be shared by a fish, Fries' goby (*Lesuerigobius friesii*). Few other animals live on this mud, but the anemone *Sagartiogeton laceratus* is quite characteristic of this habitat, attaching itself to pieces of shell buried in the mud.

Management of the Lough As a result of several gifts and purchases of land, the National Trust has now acquired control of all the foreshore and several areas of land adjoining the Lough, together with two important country houses, Castleward and Mountstewart. This means that the Trust can largely control development and sporting activities on the Lough, which it does through its Strangford Lough Wildlife Scheme. A committee representing the various interests

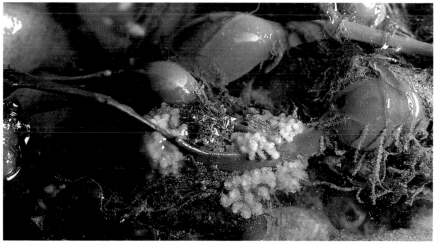

in the Lough meets regularly, and is able to balance the interests of conservation, wildfowling and sport to the benefit of all who use it.

Fishing pressures on the Lough are minimal at present. There is a large oyster-culture industry developing in the north-eastern part, but this activity is not detrimental to the Lough at the present level. Occasionally large fleets of boats dredge for great scallops and queen scallops, usually when bad weather in the Irish Sea forces them to seek sheltered waters. This type of fishing is very harmful, especially to the horse mussel beds which take many years to re-establish themselves if they are damaged. Wildfowling on the Lough is strictly controlled by the wildfowlers themselves, who realise that conservation of the Lough and the bird populations is important to the future of their sport. The birds must be allowed to breed in peace and quiet so that their numbers can be maintained at a reasonably high level. There are clearly defined seasons for shooting and the quotas of

birds to be killed are carefully regulated so that no species is allowed to decline and disappear.

A recent threat to the well-being of the Lough was a proposal to build a tidal barrage across the entrance to generate electricity. It was calculated that such a barrage could supply 10% of Northern Ireland's electricity from tidal power. However the proposal would have resulted in a drastic reduction of the tidal range within the Lough, with the lower half of the present intertidal area being permanently submerged. This reduction of the feeding grounds for the wintering bird populations would probably have been the main drawback of the scheme from a conservationist point of view. Luckily the proposal has now been abandoned, but with new technology and increasing costs of energy it must remain an attractive proposal from an engineering viewpoint. It is to be hoped that Strangford Lough's unique fauna and flora will be given proper consideration and protection in the future.

Top left: Strangford Lough is a paradise for birds, especially wildfowl and seabirds. Four species of tern breed on the Lough's islands in summer, including this arctic tern.

Above: The hydroid *Clava*, here shown on seaweed, is to be seen in the Lough's somewhat murky waters.

Left: Some large animals can be found in the Lough. Record-sized tope and skate have been caught in the past and there is a large population of common seals which haul out on to rocks and islands in the Narrows. Family groups of killer whales have been seen, and porpoises (shown here) are common visitors.

THE WILDFOWL OF WEXFORD SLOBS

The Wexford Slobs, among the best known of all the ornithological sites in Ireland, have a special attraction for ducks, geese and waders—birds that find secure roosts and rich feeding on the large areas of flat, open farmland in Wexford Harbour.

summer. The sandbanks and spits at the harbour mouth are constantly evolving, most of the sandbanks being remnants of a long sand spit across the southern half of the harbour mouth. When disturbance in the 1960s displaced breeding terns from a major colony at Lady's Island Lake on the south coast of County Wexford, Tern Island in Wexford Harbour quickly became important for the birds. Access to the island was restricted and for the next ten years it was the largest ternery in Ireland, with five breeding tern species, totalling about 2500 pairs. However, Tern Island was mostly washed away in the mid-1970s; some terns have now recolonised Lady's Island Lake once more but

The 'Slobs' were reclaimed from the extensive shallow areas of sand and mudflats of Wexford Harbour (in south-east Ireland) between the years 1815 and 1849. (Sloblands in Ireland originally meant 'mudflats', but now the name has been revised to include the reclaimed farmland derived from the slobs.)

The Slobs consist of two farms of abut 1000 hectares (2500 acres) each, one north and one south of the harbour. On the seaward side they are bordered by extensive sand dunes. Rich mudflats, exposed at low tide, support important populations of wading birds, while mud and sand islands within the harbour provide winter roosts for waders, ducks and geese, together with a few breeding terns in the

Above: Greenland white-fronted geese on the North Slob. The breeding success of these birds is low and the Irish Government introduced bans on the shooting of whitefronts to allow numbers to increase. At the same time aspects of their conservation are being studied by the Forest and Wildlife Service.

Right: Two birds to watch for on the Slobs—a pale-bellied Brent goose and the rarer lesser yellowlegs.

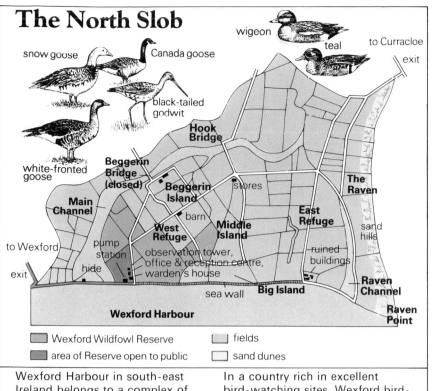

The North Slob

snow goose
Canada goose
wigeon
teal
to Curracloe
exit
black-tailed godwit
white-fronted goose
Hook Bridge
Beggerin Bridge (closed)
Beggerin Island
stores
The Raven
Main Channel
West Refuge
barn
Middle Island
East Refuge
sand hills
to Wexford
pump station
observation tower, office & reception centre, warden's house
ruined buildings
Raven Channel
exit
hide
sea wall
Big Island
Wexford Harbour
Raven Point

| | Wexford Wildfowl Reserve | | | fields |
| | area of Reserve open to public | | | sand dunes |

Wexford Harbour in south-east Ireland belongs to a complex of coastal lagoons and estuaries which includes Lady's Island Lake, Tacumshin Lake, Ballyteigue, The Cull and Bannow Bay.

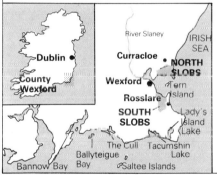

River Slaney
IRISH SEA
Dublin
Curracloe
NORTH SLOBS
County Wexford
Wexford
Tern Island
Rosslare
SOUTH SLOBS
Lady's Island Lake
The Cull
Tacumshin Lake
Ballyteigue Bay
Bannow Bay
Saltee Islands

In a country rich in excellent bird-watching sites, Wexford bird-watchers have an added bonus in their county's geographical location. Migrant wildfowl following both the east and south coasts are concentrated at the headlands and lagoons of the south east corner of the county. Whitefronted, Canada and snow geese can all be seen on the Slobs, as too can wigeon, teal and black-tailed godwit. The Great Saltee Bird Observatory (situated on the offshore island of the same name) is no longer regularly manned, but rarities are still recorded there each year by enthusiastic birdwatchers.

many are still trying to establish colonies in the harbour nearly ten years later.

Wexford geese The wildfowl of Wexford Harbour have been famous for centuries and the added attraction of the reclaimed slob-lands soon drew geese to the area. Bean geese were reputedly the first to arrive, soon after reclamation. Although some ornithologists suggest that they might have been mistaken for immature Greenland whitefronted geese, they would certainly not have been confused with the adult birds. Subsequent history is more certain. Greylag geese were common from 1900 until the mid 1940s. Their simultaneous decline on the Slobs and in the rest of the country coincided with a substantial increase in the farming of root crops in Scotland, where the Irish population of greylags is thought to have stopped over. Greenland whitefronted geese started to winter on the Slobs in the 1920s. Since their numbers increased during a period when Irish agriculture was poor, it seems likely that these geese were displaced from within Ireland by

Below: The attractive dewberry flourishes on the sand dunes at Ballyteigue. You can tell the fruits of the dewberry from those of the blackberry because they have fewer segments and a bluish waxy bloom.

loss of habitat. Recently, ringing recoveries have shown birds from Wexford and Scotland to have a common breeding range, quite distinct from the geese that winter in the Midlands and west of Ireland. So it seems that the Wexford whitefronts originally came from Scotland.

Roost requirements for wildfowl are less stringent than those for breeding terns and the fortunes of the winter flocks of duck and geese are linked instead to the changes in agriculture on the Slobs. Subsoil drainage carried out on the farmland in the 1960s was seen as a threat to their continued existence in the area and the State and the Irish Wildbird Conservancy jointly acquired 100 hectares (250 acres) of the North Slob as a Wildfowl Reserve. Fears that the wildfowl were in decline proved groundless, however, with numbers remaining fairly constant since regular counting started in the late 1960s to the early 1980s. (After protection began in 1984 numbers increased, and have now stabilised at 8000-8500 wintering birds–35% of the entire world population of this subspecies. The Wexford Slobs are, therefore, of international importance.) The geese very soon learned to exploit the large areas of stubble and root crops, and Bewick's swans started wintering on the Slobs in increasing numbers. Today the farming emphasis is shifting back to pasture because of the physical constraints dictated by poor-draining soils. The decline in root crops has been paralleled by a drop in Bewick swan numbers and, while the Greenland whitefront numbers did not decline, their competitive use of winter grass brought them into conflict with farmers.

This is not the only problem faced by the Greenland whitefronts, however. Juvenile whitefronts of all races can be distinguished from adults in the field by their lack of black belly bars and, at least in the early part of winter, by the absence of a white forehead. The proportion of juveniles in the flocks when they come back from Greenland each summer is very low–on average only 17%. This figure is much lower than for the European and American whitefronts. The Greenland geese have slightly larger broods, thus the proportion of adults that are successful breeders

is even lower than for the other subspecies. No-one knows whether the reason for the birds' low productivity lies on the wintering grounds or in Greenland, but the Greenland barnacle goose, which winters in the west of Ireland, has an even poorer breeding record. Both are thought to be unique among migratory geese in lacking staging posts between winter and summer quarters. These stages or breaks in migration are known to be important for other goose species, which time their journey northwards to coincide with the flush of spring grass so important in accumulating fat reserves for the breeding season.

Other bird species The Wexford sloblands are best known for their whitefronted geese and other species often tend to get overlooked. Particularly striking on the Slobs are large numbers of other flocking species – starlings, lapwings, golden plover, curlew, wigeon, rooks, gulls and pigeons. At times, especially in the early part of the winter, the Slobs seem alive with birds – plovers wheeling on silvery wings, noisy flocking starlings cartwheeling over each other as the group moves forward, great flocks of wigeon and mallard, raucous rooks, black-headed gulls and geese, and whitefronts wherever you look.

Up to 60,000 waders are estimated to use Wexford Harbour, mainly lapwings, golden plover, curlew, black-tailed godwit and dunlin. Consequently, a number of species of birds of prey are also found in the area. Hen harrier, sparrowhawk, kestrel, peregrine and merlin can all be seen almost daily, and a walk along the seawalls or dykes of the sloblands often reveals the plucked remains of a large number of victims.

The plants of the Slobs Both Slobs are protected from the sea by long stretches of

Above: A view of part of the North Slob in winter. Wexford Harbour, and all the other places referred to here, are within 15 miles of the port of Rosslare, which can be reached from Britain and the Continent by regular ferry services.

Below: A colony of common mussels (you can also see a few barnacles and limpets). Local boats fish Wexford Harbour and the coastal waters for mussels, which support a thriving local industry. Large flocks of scoter feed on these shellfish in the winter months.

sand dunes. Between Rosslare and the South Slob the dunes have largely been spoiled by suburban housing developments, but to the north of the Harbour, for four miles from south Curracloe to the Raven Point, the dunes are a nature reserve. The Forestry Department that used to run them effectively conserved the sand dune system by excluding farmstock and by restricting access to the public through the use of one northern gate. The well-developed series of sand dunes and dune slacks provides a great variety of vegetation types. This variety and a lack of erosion make the area unique on the east coast of Ireland.

Behind the mobile dunes are extensive communities of moss and lichen among the grasslands. These springy carpets have been modified very little by trampling and are probably maintained free from scrub by rabbit grazing. The dune slacks, characterised by dwarf willow species, support several plant species rare in Ireland – including round-leaved wintergreen and yellow bird's-nest. Up to 30 years ago the dune slacks were flooded

each winter but the plantations and improved drainage on the Slobs have caused a lowering of the water table. No indigenous woodland exists here and the plantations are principally of Corsican pine. Several of the botanically rich areas have been planted, and although most of the trees have failed, damage has been done to the natural vegetation. On the other hand, the conifers are thought to have minimised wind erosion of the mobile dunes where trampling has had an effect.

Sand and coast A superb sandy beach stretches down the strip of land (bordering the North Slob) known as The Raven. Unmarred by wooden groynes, the tip is a rare example

Above: Bewick's swans busy feeding on the North Slob.

Below left: Round-leaved wintergreen is one of the rarer plants to be seen on the dune slacks at Wexford.

Below right: A wide range of characteristic insects is present on the strip of land known as The Raven (see map). Among the butterflies found there are the grayling (shown here), the wood white and the gatekeeper. In common with some other species in Ireland, these butterflies are restricted to coastal areas, although they are found in a wider range of habitats in Britain. On the strandline of the undisturbed beaches you may also find two rare arthropods – a beetle and a woodlouse.

of a dynamic sand/shingle spit, unmanaged by man. The islands and lagoons of The Raven change dramatically throughout the winter. Here, the Greenland whitefronts have one of their two major night-time roosts. In summer ringed plover and little terns make abortive attempts to nest, disturbed only by those visitors energetic enough to make the four-mile trek from the car park. Sandwich terns have recently shown interest in nesting on the outermost spit, but it is washed by the highest tides, so no nest can be permanent.

Wexford Harbour is one of a complex of coastal lagoons and estuaries in south County Wexford – a complex which includes Lady's Island Lake, Tacumshin, Ballyteigue and Bannow Bay. The reclaimed portion of the estuary behind Ballyteigue, known as the Cull, and Tacumshin support many of the winter grassland bird flocks characteristic of the Slobs. Bewick's swans now use the Cull in preference to the Slobs and Greenland whitefronts are also found there occasionally. Lady's Island, Tacumshin and Ballyteigue were all once shallow tidal estuaries which have become blocked off from the sea by shingle and sand bars. All are now brackish water lagoons. There are extensive sand dunes on the landward side of the spits and the rare cottonweed is found on the shingle at Lady's Island Lake. The sand dunes at Ballyteigue possess a rich fauna and flora, including wild asparagus and dewberry.

All three lagoons harbour wintering wildfowl, particularly during the weeks when shooting disturbance is minimal. Both Lady's Island and Tacumshin attract a variety of waders and a surprising number of North American waders of several species are now seen almost annually. There are records of sightings of Baird's, buff-breasted and pectoral sandpipers, dowitchers and lesser yellowlegs. The mudflats and saltmarshes of Bannow Bay support large numbers of the usual wintering wildfowl and waders, including a flock of Brent geese. In terms of numbers of birds, the Bay is second in importance to Wexford Harbour and is well worth a visit since the countryside here retains a wild and rugged character.

Country code

Wherever you are in the countryside, always remember to observe the Country Code.

1. **Respect the life and work of the countryside.**
2. **Guard against fire.**
3. **Fasten all gates.**
4. **Keep your dogs under control.**
5. **Keep to public paths across farmland.**
6. **Use gates and stiles to cross fences, hedges and walls.**
7. **Leave livestock, crops and machinery alone.**
8. **Take your litter home.**
9. **Help to keep all water clean.**
10. **Protect wildlife, plants and trees.**
11. **Take special care on country roads.**
12. **Make no unnecessary noise.**

The National Parks   Names and addresses for more information

Dartmoor
945 sq km (365 sq miles)
Mr I Mercer, Dartmoor National Park, Parke, Haytor Road, Bovey Tracey, Devon TQ13 9JQ.

Exmoor
686 sq km (265 sq miles)
Mr Keith Bungay, Exmoor National Park, Exmoor House, Dulverton, Somerset TA22 9HL.

Brecon Beacons
1344 sq km (519 sq miles)
Mr M Beresford, Brecon Beacons National Park, Glamorgan Street, Brecon, Powys LD3 7DP.

Pembrokeshire Coast
583 sq km (225 sq miles)
Mr NJ Wheeler, Pembrokeshire Coast National Park, County Offices, Haverfordwest, Dyfed SA61 1QZ.

Snowdonia
2171 sq km (838 sq miles)
Mr Alan Jones, Snowdonia National Park, National Park Office, Penrhyndeudraeth, Gwynedd LL48 6LS.

The Broads
288 sq km (111 sq miles)

Mr Aitken Clark, Thomas Harvey House, 18 Colgate, Norwich, Norfolk NR3 1PQ.

Peak District
1404 sq km (542 sq miles)
Mr N Dower, Peak District National Park, Aldern House, Baslow Road, Bakewell, Derbyshire.

Yorkshire Dales
1761 sq km (680 sq miles)
Mr RJ Harvey, Yorkshire Dales National Park, Yorebridge House, Bainbridge, Leyburn, North Yorks YO6 5BP.

North York Moors
1432 sq km (553 sq miles)
Mr D Statham, North York Moors National Park, The Old Vicarage, Bondgate, Helmsley, Yorkshire.

Lake District
2243 sq km (866 sq miles)
Mr J Toothill, Lake District National Park, Busher Walk, Kendal, Cumbria LA9 4RH.

Northumberland
1031 sq km (398 sq miles)
Mr A MacDonald, Northumberland National Park, Eastburn, South Park, Hexham NE46 1BS.

Wildlife under special protection

Plants
(not a complete list)
Adder's tongue spearwort
Alpine catchfly
Alpine gentian
Bedstraw broomrape
Blue heath
Branched horsetail
Bristol rock-cress
Brown galingale
Cambridge milk parsley
Cheddar pink
Childing pink
Creeping marshwort
Cut-leaved germander
Diapensia
Dickie's bladder-fern
Downy woundwort
Drooping saxifrage
Early spider orchid
Early star-of-Bethlehem
Fen orchid
Fen ragwort
Fen violet
Field cow-wheat
Field eryngo
Field wormwood
Fingered speedwell
Foxtail stonewort
Ghost orchid
Grass poly
Greater yellow-rattle
Green hound's tongue
Holly leaved naiad
Jersey cudweed
Killarney fern
Lady's slipper
Late spider orchid

Least lettuce
Limestone woundwort
Lizard orchid
Martin's ramping-fumitory
Military orchid
Monkey orchid
Oblong woodsia
Oxtongue broomrape
Pennyroyal
Perennial knawel
Pigmyweed
Plymouth pear
Purple colt's-foot
Purple spurge
Red helleborine
Red-tipped cudweed
Ribbon-leaved water-plaintain
Rock cinquefoil
Rock sea lavender
Rough marsh mallow
Round-headed leek
Sand crocus
Sea knotgrass
Sea lavender
Sickle-leaved hare's-ear
Slender cottongrass
Small alison
Small fleabane
Small hare's-ear
Small restharrow
Snowdon lily
Spiked speedwell
Starfruit
Starved wood-sedge
Stinking goosefoot
Stinking hawk's beard

Strapwort
Teesdale sandwort
Thistle broomrape
Triangular club-rush
Viper's grass
Water germander
Whorled Solomon's-seal
Wild cotoneaster
Wild gladiolus
Wood calamint

Birds
(not a complete list)
Avocet
Barn owl
Bearded tit
Bee eater
Bewick's swan
Bittern
Black-necked grebe
Black redstart
Black-tailed godwit
Black tern
Black-winged stilt
Bluethroat
Brambling
Cetti's warbler
Chough
Cirl bunting
Common quail
Common scoter
Corncrake
Crested tit
Crossbill (all species)
Dartford warbler
Divers (all species)
Dotterel
Fieldfare
Firecrest
Garganey
Golden eagle
Golden oriole

Goshawk
Green sandpiper
Greenshank
Gyr falcon
Harriers (all species)
Hobby
Honey buzzard
Hoopoe
Kentish plover
Kingfisher
Lapland bunting
Leach's petrel
Little bittern
Little gull
Little ringed plover
Little tern
Long-tailed duck
Marsh warbler
Mediterranean gull
Merlin
Osprey
Peregrine
Purple heron
Purple sandpiper
Red-backed shrike
Red kite
Red-necked phalarope
Redwing
Roseate tern
Ruff
Savi's warbler
Scarlet rosefinch
Scaup
Serin
Shore lark
Short-toed treecreeper
Slavonian grebe
Snow bunting
Snowy owl
Spoonbill
Spotted crake

Stone curlew
Temminck's stint
Velvet scoter
Whimbrel
White-tailed eagle
Whooper swan
Woodlark
Wood sandpiper
Wryneck

Mammals
Bats (15 species)
Bottle-nosed dolphin
Common dolphin
Dormouse
Harbour porpoise
Otter
Pine marten
Red squirrel
Walrus
Whales
Wild cat

Fish
Burbot
Vendace
Whitefish

Amphibians
Great crested newt
Natterjack toad

Reptiles
Adder
Marine turtles
Sand lizard
Smooth snake

Insects
Field cricket
Mole cricket
New Forest cicada
Norfolk aeshna dragonfly

Rainbow leaf beetle
Wart-biter grasshopper

Spiders
Fen raft spider
Ladybird spider

Lepidoptera
Barberry carpet moth
Black-veined moth
Chequered skipper butterfly
Essex emerald moth
Heath fritillary butterfly
Large blue butterfly
New Forest burnet moth
Reddish buff moth
Swallowtail butterfly
Viper's bugloss moth

Worms
Lagoon sandworm
Medicinal leech

Molluscs
Carthusian snail
Glutinous snail
Sandbowl snail

Crustaceans
Apus
Fairy shrimp
Lagoon sand shrimp

Coelenterates
Ivell's sea anemone
Startlet sea anemone

Moss animals
Trembling sea-mat

Conservation sites

The aim of the conservation movement is to protect the countryside from urban, and more recently agricultural, development, and so most smaller conservation sites occur in densely populated or intensively farmed areas. In Ireland where the pressures on the land are not so great fewer protected sites exist—indeed the Irish government has only recently started designating them.

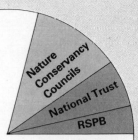

Above: A pie chart showing the proportion of sites owned by the main conservation groups. These are the Nature Conservancy Councils for England and Scotland and the Countryside Council for Wales, which aim to protect specific habitats and species, the National Trust which sets out to preserve landscapes, the RSPB—a group formed to guard areas of ornithological interest, and scores of county trusts dotted across the country.

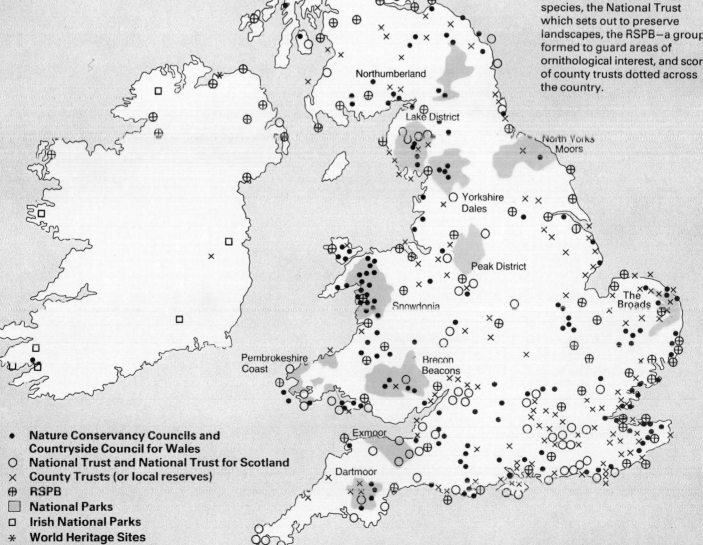

- • **Nature Conservancy Councils and Countryside Council for Wales**
- ○ **National Trust and National Trust for Scotland**
- ✕ **County Trusts (or local reserves)**
- ⊕ **RSPB**
- ▨ **National Parks**
- ▢ **Irish National Parks**
- ✳ **World Heritage Sites**

INDEX

The entries listed in **bold** type refer to main subjects. The page numbers in *italics* indicate illustrations. Medium type entries refer to the text.

ACKNOWLEDGEMENTS

Photographers' credits Penny Anderson 97, 98 (top), 100 (bottom): Heather Angel front cover, 7, 8, 17 (bottom right), 20 (middle), 22, 40 (top), 41, 42, 44 (bottom), 48, 54 (top), 55 (centre), 56, 61 (bottom), 63 (top), 64 (top), 68 (top), 76 (bottom), 77 (top left), 79 (upper middle), 81, 90 (bottom left), 91, 94 (bottom right), 98 (middle), 102 (top, bottom right), 104 (bottom), 105, 106, 109 (middle), 112, 124 (top), 127 (bottom), 129 (top), 130 (top), 134-5, 137 (top), 140, 141, 142 (top), 143, 144, 146, 147 (bottom), 148 (bottom), 149 (bottom left), 156 (top), 157, 160 (top left, middle, bottom), 162, 164 (top), 165 (bottom), 168 (bottom left), 170, 172 (middle), 173 (middle), 183 (top left), 187 (bottom left): Aquila Photographics/GG & IM Bates 104 (top): T Leach 187 (bottom right): DI McEwan 109 (top): D Platt 84 (top): N Rodney Foster 24 (top): EK Thompson 151 (bottom right): Ian Beames 84 (bottom), 124 (middle), 139: Biofotos/G Kinns 82: FV Blackburn 67 (bottom): Bob Gibbons Photography/R Fletcher 19 (middle), 125 (top), 150 (bottom): Bob Gibbons 25 (top), 33 (bottom), 35, 38, 53 (middle), 102 (bottom left): Robin Bovey 114, 115 (top, bottom), 117 (top): Bruce Coleman Ltd/J Burton 58: Udo Hirsch 23: CJ Chesney 155: Michael Chinery 86-7, 89 (bottom), 119 (right): John Clegg 78, 79 (top, lower middle, bottom), 80, 83 (bottom), 156 (bottom): Tom Cope 87 (bottom): Adrian Davies 36, 100 (top), 123: CD Deane 179, 180 (middle, bottom): Caroline Flegg 122: Jim Flegg 121 (top left): Brian Gadsby 74 (top), 75 (bottom), 77 (top right, middle): Dennis Green 49 (bottom), 62 (middle), 96 (middle), 98 (middle), 111 (top), 125 (bottom): J Gunn-Taylor 66: Peter Hawkey 88 (top), 89 (top): John Henderson 74 (bottom):

MJD Hirons 16 (bottom): CM Howson 182 (bottom): EA Janes 10, 11, 12 (top, bottom), 13: Stewart Lane 18, 19 (top), 21, 27 (top): M Leach 177: Brian Lightfoot 145 (top, bottom), 147 (top): M King & M Read/G Dore 20 (top): M King 17 (bottom left), 20 (bottom), 24-5 (bottom), 45: John Mason 26 (top), 40 (middle), 53 (bottom), 60 (top), 61 (top right), 69 (top), 83 (top), 99, 111 (middle), 120 (bottom): S & O Mathews 59 (top), 62 (bottom), 72: Richard T Mills 124 (bottom), 138 (top), 166 (top), 171 (bottom), 173 (top), 175 (top), 176, 187 (top): RT Mills/Sean Ryan 172 (top): Gosse Mitchell 16 (top): WR Mitchell 101, 104 (middle): Colin Molyneux 108, 110, 116 (centre), 128, 131, 133, 152-3: Pat Morris 42-3, 53 (top), 54 (bottom), 92-3, 118, 183 (top right): NHPA/F Baillie 64 (bottom); A Barnes 95; A Butler 161 (top); GJ Cambridge 119 (left); DN Dalton 44 (top), 52, 161 (bottom); S Dalton 71 (top); B Hawkes 14, 71 (bottom); EA Janes 96 (top); E Murtomaki 103; M Savonius 126 (top right): Nature Photographers/SC Bisserot 25 (middle), 39 (top), 46 (top), 129 (bottom); FV Blackburn 34, 75 (top); D Bonsall 100 (middle); N Brown 30 (middle); B Burbidge 30 (bottom), 69 (bottom), 166 (bottom); AA Butcher 90 (bottom right); K Carlson 60 (bottom right), 63 (bottom), 171 (top); A Cleave 130 (bottom), 185; AK Davies 39 (middle); T Ennis 181, 184, 186 (top); M Gore 55 (top); K Handford 150 (top); JV & GR Harrison 51; MR Hill 138 (bottom); D Hutton 50 (bottom); EA Janes 40 (bottom); J Karmah 76 (top); L Macnally 149 (bottom right); O Newman 29 (bottom); Mary Oates 154 (bottom); C Palmer 154; WS Paton 67 (top); D Sewell 116 (bottom), 132, 186 (bottom); D Smith 93 (bottom), 146 (top); P Sterry 33 (top); R Tidman 47 (bottom left), 60 (bottom left), 65 (top right), 68 (bottom), 88 (middle), 126 (top left), 127

(top); A Wharton 115 (middle); JB Wilson 65 (top left), 70 (bottom right): EC Nelson 167, 168 (top, bottom right), 169 (bottom): Northern Ireland Tourist Board 174 (top): DB O'Kane 178, 180 (top): AJ Panter 158, 159: Bernard Picton 182 (top): Keith Porter 12 (middle): John F Preedy 113: Premaphotos Wildlife/KG Preston-Mafham 15, 27 (bottom), 32 (top), 46 (bottom), 47 (bottom right), 59 (bottom), 94 (bottom left): Presstige Pictures/D Avon & T Tilford 142 (bottom): Richard Revels 145 (middle), 160 (top): John Robinson 19 (bottom), 32 (bottom), 49 (top), 117 (bottom), 120 (top), 121 (top right), 175 (bottom): Francis Rose 26 (middle): Scarborough Borough Council 94 (top): Ro Scott 151 (bottom left): Scottish Tourist Board 148 (top): Roger Tidman 28: Bobby Tulloch 183 (bottom): UNHA/Paul Morrison 31, 125 (middle): V Scott 164 (bottom), 165 (top): Woodfall Wildlife Pictures/AG Potts 174 (bottom): Malcolm Wright 136, 137 (bottom), 138 (middle): F Greenaway 65 (bottom).

Artists' credits Graham Allen/Linden Artists 72: Russell Barnett 134, 179 (insets): Elizabeth Dowle 36: Eugene Fleury 62 (map), 151 (map), 154 (chart): Wayne Ford title page, 39, 106: Phil Gibbs 137 (chart): Hayward Art Group 8: Richard Lewington/The Garden Studio 56: David More/Linden Artists 28: Liz Pepperell 172: Sandra Pond 45 (bottom), 67 (insets), 169 (insets), 186 (line): Gordon Riley 48: Colin Salmon (maps) 13, 17, 21, 26, 30, 45, 47, 51, 55, 67, 70, 77, 85, 90, 95, 99, 103, 112, 116, 121, 126, 131, 132, 137, 139, 147, 169, 173, 176, 179, 182, 185, 189: Helen Senior/Groom & Pickerill 162.

Index compiled by Richard Raper, Indexing Specialists, Hove, East Sussex.

Typesetting PHOTOCOMP LTD, BIRMINGHAM; Printing & Binding PRINTER INDUSTRIA, GRÁFICA S.A. BARCELONA;
Separations YORK HOUSE GRAPHICS, HANWELL; COLOURSCAN OVERSEAS CO PTE LTD, SINGAPORE;
Paper KNP MILL, HOLLAND

68-004/4